*under*EDUCATING WOMEN: GLOBALIZING INEQUALITY

feminist educational thinking

Series Editors:
Kathleen Weiler, Tufts University, USA
Gaby Weiner, Umea University, Sweden
Lyn Yates, La Trobe University, Australia

This authoritative series explores how theory/practice and the development of advanced ideas within feminism and education can be fused. The series aims to address the specific theoretical issues that confront feminist educators and to encourage both practitioner and academic debate.

Published titles:

Jacky Brine: under*Educating Women: Globalizing Inequality*
Kaye Haw: *Educating Muslim Girls*
Petra Munro: *Subject to Fiction*

Titles in preparation include:

Jill Blackmore: *Troubling Women: Feminism, Leadership and Educational Change*
Bob Lingard and Peter Douglas: *Men Engaging Feminisms*
Kathleen Weiler and Sue Middleton (eds): *Telling Women's Lives*

underEDUCATING WOMEN: GLOBALIZING INEQUALITY

JACKY BRINE

OPEN UNIVERSITY PRESS
Buckingham · Philadelphia

Open University Press
Celtic Court
22 Ballmoor
Buckingham
MK18 1XW

email: enquiries@openup.co.uk
world wide web: http://www.openup.co.uk

and
325 Chestnut Street
Philadelphia, PA 19106, USA

First Published 1999

A catalogue record of this book is available from the British Library

ISBN   0 335 19738 8 (pb)   0 335 19739 6 (hb)

Library of Congress Cataloging-in-Publication Data
Brine, Jacky, 1948–
     (Under)educating women: globalizing inequality / Jacky Brine.
         p.   cm. — (Feminist educational thinking series)
     Includes bibliographical references (p. 159) and index.
     ISBN 0-335-19739-6 (hardcover). — ISBN 0-335-19738-8 (pbk.)
     1. Working class women—Education—European Union countries.
     2. Feminism and education—European Union countries.   3. Working
     class women—Education—Economic aspects—European Union countries.
     4. Education and state—European Union countries.   I. Title.   II. Series.
     LC5056.A2B75   1998
     306.43-dc21   98-18439
                                                                                                    CIP

Typeset by Type Study, Scarborough
Printed in Great Britain by Biddles Ltd, Guildford and King's Lynn

Contents

Series editors' foreword

At the end of the twentieth century it is not a new idea to have a series on feminist educational thinking – feminist perspectives on educational theory, research, policy and practice have made a notable impact on these fields in the final decades of the century. But theory and practice have evolved, and educational and political contexts have changed. In contemporary educational policy debates, economic efficiency rather than social inequality is a key concern; what happens to boys is drawing more interest than what happens to girls; issues about cultural difference interrupt questions about gender; and new forms of theory challenge older frameworks of analysis. This series represents feminist educational thinking as it takes up these developments now.

Feminist educational thinking views the intersection of education and gender through a variety of lenses: it examines schools and universities as sites for the enacting of gender; it explores the ways in which conceptions of gender shape the provision of state-supported education; it highlights the resistances subordinated groups have developed around ideas of knowledge, power and learning; and it seeks to understand the relationship of education to gendered conceptions of citizenship, the family and the economy. Thus feminist educational thinking is fundamentally political; it fuses theory and practice in seeking to understand contemporary education with the aim of building a more just world for women and men. In so doing, it acknowledges the reality of multiple 'feminisms' and the intertwining of ethnicity, race and gender.

Feminist educational thinking is influenced both by developments in feminist theory more broadly and by the changing global educational landscape. In terms of theory, both poststructuralist and postcolonial theories have profoundly influenced what is conceived of as 'feminist'. As is true elsewhere, current feminist educational thinking takes as central the intersecting forces that shape the educational experiences of women and men. This emphasis on the construction and performances of gender through both discourses and material practices leads to an attitude of openness and questioning of accepted assumptions – including the underlying assumptions of the various strands of feminism.

In terms of the sites in which we work, feminist educational thinking increasingly addresses the impact of 'globalization' – the impact of neo-*laissez-faire* theories on education. As each of us knows all too well, the schools and universities in which we work have been profoundly affected by the growing dominance of ideas of social efficiency, market choice, and competition. In a rapidly changing world in which an ideology of profit has come to define all relationships, the question of gender is often lost, but in fact it is central to the way power is enacted in education as in society as a whole.

The books in this series thus seek to explore the ways in which theory and practice are interrelated. They introduce a third wave of feminist thinking in education, one that takes account of both global changes to the economy and politics, and changes in theorizing about that world. It is important to emphasize that feminist educational thinking not only shapes how we think about education but what we do *in* education – as teachers, academics, and citizens. Thus books within the series not only address the impact of global, national and local changes of education but what specific space is available for feminists within education to mount a challenge to educational practices which encourage gendered and other forms of discriminatory practice.

Kathleen Weiler
Gaby Weiner
Lyn Yates

Preface

For many people working in education, the impact of the range of actions of the relatively new post-war regional blocs such as the European Union (EU), are not at all clear. We hear about loss of national identity to the mandarins of Brussels or the over-production of foodstuffs induced by Euro-agriculture policies leading to butter mountains and milk lakes or seemingly crazy attempts to standardize the tomato, the banana and the sausage. We tend to hear less about how EU policy routinely affects ordinary people's lives, possibly because of the complicated nature of its legislation and bureaucracies, but also because the nation-state is still regarded by us as more important at the individual, cultural, social (and educational) level. In what ways the European Union aids or obstructs women living in different countries is also an unknown quantity to us.

For these reasons, Jacky Brine's book is an enormously important and welcome addition to the series *Feminist Educational Thinking*. She has taken on the task, begun in her doctoral thesis, of charting and rendering accessible, the emergence within the EU of a discourse of equality, and its implications – for education generally, for EU-funded training initiatives in the UK, and for the people involved, especially women. However, this book goes beyond the standard education policy analysis to offer a sophisticated and perceptive examination of the wider relationship between globalization and global trends, regionalized states such as the EU, nation-states such as France, Britain and Sweden, and at the bottom of this awesome hierarchy, the individual woman trying to improve her position in the labour market through training.

The book thus taps into a number of highly topical themes. It is theoretically sharp, drawing on a wide range of feminist, sociological, political and economic theories, though as Jacky Brine writes she 'approach[es] this book as an educationist'. It focuses on working-class women, a group ignored by male social scientists in the 1950s and 1960s and sidelined by many feminists working in the 1970s and 1980s. Working-class women have recently attracted renewed attention as a consequence of changed labour market patterns and increasing poverty following neo-liberal govern-ments, and also from feminist writers and academics who, like Jacky Brine, come from working-class backgrounds.

The book grapples with the structural features of global, regional and national policy-making yet highlights the importance of local context. In rejecting the 'coldness' of other policy analyses which are characterized by an 'absence of people', Jacky Brine shows how policy is experienced and endured by different individual and groups of women. Thus: 'in exploring globalization and global regionalization, I have tried to keep individual black and white working-class women in my mind, to ask myself what does this mean for her or her? How does this affect their lives?' (Introduction).

We are in a time, with decades of feminist campaigning and equal oppor-tunities policy-making behind us, when girls have made enormous strides in schools and in higher education, at least in western countries; when family forms have fractured and diversified, and labour market patterns have inverted and destabilized. The question Jacky Brine seeks to answer is, how can women, as educationists and as workers, meet the fresh challenges of understanding and dealing with new political and economic, global and regional formations which have replaced the equally oppressive but old, more familiar, ones? It is a pressing question for education, for feminism and for policy-making, and demands and receives lucid and comprehensive treatment in this book.

Gaby Weiner

Acknowledgements

I thank the working-class women students who have worked with me and all those people included in this book who have shared their own experiences of education and training with me.

I am grateful to Len Barton, Susan Harris, Maírtín Mac an Ghaill and Lorna Unwin for commenting on earlier drafts of various chapters. My thanks to Judith Marks for her critical debate and encouragement; to Morwenna Griffiths for discussions and comments on earlier drafts; and to Gaby Weiner for her encouragement and supportive editorship. And last, but certainly not least, my thanks to Jesse Nimorovsky for his insights and humour.

While I am grateful to all these and many other people for their discussions and support, the responsibility for the ideas expressed in this book is mine alone.

Versions of some of the ideas in this book have appeared in print previously but all have been significantly revised and the ideas reconsidered in the light of globalization. The details of these are included in the references.

Abbreviations

ACP	African, Caribbean and Pacific states
APEC	Asia–Pacific Economic Cooperation
ASEAN	Association of South East Asian Nations
CEEC	Central and Eastern European Countries
CSF	Community Support Framework
DE	Department of Employment
DfEE	Department for Education and Employment
EAGGF	European Agricultural Guidance and Guarantee Fund
EC	European Commission
EDFOR	Education Forum of the Human Resources Development Working Group
EEA	European Economic Area
EEC	European Economic Community
EO-pathway	Equal Opportunities pathway
EO Unit	Equal Opportunities Unit
ERDF	European Regional Development Fund
ESF	European Social Fund
ESF/3	European Social Fund, Objective 3
EFTA	European Free Trade Association
EMU	European Monetary Union
EU	European Union
FEFC	Further Education Funding Council
FIFG	Financial Instrument for Fisheries Guidance
GATT	General Agreement on Tariffs and Trades
ICOM	Industrial Common Ownership Movement
IMF	International Monetary Fund
ITO	International Trade Organization
JSA	Job Seeker Allowance
MAI	Multilateral Agreement on Investment
NAFTA	North American Free Trade Association

NCVO	National Council for Voluntary Organizations
OECD	Organization for Economic Cooperation and Development
OJL	Official Journal – Legislation
SDA	Sex Discrimination Act
SPD	Single Programming Document
TEC	Training and Enterprise Council
TNC	transnational corporation
TSER	Targeted Socio-Economic Research
UK	United Kingdom
US	United States
WTN	Women's Training Network
WTO	World Trade Organization

Introduction

I have frequently been asked how I came to be writing a book on globaliz-ation and the education of working-class women. My interest in working-class women is, superficially at least, easy to answer: I 'was' one. Yet this is also a complex and difficult statement to make. I can say it because I am no longer 'fixed' by it – I have other positions, some even conflicting, that also express my identity. Nevertheless, there is this unbroken link between the statement: 'I was one', and my consistent interest in the relationship of edu-cation policy to class and gender.

Yet, when I say 'was', this is not, of course, strictly true; neither can I say I 'am' one, although for the first 25 years of my life I undoubtedly was. I have in the past struggled to explain this by referring to myself as an exile or a refugee within the middle classes, waiting for the accusing hand on my shoulder – an impostor, 'passing' where I should not, yet at the same time resisting anybody who tries to stop me. Pat Mahony and Christine Zmroczek (1997: 4) say:

> class experience is deeply rooted, retained and carried through life rather than left behind (or below). In this sense it is more like a foot which carries us forward than a footprint which marks a past presence.

Pockets of feminist class analyses can be found within British social, cul-tural and education theory. For example, there have been studies of the media pathologization (Hill 1986; Kuhn 1988) and of the fantasies and fic-tions of constructed 'truths' about working-class women (Walkerdine 1990). There have been historical studies showing how working-class women have been blamed for the nation's social problems (Stedman Jones 1971; Need 1988), and of working-class girls and women within education (Purvis 1991). Thompson (1983) provides a contemporary account of working-class women and education. Wallace (1986), Holland (1988) and Bates (1990) have focused on young working-class women's transition from school to (un)employment and the classing and gendering of occupational choice.

McRobbie (1978) and Griffin (1985) have studied this transitional period in relation to constructions of working-class femininities. More recently, the contributors to Mahony and Zmroczek (1997) and the work of Skeggs (1997) have focused on the complexities of their working-class identities. While the academics of Mahony and Zmroczek struggle (as I have done) to retain (selected aspects of) their working-class identities, the students on a care course in the work of Skeggs strongly 'disidentify' as working-class. Despite the global context of the early chapters of this book and the dangers of essentializing working-class women, it is this complexity of working-class identity that I wish to hold onto and return to in the later chapters.

Nevertheless much feminist theory has ignored, or marginalized class, or more accurately has been class-blind, across all feminisms.[1] It has been mostly written from middle-class perspectives, focused on middle-class concerns, for middle-class audiences.[2] This has meant that, despite these exceptional examples, the experiences of working-class women have been undertheorized. As Beverley Skeggs says (1997: 7):

> to ignore or make class invisible is to abdicate responsibility (through privilege) from the effects it produces. To think that class does not matter is only a prerogative of those unaffected by the deprivations and exclusions it produces.

For instance, in many western countries, the 'glass ceiling' is just such a middle-class concept, which, along with the demand for 'improved access to decision-making', is applied uncritically to 'women'. My interest is not with the glass ceiling, as important as this is, but with the 'class' ceiling, the structures and processes that prevent working-class women from getting out of the cellar. Unlike the invisible glass ceiling this one is structured with harsh unbreakable materials, the kind of materials that can only be chipped at, materials that obscure the light, leaving only an odd chink filtering through here and there. Education is both the chink of light and the harsh unbreakable material – hence my interest in working-class women and education.

A key assertion underpinning my work is that working-class women (and men) are socially constructed as 'low educated' – they are *under*educated. Low educational attainment is not necessarily a consequence of pathology, or basic intelligence, but a multifaceted social construct that is directly related to Bourdieu's (1997) three guises of capital: economic, cultural and social. While education increases the choices of a few working-class young women, it effectively places limitations on the lives and choices of many more. There are many working-class women who rise above their undereducation, either within education itself, or within business or other professions. But there are many other working-class women who spend their entire lives believing themselves to be 'stupid', believing themselves to be not capable – yet at the same time investing all their own thwarted intelligence and ability on their children.

Neither am I saying that improved compulsory education would lead to employment. But, I am saying that without it, they stand very little chance in the *competition* for jobs; without it they are less prepared for the tedium and the poverty of unemployment; and without it they are, as Freire (1972) has shown, hampered in their understanding of the world and consequently their ability to change the world.

My interest in globalization is more difficult to explain. I trace this back to the early 1980s when I was employed to manage a training project for unemployed women which was funded by the Commission of the European Union (EU). I was at that time an adult educator who had already worked a great deal with unemployed, generally undereducated, adults and young people. This work with unemployed women led me to question the extent to which the training being offered did actually meet their needs. During the late 1980s I took the opportunity to research the education and training policy of the European Union. I found this policy to be intricately linked with a discourse of equality which, infused with gender and class assumptions, trained working-class women for jobs that did not exist (Brine 1992).

I later became interested in the involvement of education, training and equality policy in the construction of the European Union as, I shall argue, a regionalized 'state'. This subsequently led me to explore the policies of other regionalized blocs such as the Association of South East Asian Nations (ASEAN), the Asia–Pacific Economic Cooperation (APEC) and the North American Free Trade Association (NAFTA). This construction of regionalized blocs is also known as global regionalization. Global regionalization is part of the process of globalization, both of which are firmly located within the latter half of the twentieth century. Although in Chapter 2 I will consider the debate on globalization versus internationalization, global regionalization is directly linked to both the global economy and to the geopolitical need for peace and stability between previously warring nations. These discourses of economic growth and peace dominate the construction of regionalized blocs and are two of the dominant themes of this book.

Globalization can, to varying degrees, appear far removed from our everyday lives, yet at the same time one of its defining features is the 'global village' where an event on one side of the world has an almost immediate effect on the other. As Giddens (1990: 64) has said:

> Globalization can thus be defined as the intensification of world wide social relations which link distant localities in such a way that local happenings are shaped by events occurring many miles away and vice versa.

Yet, what relevance does the workings of a global economy have for education and training? What relevance does it have for women, particularly for working-class women? These are the questions I explore. I argue that these global changes are gendered, racialized and classed, and as such they continue to restrict and constrain (but not determine) the lives of women from the working classes within ASEAN, APEC, NAFTA and the EU.

I approach this book as an educationist and not as a political theorist, an economist or a labour market theorist, although I draw on the understandings of all of these. Although this book is written primarily for educationists, other social and political scientists will also find it of interest. My aim is to explore the complex relationship between the late twentieth-century global economy and the classroom – particularly in as much as both compulsory and postcompulsory education and the labour market are gendered, classed and racialized. I partially agree with Andy Green's (1997) interesting concluding chapter in which he explores the relationship between education, globalization and the nation state, particularly in relation to education in the formation of the state – economic development, social cohesion and national identity. He points out that the nation state has always existed within the international context despite what he sees as increasing internationalization, argues that the nation state will continue as an important player within the international context and that state interest in and control of education as a key instrument in social cohesion and civic identity will increase. Although Green's understanding is clearly borne out by the UK's new Labour administration, in the following chapters I question such belief in the power of the nation state in relation to global economics and international relations, focusing instead on the tension between the policy interest of the nation state and the economic and cultural forces of globalization. These are complex, multilayered, constantly shifting and directly linked to volatile struggles of power, compliance and agency.

Although Green touches, briefly, on the regionalized state, he sees European education policy (for example) as being *inter*governmental, and by so doing avoids the emergent area of governance between the economic and cultural forces of globalization and that of the nation state and its control of education. My own argument is first, that within the formation of the regionalized 'state' education is playing a similar role to that played in the nation state, and second, that this role maintains the existing gender, class and race power-relations.

There are of course dangers in straying into other areas of research, for instance, the theoretical basis may appear wide and thinly spread, but this can be necessary to the research process. From my feminist education perspective I have focused, as Bauman (1992) has suggested, on the social spaces *between* nation states, concentrating on the connections between economics, international relations, political science and education. And all the time, at the centre of the study, are working-class women.

As a feminist educational researcher, I search amongst the preponderance of male research on political science, international relations and economic theory for feminist analyses and understandings. There are very few, but those I find, for example Nancy Folbre (1992), Wendy Harcourt (1994), Kimberley Hutchings (1996) and Ankie Hoogvelt (1997), provide both a much needed critique of the supposedly gender-free (male) analyses, while at the same constructing new feminist theory.[3] Another difficulty arises as I search postcolonial theory, for while feminists are far more easily found here, the focus of their study (and that of male postcolonialists) tends more towards literature and art than sociology. Finally, I draw gratefully on the work of those few feminist educationalists concerned with the relationship of education to globalization (see for example, Seddon 1994; Cruikshank 1995; Ghosh 1996; Willis and Kenway 1996; and Blackmore 1997).

Although the global context of this book may appear all-encompassing, its focus is in fact quite specific. For example, in choosing the regionalized blocs of APEC, NAFTA, ASEAN and the EU, I necessarily exclude many other countries, such as those of Africa, the Indian subcontinent, South America, eastern Europe and the Middle East. Furthermore, in the European Union section of this book, I continue to restrict my concern to education and training policy, resisting the temptation to wander further than is necessary into the adjoining field of social policy. I omit what, from my educational perspective, are less pivotal documents, and may therefore appear to minimize the influence of some social policy, or of policy-making and policy-influencing actors, because my interest here is not actually with the policy-making process nor with the policy makers and influencers (such as those focused on by Ball 1994a) but with the relationship between education and training policies, the construction of regionalized blocs and globalization.

The language of globalization is particularly difficult and unwelcoming, for it is predominantly that of economics, political science and international relations. It is a patriarchal language that tends to exclude people, and where they are included, with the obvious exception of the rare feminist in these fields, such as Hutchings (1996), Peterson (1992) and Tickner (1992), people means 'men'. Furthermore, the language of regionalized blocs include numerous acronyms and I although I try to keep these to a minimum, they, unavoidably, remain peppered throughout the text. An aid is provided in the abbreviations list. I try, where possible, to 'translate' the language of policy, which is often dense and obscure. I struggle with it, searching for the gaps, the silences and the slight textual movements that signify shifts in policy, for it is these slight textual shifts that consequently affect the education and training provision, the opportunities and choices available, and the arenas for agency and struggle of the unemployed working-class women.

In exploring globalization and global regionalization, I have tried to keep individual black and white working-class women in my mind, to ask myself what does this mean for her or her?[4] How does this affect their lives? Does it restrict it? What are the opportunities within it? And, of course, how can they resist, adapt or use it for themselves? There have been times when the enormity of globalization, the dominance of economic analyses, the absence of people, the coldness of the language, have made it difficult to maintain this link to the individual – reaching out through the fog for contact. There have been other times when the presence of individual working-class women has been a strong sustaining and critical force, with me as I read or write.[5]

Globalization and women of the working classes

One of the effects of globalization is increased unemployment and an increase in unstable, insecure, employment (Bergsten and Noland 1993; Harcourt 1994). Working-class women provide a never-ending global supply of the cheapest, most 'flexible' labour. The impact of these changes has not been confined to the 'working classes', or to low- and undereducated people. Within Britain, for example, there has been a steady increase in graduate unemployment, especially amongst the black working classes (HMSO 1996; Pool 1997). It is nevertheless, low- and undereducated people, and people with disabilities, migrants or immigrants that represent the largest categories of the long-term unemployed, with intense concentrations found in particular impoverished regions, and particular impoverished and ill-resourced areas of cities (Brown and Lauder 1992, 1997). In some regions and cities of the early industrialized nations, long-term unemployment is now a generational problem.

Reports, including the Council of Europe (1992) and the OECD (1992), have all shown that the undereducated and those with low educational attainment are most likely to become the long-term unemployed. The long-term unemployed are most likely to experience poverty and to be excluded from other areas of social, civil and political life (Ramprakash 1994). The racialized and classed occupational gendering of the labour market, combined with gendered, classed, state welfare policies, increase the likelihood of impoverished unemployment amongst women of the white and black working classes, of women with physical and learning disabilities, chronically ill women, and women migrants and immigrants.

I use the term 'undereducated' to signal first, a deeper educational consequence than that indicated by 'low- or underqualified' – a consequence that relates to the educational 'process' as well as to the quantifiable outcome, and second, to distinguish it from definitions and statistical indicators of functional illiteracy. Many young people, throughout the regionalized blocs, leave school with no, or few, qualifications, and increasing numbers are excluded from state schooling, or have no access to it in the first place (Wong and Cheung 1987; King and Hill 1993; Sewell 1994; Apple 1996). Young women, leaving school at the earliest opportunity with no or few qualifications, may, if they are lucky, find legal, paid employment. However, given their lack of qualifications, skills and experience, such employment within the global labour market is likely to be in service industries, to be very low paid, to have very little opportunity for further training or promotion, and to have very little security (Mitter 1986; Social Europe 1993, 1994a; OECD 1994).

Working-class women are a necessary part of the labour force; they provide cheap, flexible, easily discarded labour: from those women working in the horrific conditions of the free trade zones of the Philippines to those experiencing comparatively better conditions in the insecure, low-waged employment of the southern Welsh electronics factories. Despite the increasing provision of postcompulsory education and training for women, the relative and actual position of undereducated women of the working classes changes little. When referring to unemployed women I mean women who do not get paid legally for their labour – irrespective of the official unemployment classification of their country.

Although, for ease of reading I sometimes refer to 'working-class women', I try, wherever possible, to use the plural, 'women of the working classes', to refer to the numerous economic, cultural, national and social differences that exist between working-class women. In addition, woven across these are further significant differences based on (un)employment; not all working-class women are unemployed, and not all unemployed women are working-class. For instance there are differences between women in paid employment and those who are unemployed – differences between the numerous shades of economic activity whose distinctions are highly significant to the women concerned. Although within different countries these distinctions will reflect different common understandings and values, it is nevertheless possible to provide an understanding of the range of distinctions within working-class women's labour. Distinctions can be made between traditional and contemporary gendered working-class 'legal' employment, whether it is 'clean' or 'dirty' – office, factory or cleaning. Distinctions are then based on whether or not this is permanent, temporary, casual, shift, formal or informal employment, and whether it is full-time or part-time. There are as many distinctions to be made between the labour of unemployed women, based for example on whether the woman is engaged in paid work and whether this is informal, 'illegal' or semi-legal work, or unpaid work such as caring for dependants or neighbours, voluntary work or domestic work. Then there are women who are chronically ill or disabled and who may be unable to work, and finally there are women who are involved in education, training, or other pursuits and activities. However, despite these important distinctions, there are nevertheless, common characteristics such as undereducation, absence of economic and cultural capital, and, for those focused on in this book, unemployment.

Following her participation in a training programme, an unemployed woman may find legal, paid employment – generally within the service sector or the electronic manufacturing industries. For the majority of those who do, in all countries such work is, relative to that particular country, low-paid, insecure, generally part-time and with little prospect of advancement (OECD 1994). More often, however, the 'trained' unemployed woman will remain unemployed: training policies and programmes themselves do not *create* jobs, (Brine 1992; Nicaise *et al.* 1995). Unemployed single women, dependent on ever-decreasing rates of state welfare, from the most wealthy to the poorest of nation states, are undoubtedly poor. If living with or supported by a partner, women are dependent upon their partner's earnings and their own economic status may or may not reflect that of their partner. Unemployed working-class women frequently turn to other informal or illegal means of earning money such as cleaning, childcare, prostitution or drug dealing. Such women, along with unemployed (particularly working-class) men, are pathologically located within a concept of dependency (Fraser and Gordon 1994). Lone parents, certainly within the UK and the US, are a particular target for training programmes such as Welfare to Work and Workfare that are linked to benefit entitlement. Furthermore, within the EU, US, Canada, Australia and New Zealand (that is the colonizer and settler-colonized states) this gendered, racialized and classed concept of dependency is intricately linked not only with postcompulsory education and training policies but also with the discourse of equality. The discourse of equality is a dominant thread, to which, in the following chapters, I repeatedly return before finally drawing dependency, lone parents and equality together again in my conclusion.

Globalization and global regionalization

As I explore the concept of globalization I gingerly tread a path though the quicksand of economic determinism. The structures and processes of economic and cultural globalization and regional globalization are evident both nationally and locally. As I witness and even experience the constraining, and power maintaining, effects of economic globalization I also perceive and experience the struggle against it, and can even occasionally attest to and experience its benefits. Throughout this book I argue that neither regionalized blocs, nation states, educational providers nor individual women are passive to the forces of globalization, but actively struggle with, resist, accommodate, side-step, and even positively use, as well as sometimes collude with, its forces and effects. Policy, including that of the regionalized blocs, is not solid and absolute, but is shaped, manipulated, chiselled even, by the agency of policy makers, educators, groups and individuals (Blackmore and Kenway 1993; Ball 1994b).

In Chapters 2 and 3 I focus on differing definitions of globalization, and explore their connection with neoliberalism and neocolonialism. Whereas postcolonialism relates to the period after colonialism, and to an underside of colonialism, neocolonialism expresses a reworking of colonial relationships. In these new forms the state acts in its own colonization, facilitating the globalized exploitation of its labour and national resources. As well as encompassing the power structures between capital and state, and between state and state, neocolonialism also includes the power structures within regionalized and nation states. Within globalization, neocolonialism is intertwined with the free-market justifications of neoliberalism, and the impoverished position of working-class women, from the US to the Philippines, is maintained. Globalization is a gendered, classed and racialized process: a process that systematically subordinates different women in different ways.

Common features of globalization include economic and cultural globalization, global technology and global capital. In this book I focus on the gendered/classed social effects of globalization, and specifically on the spaces generated by the tension between economic globalization and the political agency of the state. For, as Bourdieu (1997) has said, different types and subtypes of capital structure the social world, constrain and inscribe its reality and govern its functioning. It is here that globalization becomes a contested concept. Globalization is frequently taken to imply the demise of the nation state, an economic determinism where overarching power is held in the hands of the transnational corporations (TNCs). Alternatively an understanding of the internationalization of capital maintains the nation state as a key player. I argue that, despite this contested terminology, the transnationalization of capital and the whittling away of many economic powers, the state (both regionalized and nation) continues to play a key role within the global economy – and within the lives of working-class women.

Neoliberalism legitimates the globalized free market and, at the same time, promotes the construction of a strong state. As the state's control of economics dwindles, so the need for its hold on social policy increases, especially in areas of welfare and education. This is one of the main reasons why nation states have entered into voluntary agreements with other nation states to form regionalized blocs. I discuss this, and other possible reasons, in Chapter 1. Global regionalization covers a spectrum of agreements from those simply of free trade agreements, such as the European Free Trade Association (EFTA), to that of the European Union (EU) which already includes social policy and European citizenship and is currently deciding on monetary union and military union – key functions of the nation state. Other blocs include those that I focus on in Chapter 1: the Association of South East Asian Nations (ASEAN), the North American Free Trade Association (NAFTA), and the Asia–Pacific Economic Cooperation (APEC).

Contemporary debates on education, training, unemployment and equality are framed by these global changes of the latter half of the twentieth century. There have been widespread demographic changes in both western and Asian–Pacific countries (Hao Li 1987; Eurostat 1992). Moreover, we are in the midst of a major technological revolution in which the ubiquitous impact of new and information technology has been felt globally, throughout the manufacturing, service and financial sectors (EC 1987a), causing a change in the means of production equalling that of the first western industrial revolutions (EC 1993a). These technological changes have generated a global change in the flow, and hence control, of capital – a change to 'late capitalism' related, Jameson (1984) argues, to postmodernism. Such changes in capital and production are key factors in globalization. This economic globalization is the context within which post-1945 global regionalization takes place. Moreover, it is these processes and effects of globalization that frame contemporary education provision – both compulsory and post-compulsory.

From their inception, regionalized blocs have expressed their need to develop a common education and training policy – initially within the post-compulsory sector, but later, as in the EU, moving into the compulsory sector as well. At first, education and training policy is framed by the 'human resources' argument of the economic discourse, that is the need to educate and train people for the needs of the labour market. This discourse is weakening as education and training policy is used as part of the bloc's overall social policy for addressing the effects of globalization – their increasing fear of 'social unrest'.

The structure of the book

My intention is to explore the connectedness between the themes of this book, rather than to go into any one of them in depth. From the opening focus on globalization, global regionalization and neocolonialism, I move to a more focused exploration of the education and training policies of the European Union, paying particular attention to the agency of femocrats (Eisenstein 1990), training providers, feminist activists, and individual unemployed women. There is a continual narrowing of focus, from the early chapters' concern with globalization, onto the regionalized bloc, then the nation state, training providers and unemployed women. In the final chapter I zoom out to reconsider the wider picture, to work towards an understanding of the relationship between globalization, global regionalization, education and training and working-class women.

Chapters 1 and 2 explore the theoretical background to globalization. I consider the debates surrounding the origins of globalization, the definitions of terms, and pull at some of the threads of globalization, regional globalization, neoliberalism and neocolonialism. These chapters will be particularly useful for those unfamiliar with the economic and political perspectives.

In Chapter 1 I begin by focusing on global regionalization. As I suggest by the title of this chapter, 'The unpeopled planet; global regionalization', people, both women and men, are surprisingly absent. I sketch a brief history of the development of ASEAN, APEC, NAFTA and the EU; developments that include the geopolitical as well as the economic. I follow this by considering the dominant discourses of economic growth and peace, focusing particularly on the shifts that have taken place within that of peace. I argue that it is in the interface between the discursive shifts of peace and economic growth that the regionalized bloc's social policy is generated – a social policy that includes education and training policy.

Chapter 2, 'Gendered, classed and racialized: globalization and neocolonialism', contains an exploration of the relationship of nation states, both within and between regionalized blocs. I begin this chapter by introducing the concept of globalization. I then turn to neocolonialism. Theories of neocolonialism provide a theoretical framework in which to explore the 'new' forms of power-relations between nation states as well as the racialized, gendered and classed relations within them. I begin the exploration, continued throughout this book, of a feminist perspective on neocolonialism. In the next section I consider the colonial history of regionalized blocs, and then I focus on the relationship between transnational corporations, the nation state and the regionalized bloc. I end this chapter by looking briefly at the global, gendered, labour market. Although I remain ambivalent as to whether or not the regionalized bloc is an attempt by nation states to collectively manage the effects of global capitalism, or whether it is an attempt by global capitalism to manage the nation states, the fact remains that the exclusively profit-centred focus of TNCs allows gender, class and race oppressions to flourish, between and within the nation state, having particularly vicious consequences for undereducated working-class women, consequences that are further compounded by race, ethnicity and disability.

Chapter 3 forms a bridge between these early theoretical chapters and the subsequent focus on the European Union. This is a key chapter, in which I introduce themes that are developed throughout the rest of the book: the welfare state, the pathologization of 'the unemployed' (linked to the concept of dependency) and most importantly, the discourse of equality – a key theoretical thread throughout the remaining chapters. In Chapter 3, 'The regionalized 'state' and working-class women', I explore the social consequences of globalization and global regionalization and reintroduce people, especially working-class women, into the picture. I begin this chapter by drawing on feminist theories of the state to consider the construction of the regionalized bloc as a 'state' – the regionalized state. In considering the transfer of powers from the nation state to the regionalized state, I explore the concepts of the imagined community, citizenship and nationalism. From here I focus on the social 'welfare' policy of this regionalized state, especially its relationship to unemployment, and in particular the pathologization of 'the unemployed' and the gendered, classed and racialized concept of dependency. I then turn to the education, training and equality policies of the regionalized state.

The European Union provides the focus for Chapters 4 and 5. They provide an in-depth analysis of the more theoretical concerns discussed in those early chapters. They are also the first steps in a trajectory analysis of European policy that continues through to Chapter 7. In Chapter 4, 'Educating unemployed women: the EU 'state', its discourses and competencies', I draw on the discourses of economic growth and peace that I introduced in Chapter 1 to explore the ways in which education and training policies are used in the construction of the EU. I argue that the European Union exists only through its discursive construction and that this construction remains fragile, particularly in the areas of tension that exist between the European Commission and the member states and between individual member states. The chapter includes an introductory exploration of two areas of EU legal competency that have a direct impact on the education and training policy for undereducated, unemployed women: first, the competencies for education and training (which includes the main training funded programme, the European Social Fund) and second, the competency for gendered equal opportunities. This leads me into an exploration of the discourse of equality in which I consider the difference between formal and material equality, the debate surrounding similarity and difference, and the relationship between unemployment and shifting equality discourse.

Chapter 5, 'Education, training and gender equality in the EU', provides a gendered/classed analysis of EC policy texts during the latter half of the twentieth century. This account of policy does not present an unproblematic historic progression but a series of changes that reflect many, often conflicting, interests, full of contest and compromise. I begin this chapter by focusing on the 'femocrats' who work within the European bureaucracy – particularly those of the Equal Opportunities Unit. In the following section I highlight the way in which each shift in the discourse and the policy represents a highly contested site. Yet, at these sites, the struggles for opportunity, and those of resistance, point not only to the agency of people but also to a shadow image of the constraints of the policy. My focus is then turned on the European Social Fund, which although the main source of funding for European unemployed women, is, I show, simply giving women the crumbs from the bakery. In the main section of this chapter I provide an historic overview to the development of European education and training policy, with, running alongside each of the four identified periods, an analysis of the impact of the equality discourse.

In Chapters 6, 7 and 8 I continue the trajectory analysis of the previous chapters by turning my focus away from the regionalized bloc and onto the nation state to consider the effect of the UK government on European education and training policy. The UK provides a useful example of the neoliberal state, for, with the exception of the US, it has, at the time of writing, the most deregulated and unprotected labour market of any of the OECD economies. Chapter 6, 'The "agency" of the nation state', is structured into the same four periods of policy as Chapter 5. I conclude each period with an analysis of the implications of the policy for British working-class women.

Chapter 7, 'Marginalizing women's training', is a case study of nation state implementation of policy in 1996, in which I focus on the agency of five UK administrative sectors to explore the discursive drift towards the marginalization of women's training.

In 'Gaps, spaces and complexities: educating feminists' (Chapter 8), I explore the agency of British women: the women providers of European-funded training and the unemployed working-class women who are students on these projects. In this chapter I concentrate on the 1983–93 period, and drawing on case studies of three separate projects I consider the role of feminist educators, and their involvement in basic and radical education. Feminist educators are not a homogeneous group and neither do they exist in a simple relationship to either the students or the state. The first half of this chapter considers their impact on the curriculum. In the second half I explore some of the differences and power-relationships that exist between these feminist activists: differences of class, sexuality, race, education and occupational status. Finally, the trajectory analysis of policy leads to unemployed working-class women, first through the workers' perceptions of them, and second, through the understandings of unemployed women themselves. The women of this chapter are contextualized by both the global and the local, yet they are passive in neither. They struggle with a shifting complexity of identities and power-relations, taking whatever opportunities are offered, often in ways unforeseen by the policy makers and interpreters. These women, workers and students, express their agency by finding the spaces and gaps in the policies and structures of the European and British state.

Finally, in 'Globalization, education and unemployment' (Chapter 9), I return to the theoretical concepts introduced in Chapter 2. Here I repeat my argument that, despite the overwhelming force of globalization, we should not be led into a deterministic reading where we ignore the many conflicting and collaborative interests, and the possibilities for opportunity and change as well as resistance. Although this includes recognizing the agency of the regionalized and nation state, there has been a strong argument throughout the book that suggests that the job of the state is to manage the unequal economic and social effects of globalization – to prevent the lid blowing off. It is from within this understanding that I return to the welfare state and the concept of dependency that I introduced in Chapter 3. I now explore the connection between education and training policy and the welfare state – particularly in respect to benefit-linked compulsory training programmes such as Project Work, Welfare to Work and Workfare. In the light of the continual patterns of unemployment resulting from globalization, and the predictions of even higher levels of structural unemployment (Rifkin 1995), I question the intention of such training programmes and conclude that not only, by continuing the discourse of dependency, are they punitive, but that they also enable the state to control its unemployed people. I focus on the recent state targeting of lone mothers to pursue a gendered analysis of such benefit-linked training programmes. The discourse of equality is found, yet again, to be a key player in the repositioning of lone mothers amongst the 'undeserving' poor.

I conclude the chapter and the book by considering the possibilities of future educational responses to globalization, arguing that the neoliberal emphasis on educational standards and quantifiable qualification outcomes is in itself no answer, for even if all people left compulsory education extremely well qualified, other criteria would be used in the distribution of what, undoubtedly, will remain limited employment. Moreover, the evidence suggests that such criteria would continue to maintain and reflect the existing gendered, classed and racialized power structures. My conviction is that the social structure is neither a given, nor inevitable; it is a structure made of choices – and because this is so, such choices can be challenged. Therefore the task of educators is to encourage a critical engagement with, and questioning of, our world, and to demand accountability for the choices and decisions that are made.

Notes

1 See Gaby Weiner (1994) for an overview of feminisms and education.
2 Similar arguments on the white dominance of feminist theory have been made by black women (hooks 1982).
3 I take the feminist concept of 'critique and construct' from Sneja Gunew (1990).
4 In the struggle against long lists of descriptors I have decided on the expression, 'black and white'. While this would of course be totally inappropriate as a descriptor of the many racial and ethnic global differences between women, I prefer it to the potentially essentialist use of 'woman' in the hope that it will repeatedly signal racial and ethnic difference and power relations.
5 Skeggs (1997: 167) refers to this as the 'dialogic other'.

I The unpeopled planet: global regionalization

I begin my exploration of the theoretical background of globalization by focusing on global regionalization: the groupings of nation states which mutually agree to enter a voluntary relationship with each other in order to foster their joint economic and geopolitical interests. The first section of this chapter introduces feminist theories of international relations. In the following section I sketch a brief history of the development of regionalized blocs, which leads me to consider the dominant discourses of economic growth and peace. I then focus on the discursive shifts that have taken place within this discourse of peace. I conclude by exploring the interface between the shift in the discourses of peace and economic growth, arguing that it is here that the social, education and training policy of regionalized blocs is generated.

Feminist theories of international relations

As the title of this chapter suggests, within international relations people are surprisingly absent – we appear to inhabit an unpeopled planet. Kimberley Hutchings (1996), however, is not surprised by this. She traces the philosophical basis of the discipline of international relations back to Kant and his distinction between morality and politics. From this she argues that international relations theorists have tended to fall into two camps: the realists and the idealists. The realists believe that in an amoral and anarchic world the relations between nation states are based on self-interest and struggles for power and security; the idealists see an eventual world order of peace and cooperation within which interstate relations change as we progress towards the ideal. Postmodern and critical theorists critique both, while at the same time accuse each other of continuing the tradition of postmodernists as realists, and critical theorists as idealists. Yet Hutchings argues that they have all dismissed the work of feminists working in this field, presenting international relations and its concepts as ungendered, and assuming that the gendered identity of theorists is irrelevant.[1] On the other hand, feminist theorists, such as Hutchings (1996: 179) argue that:

> inter-state relations are governed by a complex of economic, social, legal and political relations which are structured in ways that confirm women in positions of subordination and are, in turn, kept in place by that subordination.

Hutchings identifies three conceptions of feminist theory of international relations. The first adds a feminist perspective to the existing masculinist one, as in the work of Tickner (1992). The second, such as Brown (1988) uses gender as a means to analyse the deep underlying structures of global inequalities. Peterson (1992) provides an example of the third perspective which focuses on the differences and power relations between women. Echoing my own thoughts, Hutchings (1996: 183) states:

> the idea of a single feminine gendered identity as a basis for either understanding or practice simply does not make sense. Moreover, the claim to such an identity both masks and confirms global hierarchies of power.

While my attempt to place women (especially working-class women) and social policy (especially education and training policy) within the global context is pursued throughout this book, in this particular chapter it is unavoidable that women are, for the most part, absent. This reflects the academic discipline of international relations, the operations of global economics and finance and the gendering of global power. The vast majority of world leaders, of governments and officials, of the presidents and boardrooms of transnational corporations are men. While, on one hand, my title for this chapter – unpeopled – is correct, it is also misleading. The actors behind the construction of regionalized blocs are overwhelmingly male. While it may appear unpeopled, it is nevertheless, heavily gendered.

Global regionalization

The story begins in the immediate aftermath of the Second World War. In the 1940s, an attempt was made to set up an International Trade Organization, (ITO). Evident within this embryonic ITO are the two dominant discourses within regionalized blocs: economic growth, in this case global, and peace between previously economically competitive and warring nations. The ITO itself did not materialize, but the General Agreement on Tariffs and Trades (GATT) set up as an interim measure, still exists to promote global free trade. Although the GATT can be seen as a postwar modernist attempt to construct unifying rules and regulations for the global economy, the postwar global economies have not developed as one grand design but are complex and diverse, reflecting differing stages of industrialization and economic growth and differing philosophies and ideologies. Underlying both GATT and regionalization is the post-1945 recognition of global economic inter-dependence. Although currently the GATT aims of multilateralism and global free trade are experiencing difficulties, global regionalization is increasing along with additional trade agreements between blocs, such as, for example, the EU–ASEAN agreement, signed in 1980.

Regionalization rarely involves only newly industrialized countries, relationships generally being formed between newly industrialized and highly industrialized countries – a contemporary power-relationship that reflects, as I will explore in Chapter 2, their colonial past. The following thumbnail sketches of each regionalized bloc shows the dominant discourses of economic growth and peace each playing a major part in their construction. Appendix I shows the countries involved in each of these blocs.

The European Union (EU)

Postwar Europe wanted to rebuild the devastated economy and prevent a third European war. The European Economic Community (EEC) was the first agreement (EC 1957). Several countries, including the UK, Sweden and Switzerland which had not joined the EEC, established instead the European Free Trade Association (EFTA 1960). There has been a steady decline of EFTA as countries have left to join the EEC, and in 1993, those remaining EFTA countries joined with the EU to form a joint European Economic Area (EEA). The expansion of the EEC from its original six member states (see Appendix I) has continued to its present membership of 15, and it is pre-dicted that by the early twenty-first century the now renamed European Union could consist of 25 member states or more (EC 1997a).

There are interesting differences between the EEC and EFTA. EFTA is a free trading area. On the other hand, while the EEC's concern was also econ-omic, there was also, from the beginning, a concern for social cohesion: interstate equality as a means of maintaining peace, a 'preoccupation with collective security and geopolitical stabilization . . . especially *vis-à-vis* Ger-many' (Wallace and Wallace 1996: 17). As well as this concern with inter-state peace, the EEC was also concerned with maintaining peace with non-EEC states, especially the communist states of Eastern Europe.

Association of South East Asian Nations (ASEAN)

In 1967, in the Asia–Pacific region, five countries established ASEAN: Indonesia, Malaysia, the Philippines, Singapore and Thailand. ASEAN has now expanded to a membership of seven countries with Brunei Darussalam joining in 1984 and Vietnam in 1995, and the possibility of further expansion to ten. Significantly, amongst regionalized blocs, the countries of ASEAN are all emergent, newly industrializing countries that do not include the three strongest economies of the region: Japan, Taiwan and Hong Kong. The three main objectives of ASEAN again reflect the dominant discourses of economic growth and peace (internal and external). These objectives are: economic growth, protection from larger or more affluent capitalist or communist powers, and the peaceful resolution of differences between member countries.

North American Free Trade Association (NAFTA)

In 1992 the North American Free Trade Agreement was signed by Mexico, Canada and the US. Although initially NAFTA appears concerned only with economic growth and free trade, the discourse of peace is nevertheless also present, but it takes a different form to that of ASEAN and the EU. Unlike the EU, NAFTA does not attempt to address the inequalities between its member states, but instead formalizes it – building, as will be seen in later discussions, the inequality that exists between Mexico and the US/Canada into its structure. Despite promoting economic growth and political pluralism in Mexico, the discourse of internal peace operates, for example, by strengthening the Mexican borders.

Asia–Pacific Economic Cooperation (APEC)

Established in 1989, the Asia–Pacific Economic Cooperation, is emerging as the most likely, and to date the most powerful, of the Pacific blocs:

> APEC's great potential rested on the fact that its membership included not only the small economies in the region, but also the three giants [US, China and Japan], whose economic performance and triangular relationships would greatly affect all, regardless of any institutional configuration. In addition, APEC provided the United States – which remained a major source of dynamism in the region – a mechanism to focus its renewed interest in East Asian economies and involve it in Pacific affairs.
>
> (Janadas 1994: 61)

APEC is important because it includes all the major countries of the region and the most dynamic and fastest growing economies in the world. Its objectives, as stated in the Seoul 1991 Declaration, are exclusively economic: to reduce trade barriers amongst APEC members, and then amongst the rest of the world (APEC 1991). Although it refers to the free flow of goods, services, capital, investment and technology, like NAFTA, it does not refer to the free movement of people. Three years later, APEC recognized the need to address the economic inequalities between the member countries (APEC

1994). Some theorists such as Hufbauer and Schott (1993) predict a global economy focused around two major competing blocs, the EU and APEC, whereas others, such as Roger Thompson (1994) are less convinced. Although the discourse of economic growth is a strong feature within APEC, I will argue later in this chapter that the discourse of peace is also a major force, expressed primarily through the US presence within the region.

The dominant discourses of economic growth and peace

It is neither possible nor desirable to make straightforward comparisons between the different economic blocs, for each contains a variety of cultures and histories, conflicts and agreements. Even the expression of capitalism itself differs within the blocs as well as between them (Whalley 1993; Hutton 1995). Yet there are certain characteristics that they all address, albeit in different ways and at different times within their development.

Throughout this foray into global regionalization, the spectres of the twentieth century lurk amongst the language of economic growth, free trade, peace and cooperation: the fear of communism and postcommunism, the fear of fascism, the legacies of global colonial history and US economic and cultural expansionism.

It is useful to imagine a continuum of global regionalization with exclusive trade agreements at one end (for example EFTA) through to social, political, and monetary union at the other end (for example the EU). While each regionalized bloc makes repeated early reference to economic growth, I argue that this is not the sole determining factor in their development, for as Devan Janadas (1994: 65) writes:

> there was hardly anything 'economic' about regional economic groupings. Regional groupings were formed primarily for geopolitical and security reasons, with economic cooperation functioning as a means rather than an end.

Whether these blocs are economically or geopolitically determined, they are clearly interlinked. A useful definition of the discourse of peace includes geopolitical and security/defence interests. The powerful Second World War powers of Japan and Germany have since developed into major economic powers within the Asia–Pacific region and Europe. Similarly, the Asia–Pacific region and Europe have been bordered by powerful communist states. The Second World War and the Cold War have been factors in the development of both regions. Therefore, as well as concerns of external peace, the discourse also includes internal peace, that is, between the member states. Thus, at the heart of global regionalization are these dominant discourses of economic growth and peace. It is at the interface of these that education, training, equality and other social policies are generated.

This concern with external peace, and interstate internal peace is evident in the EU and ASEAN. These, along with APEC, are now considered.

The European Union (EU)

Within Europe, a major concern of the EEC in the immediate postwar period was the perceived external threat from the eastern communist states and, following the tearing down of the Berlin Wall in 1989, the internal need to integrate the Federal Republic of Germany. The founding Treaty (EC 1957) was concerned that no one member state should gain unfair economic advantage over another, the aim being cohesion between member states, with the European Commission (EC) redistributing finances to support the development of the less industrialized or economically threatened countries, regions and social groups.[2] However, despite this intention, significant differences in labour costs are present between the member states, where workers in Germany and Denmark are paid, on average, more than three times as much as those in Greece, five times that of Portugal, and UK workers receive approximately two-thirds that of Danish workers (Ramsay 1995). Women workers in all these countries continue to earn approximately two-thirds of their male equivalents (van Doorne-Huiskes *et al.* 1995).

Association of South East Asian Nations (ASEAN)

While the original peace discourse of ASEAN acknowledged the threat from neighbouring communist countries including the Soviet Union, this threat was not seen by those in the region to be as great a threat as was supposed by the Europeans (Wanandi 1987: 164). Of at least equal concern to ASEAN was the US presence – military, cultural and commercial. It is argued that the primary purpose of ASEAN was political, a consequence of the Cold War, in which economic cooperation was used to serve the overriding objective of regional security. Economic cooperation was, it is argued, a means and not an end in itself (Palmer and Reckford 1987; Janadas 1994).

Asia–Pacific Economic Cooperation (APEC)

Post-Cold War, in the EU and ASEAN, the discourse of external peace has, to some extent, decreased. However, it may be that it is the perceived *absence* of the external Cold War threat, rather than its presence, which has been a significant factor in the development of APEC. Previously the Cold War had provided the US with a reason for its post-1945 presence in the area, and with this removed, a new rationale is constructed for its continued presence. Furthermore, the expansion of Japan has increased its tension with the US, and has led Thompson (1994) for example, to question Japan's future acceptance of US leadership in the region. It is this need for peace *between* the countries of APEC which, given its size and the power of several of the countries involved, is one of the key features of its construction, particularly in relation to the history, the nationalism, the economic power of Japan and their past relationship with the US. While cultural diversity is, of course, a factor in both ASEAN and the EU, the cultural diversity within APEC is considerable, and the criteria for membership is questionable. Australia and New Zealand are undoubtedly, geographically, part of the Asia–Pacific region, yet their membership of APEC has been questioned both by other APEC members such as Malaysia who question their appropriate 'Asian-ness' and, on the other hand, by an emerging anti-Asian discourse within Australia itself. Peace *between* the member countries is, at this early stage, the dominant peace discourse of APEC.

The shifting discourse of peace: from external to internal

Towards the end of the twentieth century the dominant peace discourse in the EU and ASEAN is that of internal peace within and across their member states, whereas that of the much newer APEC is concerned with peace *between* the member states.

The European Union (EU)

Towards the end of the 1980s the EU became concerned at the possible threat of social unrest from within and across the member states. Key policy documents of the early 1990s highlight the perceived direct relationship between economic growth and social stability.[3] Policies begin to address the social consequences of long-term unemployment, poverty and regional inequality. Furthermore, this initial concern with internal social unrest is now linked to the reshaped external threat to peace: the rise of fascism, from within both the postcommunist states and the EU (Hockenos 1993; EC 1994a; Social Europe 1995).

Association of South East Asian Nations (ASEAN)

Whereas in the late 1960s, the internal peace of postcolonial ASEAN had been threatened by insurgencies, subversion and infiltration from separatist, religious or communist movements (Wanandi 1987: 144), the current threat to peace is, ironically, successful economic growth. This new threat arises partly as a result of people's demand for an improved lifestyle, better education and increased involvement in democratic processes, and partly from the poverty that accompanies economic growth.[4]Economic growth has affected ASEAN's demography; it has led to an emergent and vocal middle class, a very high rate of urbanization, and growing urban poverty that is particularly vicious towards women (WIDE 1996).[5] There is increased internal unrest, increased differentials in health and mortality rates, and an unequal distribution of resources closely linked to ethnic difference:[6]

> Given the ethnic diversity in the region and the past history of ethnic conflicts that have periodically erupted into violence, the spectre of economic slowdown is indeed a very dark cloud on ASEAN's horizon.
>
> (Wong and Cheung 1987: 34)

The inequalities in the distribution of wealth within and between the member states is leading to demands for social and political intervention at the ASEAN level and also to a change of interest in education and training policy. A greater emphasis on cultural and racial tolerance is replacing the earlier focus on 'human resources'.

From mid-1997 the region's fears of a stagnating economy leading to serious unrest are increasing as the domino effect from Thailand's forced currency devaluation in July sweeps through the region, leading in November to South Korea's reluctant request to the International Monetary Fund for help, to the collapse of one of Japan's strongest financial institutions, Yamaichi, and to subsequent fears of a global recession.

Although there are definite similarities between the concerns of ASEAN and the EU over possible social unrest, it does not mean that ASEAN will mirror the development of the EU, but rather it will reflect, albeit within the global economic and political realities, the particularities of the ASEAN countries. The greater cultural, philosophical and ideological diversity within the Asia–Pacific region may be compared with the EU, which is seen as sharing 'a common cultural core and geographical proximity [which] make political and economic integration a greater possibility' (Hao Li 1987: xvi).

Asia–Pacific Economic Cooperation (APEC)

The concern with internal unrest is also part of APEC's discourse. At the second meeting of its leaders, held in Bogor, Indonesia (APEC 1994), diversity among member states was discussed. The industrialized countries pledged 'opportunities' in which the newly industrialized countries could increase their economic growth, for which, they in their turn pledged to aim for high growth rates (APEC 1995). APEC is a young organization. It includes countries diverse culturally, economically and ethnically. The peace discourse is in its early stages and, recognizing the economic differences between the member countries, it attempts to address the more obvious inequalities that might threaten peace. Although APEC's discourse of peace does not, yet, include the threat within and across the member states, racial and ethnic unrest, linked to migration, unemployment and neocolonial relations, is a growing problem within individual member states – for instance, within some of the ASEAN members of APEC, the US and Australia. Pauline Hanson's Australian nationalist campaign against Aboriginal positive action and Asian immigration is both gaining increasing support and provoking heated, and sometimes violent, protest.[7]

The shifting discourse of peace

This change in the discourse of peace from the initial focus on difference *between* member states, to inequality *within and across* them, is linked to the dominant discourse of economic growth, and the resulting processes of industrialization and urbanization. 'Successful' industrialization and economic growth not only creates wealth and a middle class, but also generates social inequality and poverty. The extent and depth of such inequality is the basis of social unrest, and social unrest threatens economic growth, hence the concern of nation and regionalized states. Per Magnus Wilkjman (1993) sees greater involvement in social and political policies as a 'deepening' of the regionalized bloc. Such deepening is a response to the dominant discourses of both economic growth and peace.

Addressing internal, or external, threats to the regionalized blocs, is reliant upon a hegemonic base – a shared philosophy or ideology, enough common ground on which to develop and ratify a collective social and political strategy. The extent to which the bloc moves along the continuum, away from a pure trading association towards social and political unity, is possibly linked to the degree of shared industrialization as well as a common history and understanding of the culture of the countries involved.

Conclusion

I have concentrated in this chapter on the construction of regionalized blocs. There are two themes that emerge: first, their global context, and second their dominant discourses of growth and peace. Regionalized blocs are seen as both a reaction to, and a constitutive part of, globalization. They are as concerned with geopolitical security (between and beyond the countries of the bloc) and the maintenance of neocolonial power, as they are with economic free trade and growth.

The dominant discourses in the construction of regionalized blocs are those of economic growth and peace. There is a tendency, in the discourse of peace, for a shift from the original concern with external peace (including peace between the bloc's own member states) to a growing concern with internal peace – that is peace within and across (rather than between) member states.

The education and training policies of regionalized blocs are located in the interface between the dominant discourses of economic growth and peace. Moreover, it is the shifts in the discourse of peace that reflect and constitute the bloc's increased involvement in social, education and training policy. Chapter 3 returns to these regionalized blocs to explore their increasingly interlinked policies, and to consider their implications for undereducated women of the working classes.

Notes

1 Hutchings (1996) lists the following feminists theorizing international relations: Brown (1988); Enloe (1989); Grant and Newland (1991); Peterson (1992) and Tickner (1992).
2 The European Social Fund is the Structural Fund targeted on people, and this is explored in depth in Chapter 5 of this book.
3 These key documents include the White Paper on Growth, Competitiveness, Employment (EC 1993a), the White Paper on Social Policy (EC 1994a) and the White Paper on Education and Training (EC 1995a). I consider these Papers in Chapter 5.
4 The effects of economic growth within ASEAN are described by Hao Li (1987), Martin (1987), Wanandi (1987) and Wong and Cheung (1987).
5 For example in the Philippines, in 1990, women earned only 30 per cent of the total income (Network Women in Development Europe (WIDE 1996)).
6 For an example of the diversity within an individual ASEAN country see Floresca-Gawagas (1996) for an account of the Philippines.
7 In the 1996 Federal Elections Pauline Hanson was elected for Oxley, Queensland. She made her maiden speech to Parliament on Tuesday 10 September 1996 and formed her own One Nation party the following April. Numerous branches of the party have since been established across Australia. The prime goal of the One Nation party is to stop all immigration to Australia, except that related to investment, until all Australian unemployment is solved, and to abolish divisive and discriminatory practices, such as those attached to aboriginal and multicultural affairs. An up-to-date account of the One Nation party and of opposing views can be found by searching 'Pauline Hanson' on the internet.

2 Gendered, classed and racialized: globalization and neocolonialism

In this chapter I explore the relationships of nation states, both within and between regionalized blocs. Globalization links distant localities together so that an occurrence in one part of the world can have a direct effect on another part (Giddens 1990). Common features of globalization include economic and cultural globalization, global technology and global capital. At any time, different types and subtypes of capital structure the social world, constrain and inscribe its reality and govern its functioning (Bourdieu 1997). While this chapter focuses on these and related structures of economic globalization, it gingerly treads a path though the quicksand of economic determinism. Although in subsequent chapters I will argue that, within the context of economic globalization, nation states, educational providers and unemployed women are active agents, at times struggling, accommodating, using and side-stepping the structures of economic globalization, it must be conceded that the threat of economic determinism continues nevertheless to lurk within this chapter.

It begins by introducing the concept of globalization and is devoted to theories of neocolonialism which I have found to be a useful theoretical framework for understanding the social aspects of globalization and from which to introduce a gendered analysis of education and globalization. The colonial history of regionalized blocs is the subject of the third section, which is followed by a discussion on the relationship between transnational corporations (TNCs), the nation state and the regionalized bloc. It considers the state within globalization, and more particularly the role of the regionalized 'state', and finally the global, gendered labour market.

Globalization

Anthony Giddens (1990) identifies two main strands of literature relating to globalization: first is that of international relations where the emphasis is on the nation state as an actor and where social relations can only take place between such actors. As Chapter 1 has shown, the field of international relations is generally assumed by the dominant male theorists to be an ungendered field of study. Second is the literature that develops a theory of a world system, a world capitalist economy in which capitalism is always linked to the world economy rather than linked to nation states. This latter approach focuses solely on economic influences and, ignoring nation states, treats the TNCs as the dominant actors. It is in this arena, emerging from the tension between economic globalization and the political agency of the state, that we can, as Bauman (1992) suggests, sociologically explore the spaces between nation states.

Giddens identifies four interlinking dimensions of globalization: the world capitalist economy, the international division of labour, the world military order and the nation state system, to which he subsequently adds cultural globalization. Each of these four dimensions are male dominated, especially within the power-holding and decision-making positions, with women generally playing at best a supporting role but more frequently restricted to minor and subservient positions.

Building on the work of Benedict Anderson (1983) and focusing primarily on the global cultural economy, Arjun Appadurai's (1993) exploration of globalization as a complex transnational construction of imaginary land-scapes provides a welcome alternative to the theories of international relations and global economics. Moreover, these landscapes, it is argued, can be contested and even subverted. The five landscapes are: ethnoscapes, technoscapes, finanscapes, mediascapes and ideoscapes, relating respectively to people, technology, finance, media and ideologies.

Appadurai (1993) argues that these perspectival landscapes reflect the history, language and politics of the different actors, from nation states, TNCs, diasporic communities, social groups and individuals. A messy, chaotic picture is drawn, where overlapping and conflicting interests shift, accommodate and struggle against each other in varying ways, at varying times and in different locations. This messy picture shows that although globalization uses many instruments of homogenization it does not actually or unproblematically result in homogenization. Moreover, capital itself is not a straightforward organizing structure, but is 'disorganized', or as Will Hutton (1995) calls it, 'unfettered'. Appadurai (1993: 328) defines it as:

> a complex, overlapping, disjunctive order which cannot any longer be understood in terms of existing centre-periphery models (even those which might account for multiple centres and peripheries). Nor is it susceptible to simple models of push and pull (in terms of migration theory), or of surpluses and deficits (as in traditional models of balance of trade), or of consumers and producers (as in most neo-Marxist theories of development).

The five landscapes are intricately interwoven. Technological globalization (omitted from Giddens's model) results from changes in the means of production and in the movement of capital (Hutton 1995; Amin 1997) and is intricately intertwined with the economic and the cultural.

It is important, at this point, to consider the multifaceted complexities of cultural globalization, referred to by Schiller (1976) as cultural imperialism. Cultural imperialism ensures that postcolonized nations remain attached to their colonizers, the old forms of inequality reinforced not only by the TNCs but also by less tangible means. In their critical overview of the study of cultural imperialism, Phil Golding and Phil Harris (1997: 7) see the dynamics of such imperialism as highly complex, but conclude that in its various forms it nevertheless remains 'deeply and starkly inegalitarian', simply 'papering over' the inequalities of race, ethnicity, gender and class.

While it is possible to identify various aspects of cultural imperialism, in practice they are not such distinct features and all are closely interwoven with economic globalization, technology and global military powers. First, and probably the most visible aspect of cultural globalization is that of the media: films, TV programmes, music (pop and classical) and, of course, advertisements. The media constructs not only the global market but is also a major aspect of the hegemonic (essentially US) and predominantly youth, culture. The second aspect of cultural globalization relates to the actual depiction of the world: the maps we use, especially the Eurocentric Mercator's projection where the boundaries themselves reflect intercolonial rivalries and deals.[1] Third is ideology, which is often directly political and is generally related to the nation state or to counter-ideologies trying to vest state-power.

All these aspects of cultural globalization, particularly ideology, are closely linked to neocolonialism and US imperialism. Golding and Harris (1997) argue that global culture is in fact simply the transnationalization of a very national voice – that of the United States. Marxist theorists such as Chronis Polychroniou (1995) see US imperialism as an attempt at global supremacy, a part of their desire for overseas expansion. Two of the crucial and frequently used structures in the post-1945 development of US imperialism are the World Bank (1944), which gave the US increased financial control, and the Truman Doctrine (1947), which gave it 'the right to intervene in order to protect "free" peoples from communist subversion' (Polychroniou 1995: 59). Philip McMichael (1995: 39) suggests that in using GATT, the World Bank and NAFTA, the US has attempted to 'consolidate a post-national order', where other nation states 'submit to the rules and culture of the global market on a world scale'. The current key debate between economic globalization versus the interests of the state is focused around these concerns of neocolonialism and US imperialism.

Education (Gramsci's (1971)'domination by consent') is the fourth aspect of cultural imperialism and is a major component of neocolonialism and imperialism. Thus education, Philip Altbach (1995) argues, contributes to the continuing inequality between colonizing and colonized states, but is frequently ignored. Annabelle Sreberny-Mohammadi (1997) adds that western 'knowledge', values, culture, and taste for western lifestyles is exported/ imported through education where it is felt most keenly at the level of university education, and increasingly through 'distance education' and the transfer of western notions of 'professionalism'. The language of neocolonial education is overwhelmingly 'English' – within the curriculum, within international journals and during international conferences.[2] For example, even within the EU the dominance of English is both highly evident and highly contested. Adopted by the EU as a dominant working language along with French and German, English continues to dominate European academic conferences.[3] Similarly, 'English' is the language of the media, of products and of the internet.

The final aspect of cultural imperialism relates to what Appadurai (1993) called the ethnoscape, the landscape of persons who 'constitute an essential feature of the world and appear to affect the politics of (and between) nations to a hitherto unprecedented degree' (p. 329). These persons include, for example, immigrants, refugees, guestworkers, tourists, business people, academics, students, and frontier workers – some of whom are welcomed and some are not. Cultural imperialism within the ethnoscape is a concept soaked in xenophobia and racism. Floya Anthias (1995: 290) defines racism as being 'forms of ideology and practice that serve to inferiorize and exclude (or include in subordinate positions) all groups whose boundary is defined in terms of an ethnic or collective origin'.

The promotion of racial/ethnic exclusion is a key aspect of the construction of regionalized blocs; it is directly linked with economic globalization, and moreover, is a heavily gendered and classed practice. For example, within the landscape of people, cultural imperialism can lead, on one hand, to exclusion, or, as in the case of immigrants and guestworkers, to subordinated inclusion, and, on the other hand, to restricted invitation through tourism. Neocolonial tourism results in the commodification of 'traditional' culture where the ownership of 'the pleasure periphery' is held in Europe, North America and Japan (see Sreberny-Mohammadi (1997) for further analysis). A particular gendered feature of this expanding area of neocolonial tourism is the sex-tourism industry. For example, Swasti Mitter (1986: 65) argues that the process by which ASEAN women are sold to the West is yet another form of colonization. Working-class women of South-East Asian countries are advertised to western, especially European, men. Sex-tours provide the second or third most important source of foreign exchange in Thailand and the Philippines. In addition, particularly in European countries, South East Asian women are sold through illustrated colour catalogues from 'marriage bureaux'.

Moving away from a simple economic reading of globalization towards the greater complexity offered by Appadurai introduces other (albeit economically linked) aspects of globalization that affect working-class women's lives – notably restricted movement and prostitution. The oppressions of colonialism and patriarchy are interwoven with those of global capital, and reinforced by technological and cultural globalization, individually and jointly serving the interests of the rich and powerful. In this account of globalization, beneath the new drapings of global capitalism, cultural imperialism, global technology and the military, are the barely touched skeletal structures of patriarchy and colonialism. No matter which thread is pulled, it unravels to show the established sets of power relationships based on patriarchy, colonialism and imperialism.

Neocolonialism

Throughout the twentieth century, particularly the latter half, the vast majority of colonized nations have gained political independence. At this level then the nineteenth-century period of colonialism appears to have ended. However, the economic and political power of the colonizers remains, aided and abetted by economic and cultural globalization and by military and financial power. Theories of neocolonialism provide a means for understanding the late twentieth-century power structures that exist between supposedly free and independent nation states. McMichael (1995: 37) considers neocolonialism to be a postnational phase of world capitalist history, one in which the 'late twentieth century *nation*-states, the regulators of territories and peoples, are being colonized' – colonized by capital. From his perspective as a political economist he argues that postcolonized nation states have surrendered their powers of economic control and have collaborated in dismantling public assets and facilities.[4] This undermines their control of social democracy and exposes their political processes and economies to the global market. This also leaves them vulnerable to both internal ethnic separatism and external pressures from the TNCs and other states. As their nation state control subsides, the power of the major economic nations such as the US, Japan and Europe, increases. This means that the postcolonized states now face a new form of colonization, quite different from that which preceded it. Moreover, the state itself increasingly facilitates the exploitation of its national labour and resources.

Vijay Mishra and Bob Hodge (1993) distinguish between two of the main perspectives on late twentieth-century colonialism: post-colonialism and postcolonialism (unhypenated). In their usage, post-colonialism relates specifically to the period after colonialism, whereas postcolonialism is an always present underside of colonialism, which is neither an homogeneous category nor a static one, but is always in the process of change. Preferable, however, is the concept of neocolonialism, first because it suggests the significant ending of an earlier form of colonialism (overt, military and civic occupation) and its replacement by a 'new' political and economic form in which the postcolonized state maintains the supply of labour, the production of goods, social stability and market place for consumption. Second, it recognizes the complexity within colonial relations, for as well as describing these new forms of power-relations between nation states, it also describes the racialized, gendered and classed relations within them. In this way it recognizes the lack of homogeneity between and within nation states and provides a theoretical framework with which to study the neocolonial relationship between states and the neocolonial relationships within the diversity of states such as the UK and US. Third, neocolonialism shares some important characteristics with theories of feminism. They both have distinct political agendas for social change and they both have a theory of agency that allows them to go beyond postmodern deconstruction into the realms of social and political action. Yet neocolonialism provides only a partial theory of global gendered power-relations and therefore needs to incorporate other perspectives, such as that of feminism.

From this emergent feminist neocolonial perspective, it is possible to discern a multidimensional, ever-shifting dance of power, struggle, accommodation and resistance between regionalized blocs and nation states and within individual states; the numerous dancers move, coming together variously, in the guise of states, groups and individuals, at different times and for different reasons.

The colonial history of regionalized blocs

The legacies of global colonial history and US economic and cultural expansionism stalk the study of global regionalization. Although each regionalized bloc reflects its geographical location, and although this may, at first, appear unproblematic, evidence of colonialism nevertheless persists. In the immediate post-1945 literature, countries such as Indonesia, Malaysia, the Philippines and Japan were located within east Asia, and their own self identification was with south-east Asia, an identity reflected in ASEAN – the Association of South East Asian Nations (see Figure 2.1). In the early 1990s, NAFTA (see Figure 2.2), looking towards the Pacific from its eastern edge, perceived the location of the countries of ASEAN and Japan as the western Pacific and not south-east Asia. This perception links the countries of ASEAN and Japan across the Pacific to its eastern edge, to the west coast of America, and away from Asia – away from China to the north and India to the west. The subsequent development of APEC includes the remaining countries of the south-west Pacific, New Zealand, Australia, China and Papua New Guinea and, from the south-east Pacific, Chile. Figure 2.3 shows the countries of APEC circling the Pacific Rim, with the US Hawaiian Islands strategically located in mid-Pacific.

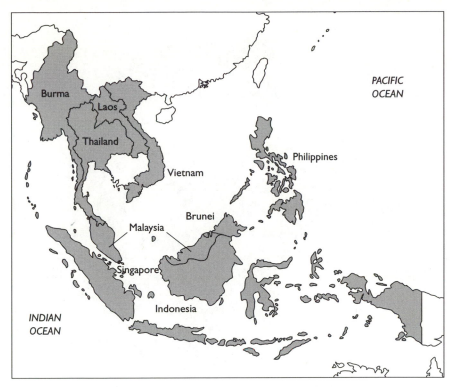

Figure 2.1 Association of South East Asian Nations (ASEAN)

While APEC looks out from its land masses across the Pacific ocean, the EU is, at first sight, unproblematically defined by the continent of Europe. However, this too is an indistinct area, with Turkey, a geographically non-European country an applicant for membership, and Israel, also geographically an Asian country, while not pursuing actual membership, nevertheless developing a close relationship.[5] Following the completion of the Intergovernmental Conference in 1997, several other countries, primarily from eastern Europe, were having their applications for membership considered.[6] This is illustrated by Figure 2.4.

The expansion of the European preferential trading area continues in other directions. For example, in 1997 the second Euro-Mediterranean conference was held, with the aim of further developing 'a framework for political, economic, cultural and social ties between the partners' (EC 1997b).[7] The broader Lomé Convention included a succession of treaties agreed during the previous 20 years or so between the European Union and 70 developing countries known collectively as the African, Caribbean and Pacific (ACP) states (Appendix II). The aim of this Convention was 'to promote and expedite the economic, cultural and social development of the ACP states, and to consolidate and diversify their relations in a spirit of solidarity and mutual

Figure 2.2 North American Free Trade Association (NAFTA)

interest' (EC 1996b). Unlike the imbalanced US–Mexico power-structure of NAFTA, the trade concessions within the Lomé Convention granted free access to the EU market, with further preferential treatment for the export of certain agricultural goods, such as sugar. However, this seemingly one-way flow of trade does not mean that these exporting countries are wealthy, in fact the reverse, as it is the importing countries of Europe, North America, Japan, and to a lesser extent, Australia and New Zealand, that benefit from the wealth of production in the ACP and ASEAN states. The ACP pact can thus be seen as another aspect of what Wanandi (1987: 162) describes as an 'international division of labour in industrialization, [where there are] deteriorating terms of trade for countries producing primary commodities'.

Prior to its anticipated twenty-first century expansion, the European Union was essentially a bloc of highly industrialized countries, the majority of whom were ex-colonial powers with a direct historic relationship to almost all other countries involved in ASEAN, NAFTA, APEC and the ACP. With the excep-

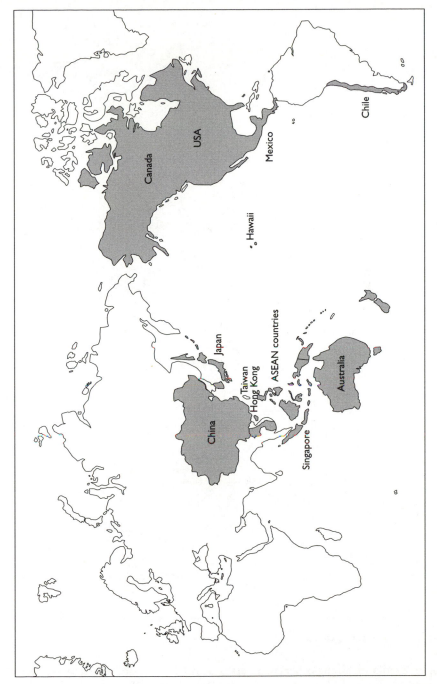

Figure 2.3 Asia-Pacific Economic Cooperation (APEC)

Figure 2.4 The European Union (EU)

tion of Thailand, all the other members of ASEAN were colonized by western countries, and with the exception of the Philippines, which gained independence from the US in 1946, the remaining five countries were colonized by

European countries: Indonesia gaining independence from the Netherlands in 1945–49, Vietnam from France in 1945; Burma, Malaysia and Brunei Darussalam gaining independence from Britain in 1947, 1963 and 1984 respectively. When Malaysia was left with a scattered federal system of 13 smaller states, its principal challenge was that of 'race relations' as a country consisting of 'a complex mix of races, religions and contending regional elites in what had been independent chiefdoms and sultanates' (Palmer and Reckford 1987: 30). In addition to colonization between Europe and the countries of ASEAN and APEC, there is also a history of colonization between ASEAN and APEC countries, such as the relatively recent (1905/10–1945) colonization of Korea by Japan.[8] The relations of colonialism must thus be related to an analysis of the current debate concerning globalization and the demise of the nation state.

The transnational corporation, the nation state and the regionalized bloc

A major concern within economic and political studies of globalization is the power relationship existing between transnational corporations (TNCs) and nation states. Some, such as Mitter (1986) and Ohmae (1990) see TNCs operating, with no allegiance, beyond the state. Will Hutton's (1995) 'unfettered capital' is 'virtually zapped' by computers around the money markets of the world, beyond the financial controls of the state. Such capital is mobile and will locate itself wherever it is able to gain the greatest economic return. Yet, whereas capital is mobile and 'free' of the state, labour remains located within the state, and high costs and protective legislation will result in unemployment as the TNCs go elsewhere. Theorists who identify global economic power in the hands of international finance markets and TNCs see their potential to dominate the world order, to subsume state economies within the global one. The most extreme arguments of globalization depict the demise of the nation state. Here, identifying exhaustive powers in the TNCs leads to a form of global economic determinism: a global order in which the nation state is inevitably malleable to the will of the TNCs.

Paul Hirst and Grahame Thompson (1995, 1996) and Philip McMichael (1995) however, dispute this concept of globalization and argue instead for a process of internationalization. They see labour and the market as global, but not the ownership and control of TNCs or the territory of the state. Phillip Brown and Hugh Lauder (1997) suggest that the relationship of TNCs to particular nation states is especially dominant. They argue that during the 1980s an estimated 700 American companies employed more than 340,000 workers in Singapore, Mexico and Taiwan alone, and similarly, 40 per cent of jobs created by British TNCs were overseas. The growth of TNC profits has been at a greater rate than even that of the US economy:

In 1975, the fifty largest industrial corporations worldwide had sales of $540 billion, and received $25 billion in profits. In 1990, sales figures for the top fifty had climbed to $2.1 trillion and their profits had reached $70 billion.

(Brown and Lauder 1997: 173)

Hirst and Thompson argue however that the international economy is governable and the economic processes and policies of the nation states are central to this. They see an 'internationalized economy' – one in which the companies trade from within a distinct national economy, and are therefore reliant on the state's regulation and protection of trade. Giddens (1990) also acknowledges the decreasing economic power of the state but sees it maintaining its power in the key areas of territory and military/policy power. TNCs are therefore closely linked and identified with the neocolonial order.

However, despite such important critiques of global TNC economic determinism, those who argue for internationalization also see the role of the state as a changed one, a role in which the state control of the economy has significantly decreased, to be increasingly relocated in the hands of the TNCs.[9] The Multilateral Agreement on Investment (MAI) that surfaced from its cloak of secrecy in 1998 will considerably increase the powers of TNCs and decrease those of the state (Rowan 1998). Developed through the Organization for Economic Cooperation and Development (OECD) the MAI is a new set of investment rules that grant TNCs the right to buy, sell and move their operations wherever they wish around the world, without government regulation. As though the world has gone into a reverse image, the TNCs will be able to sue governments for any profits lost through any laws that discriminate against them. On one hand, the state can be seen as being left with the task of servicing the TNCs with an adequately educated, relatively healthy, compliant and flexible labour force. On the other hand, the state can be seen as mopping up the social and economic after-effects of TNC global power and national involvement: unemployment, poverty, social exclusion and possible unrest.

Whereas it may be uncomfortable to suggest global economic determinism, I see the state as involved in a process of struggle within the global economy. Such a struggle is not new, but this is the turn of the century manifestation of it. Although not totally passive to economic globalization, a change in fortunes such as that witnessed in the south-east Asian financial crisis of 1997/8 can considerably restrict the choices open to the state. For example, the International Monetary Fund (IMF), backed by the military strength of the US, forced the Indonesian and South Korean governments to comply with their demands. The global role of the United States was significant in this particular global–state struggle, and epitomized the relationship between global capitalism and neocolonialism. When the US President Clinton gave South Korea two days in which to agree to the IMF, there were 37,000 US troops stationed in South Korea. The IMF agreement was signed (Higgins 1998).

Within this complex understanding of global–state relations Hirst and Thompson's analysis of the TNC–nation state relationship is particularly useful, for it not only allows for state participation and agency (and by implication, the agency of education providers and unemployed women) but also because they provide a model that describes the involvement of the regionalized as well as nation state. They see the state's involvement with the global economy as operating through five levels of governance (see Table 2.1). First are the major nation states, the 'G3': Europe, Japan and the US; second are the international regulatory agencies such as the World Trade Organization (WTO) and GATT; third are the regionalized blocs; fourth the nation state; and fifth regional level governance.

The first and second levels of governance relate most closely to the preceding discussion on neocolonialism. The third, fourth, and to a lesser extent fifth, levels are the more detailed concern of the following chapters. First, however, we consider their view of the state and globalization.

Globalization and the state

Hirst and Thompson argue that national economic processes remain central, but ascribe to them a management rather than an autonomous macroeconomic decision making role. They see the national government not only as a representative of the population, but more crucially, as a source of legitimacy for new forms of governance. Power is thus distributed from the nation state upwards to the international level and downwards to subnational and regional agencies; nation states are 'the sutures that . . . hold the system of governance together' (Hirst and Thompson 1995: 423). This then is a crucial

Table 2.1 The five levels of governance

Level 1	Major nation states	G3: Europe, Japan, United States
Level 2	International regulatory agencies	World Trade Organization (WTO)
		General Agreement on Trades and Tariffs (GATT)
Level 3	Regionalized blocs	Asia–Pacific Economic Cooperation (APEC)
		Association of South East Asian Nations (ASEAN)
		European Union (EU)
		North American Free Trade Association (NAFTA)
Level 4	Nation state	e.g. Australia, Belgium, Canada, Denmark, Poland, New Zealand, UK, US
Level 5	Regional level governance	e.g. California (US), New South Wales (Aus), East Midlands (UK)

Source: Based on Hirst and Thompson (1995)

part of the relationship of nation states to regionalized blocs, the regionalized bloc being the new form of governance which only has legitimacy (and democratic accountability) through the channel of the nation state government. The state's legitimacy lies in this democratic accountability. Democracy, Hirst and Thompson argue (1995: 423), 'requires a substantial measure of cultural homogeneity (or publicly recognized cultural difference within some overarching political identity) if it is to be tolerable'. Such homogeneity is, at present, not realizable beyond the level of the nation state – hence, for example, the apparent limited accountability of the European Parliament.

The final, and key, role of the nation state is its retention of territorial control. Giddens (1990) asserts that nation states do not act as economic machines but are in fact jealous of their territory and are concerned with maintaining strategic geopolitical relations with other states. Furthermore, such territorial control is not simply the control over a defined and agreed area of land, but also effectively, the regulation of populations. Chapter 1 showed that the European Union was the only regionalized bloc, to date, to allow the free movement of people along with that of goods, money, ideas and knowledge. With such apparent freedom of movement, there has been only limited success in reducing, through the Schengen Agreement, the internal border controls within the EU (Wallace and Wallace 1996). Free movement applies to business personnel, academics, European bureaucrats and 'experts', and also to inter-European tourism, yet the free movement of the general population to live and work in another member state has remained fraught with those bureaucratic and financial difficulties connected not only to state welfare, health and benefit systems, but also to characteristics of race, ethnicity, nationality, class, age, health and disability, and gender. The free movement of people is thus a heavily racialized, classed and gendered concept and is frequently linked, as will be seen in the next chapter, to the concept of citizenship. People therefore remain 'nationalized', their movements and their social and legal rights regulated by the nation state. This issue of mobility and migration will be returned to in Chapter 3.

The global, gendered, labour market

While the literature of ASEAN, NAFTA and APEC makes little, if any, reference to people as actors, there is an occasional mention of 'labour'. Similarly, the language of male economists such as Gary Hufbauer and Jeffrey Schott (1993) is of 'labour' being 'displaced', and never 'people' being made 'unemployed'. Within this dominant global discourse unemployment tends to be distanced from the economy, and the problem of being unemployed is located at the level of the unemployed person. My concern with *unemployed* women of the working classes therefore needs to be contextualized by an understanding of the position of women in paid employment.

The main post-1945 trend within the global labour market has been the reduction of heavy manufacturing by the early industrialized nations and their relocation as newly industrialized states, with a widespread increase of light, mainly electronic, manufacturing. Within the entire manufacturing sector, technological changes have raised the levels of production, and simultaneously reduced the need for labour. Within the global labour market, the manufacture of goods is increasingly located within those countries where the costs of labour and other overheads are cheapest (Mitter 1986; Hart 1992; Harcourt 1994; Ramsay 1995). At the same time, the service sector, usually dependent on women's part-time, low skilled, 'flexible' labour, has increased, particularly in Europe, the US, Canada, New Zealand and Australia. This can be seen as a trend towards an apparent 'uniformization and convergence' (Women of Europe 1992). This trend in which the gap between the economic activity of men and women is, allegedly, narrowing, is often referred to as the 'feminization' of the labour market. However, the Women of Europe (1992) report on women in the labour market argues that this process is far less a result of women taking men's jobs than of increased job creation in women's traditional sectors of work combined with the lower labour costs involved in employing women, not only in the newly industrializing countries but also in those early industrialized countries of the European Union, North America and Australasia. This apparent increase in women's employment and decrease in male employment has nevertheless barely touched the occupational gendered segregation of the labour market or its more contentious hierarchical segregation[10] (EC 1992b; Social Europe 1993, 1994b). For example, Elizabeth Eviota's (1992) study of the gendered impact of new technology within a multinational jeans making factory in the Philippines found that whereas 95 per cent of the workers were women, all middle and senior managers were men. Similarly, the best paid factory-floor occupations such as cutting, pressing and zipping were gendered as male.[11]

This section provides a gendered analysis of the labour market, however, the intention has not been to write a gender-essentialist account, but rather I wish to stress the national, class and race differences within this gendered analysis that are based on the premise that divisions within the labour market sustain neocolonial power structures between nation states and groups. It is not simply the result of differing experiences of education, training and employment opportunities.

While Marx and Weber provide the starting points for many analyses of the labour market, it is to feminist analyses that I have been compelled to turn to discuss women in the labour market. Some feminists emphasize the sex-typing of occupations, arguing that people make choices based on traditional notions of masculinity and femininity, which in turn can be changed by challenging sex-stereotypes and increasing access to non-traditional occupations (Oppenheimer 1970; Barron and Norris 1976). Others believe that women are in low-skilled, low-paid jobs because they have less human capital with which to enter or re-enter the labour market (Beechey 1978). The argument here is that, by improving education and training, women's 'human capital' would increase and then intervene in the sex-segregation of the labour market. Yet others have constructed theories around the concept of a gender (rather than sex) segmented labour market. Here, gendering is seen as a political process through which identifiable structures emerge, are constructed and then maintained for the benefit of both capitalism and patriarchy (Mies 1986; Walby 1986, 1988; Cockburn 1990).

Some feminist theorists have studied the global labour market (Mitter 1986; Folbre 1992) and others have focused specifically on the EU, both in relation to globalization (Harcourt 1994)[12] and with regard to the specific position of women (van Doorne-Huiskes *et al.* 1995). Swasti Mitter (1986) is particularly relevant here, for her concern with the TNCs leads her to explore the gender and race-based oppression of women across the whole of the global economy, in both the newly industrialized and the early industrialized countries.

Mitter describes the late twentieth-century use of free trade zones and export processing zones within newly industrialized countries, and also the enterprise zone sweatshops and outworking systems of the increasingly deregulated industrialized countries. Common to both is the exploitation of working-class women's labour, and their gendered economic, political and sexual oppression. The occupational, physical and sexual exploitation and abuse of women working in free trade zones has also led to early prostitution and drug dependency. In the western industrialized states, women working within the unregulated sweatshops are overwhelmingly 'ethnic minority' immigrants, trapped, Mitter (1986: 123) says, 'between the racism of the host community and the sexism of their own [in which they] . . . offer the advantage of Third World labour in the middle of the first [world]'.

Similarly, Anne-Wil Harzing (1995: 69), in her study of 'ethnic minority' women in Belgium, the Netherlands, Germany and the UK, finds their position in the labour market worse than that of women from the 'majority culture', and adds that 'this is determined more by their belonging to an ethnic minority than by their being women'.[13] Women are the cheapest and most 'flexible' source of labour within the industrialized colonizing countries, and even more so within the newly industrializing postcolonized countries. The gendered labour market is clearly also racialized and classed. The additional significance here is that, within the globalized world, this process reflects neo-colonial power relations not only *between* nation states but also amongst social groups *within and across* the nation states.

Conclusion

I have shown that regionalized blocs provide a free trade market for member states, and also allow the pursuit of social and environmental policies that could not be pursued at the national level (Hirst and Thompson 1995). Similarly, Giddens (1990) argues that regionalized blocs both increase and decrease the power of the nation state. What is clear is that regionalized blocs are far more complex than the British manoeuvrings of Eurosceptics and Europhobes suggest. They are both an economic and a political construct; they reduce and increase the power of the nation state; they enhance and restrict the movement of people; legislation is both restrictive and enabling – not only impacting directly on the general population but also, as in the case of the European Union, providing a means of circumnavigating and contesting the legislation of the nation state itself. They represent a coming together of nation states which, voluntarily, relinquish or reduce significant aspects of their individual state policy-making powers to the collective will of the bloc. It is, as Bauman has stated (1992: 60, 61), this 'social space between the nation states' that needs to be sociologically explored, for 'we face . . . a social space populated by relatively autonomous agents who are entangled in mutual dependencies and hence prompted to interact', the problem however is that they are 'not operating in anything like the "principally co-ordinated" space, similar to that inside which all traditional sociological categories have been once securely allocated'.[14] From a sociology that has focused on and within the state, globalization is leading us to concentrate on the social spaces *between* the nation states – most particularly within the regionalized bloc, for example, the construction of joint-state social and education policy.

Finally, it is unclear whether or not the regionalized bloc is an attempt by nation states to collectively manage the effects of global capitalism, or whether it is an attempt by global capitalism to manage nation states. It is a chicken or egg question that can deflect attention away from global capitalism's effects on education, training and equality policy; for example, the exclusively profit-centred focus of TNCs allows gender, class and race oppressions to flourish, with particularly vicious consequences for undereducated working-class women, further compounded by race, ethnicity and disability.

Underpinning this chapter have been the themes of gendered, race and class oppression, economic and cultural globalization and neocolonialism. While increasingly devoid of national loyalty, the ownership and the capital investors of TNCs tend nevertheless to be located within the old colonial countries and not the colonized ones. The old colonial powers of Japan and Europe, along with the expansionist cultural and economic imperialism of the US, remain the major players as we approach the twenty-first century's reordering of the economic world.

In the next chapter I continue to focus on globalization and the regionalized 'state', but concentrate on the *effects* of economic globalization and on the development of social, education and training policy. The important question here is what does globalization mean for people – particularly working-class women?

Notes

1 See for example the work of Huggan (1995), Barnett (1997) and Sreberny-Mohammadi (1997).

2 While the dominance of English as a world language can be attributed to the British colonial past, the present US neo-imperial presence (cultural and economic) is a key factor in its continued importance. It may therefore be more accurate to say that the language of neo-colonial education is overwhelmingly that of American-English.

3 The dominance of English was challenged during the European Conferences for Educational Research held in Bath, England (1995), and Seville, Spain (1996) and the European Sociological Association conference, Essex, England (1997).

4 This surrender of economic control is not only true of postcolonized states. For example, during the past ten years, British public utilities such as gas, water, electricity and nuclear power have been privatized, and some are now owned by US companies.

5 Turkey applied for membership of the EU in 1987 and was rejected in 1989 because the Commission felt that 'membership would result in too much economic dislocation' (EC 1997a: 6). To increase the future possibilities of Turkish membership a customs union was established to aid their economic and political modernization. However although there has been economic improvement, the Commission has strong concerns about the extent of democracy and human rights in Turkey (EC 1996a).

   The earlier European tension with Israel during the oil crisis of 1973 is fully described by Stephen George (1996).

6 The applicant counties of eastern Europe are Bulgaria, the Czech Republic, Estonia, Hungary, Latvia, Lithuania, Poland, Romania, Slovakia and Slovenia. From the Mediterranean, Cyprus is also waiting to join.

7 The Mediterranean partner countries are Algeria, Cyprus, Egypt, Israel, Jordan, Lebanon, Malta, Morocco, the Palestinian Authorities, Syria, Tunisia and Turkey.

8 I draw here on Sam Jae Sung's (1997) study of Korean education.

9 An example of the TNC–nation state power relationship is provided by the Vauxhall motor company (part of General Motors) who, in October 1997, announced that unless Britain joined the EU's monetary union at the earliest opportunity they would relocate into mainland Europe. This announcement was rapidly followed by similar announcements from Rover and Ford.

10 The report, *The Position of Women in the Labour Market* (EC 1992b) not only provides a broad overview of the position of women in the EC labour market during the 1980s, it also analyses the broad labour market gendered trends of first, 'feminization' and second, occupational and hierarchical segmentation.

11 Similar observations have been made in the UK by Anna Pollert (1981) and Cynthia Cockburn (1985, 1988).

12 See also Harvie Ramsay (1995).

13 I put the words 'ethnic minority' in inverted commas in order to problematize its use. The construction and use of the term 'ethnic minority' reflects an ethnic power relationship in which 'whites' 'name' others as the minority, when numerically, they themselves are the global minority.

14 See also Waters' (1995) review of sociological theories of globalization.

3 The regionalized 'state' and working-class women

This chapter introduces the concepts of the welfare state, dependency and the pathologized 'unemployed'. It also discusses the discourse of equality – a key theoretical thread for the book. The argument developed in the previous chapters has been that regionalized blocs are being actively constructed, and while their origins lay partly in the discourse of free trade, they are also being constructed for geopolitical reasons. Furthermore, ASEAN, APEC and the EU all construct social policy, and all are involved in education and training policy. The EU, for example, is far more than a free trade area. Its legislation relates to supra-European political, monetary and social policy.

The chapter begins by drawing on feminist theories of the state to consider the construction of the regionalized state. In considering the transfer of powers from the nation state to the regionalized state, it explores the concepts of the imagined community, citizenship and nationalism. It focuses on the social welfare policy of this regionalized state, especially its relationship to unemployment, and in particular how 'the unemployed' are pathologized by the gendered, classed and racialized concept of dependency. Finally, I contextualize the education, training and equality policies of the regionalized state within the discourses of economic growth and peace.

The regionalized 'state'

Political scientists, sociologists, feminists and anthropologists have all contributed to the current debate on the definition of the state, in particular the debate on whether or not such a thing as a 'state' can be defined at all, especially in relation to the regionalized bloc, or in relation to women. As previously, my concern with the position of women within the regionalized state leads me primarily to feminist theories, this time of the state.

Feminist theories of the state

Feminists have theorized the state in a variety of ways. Jane Kenway (1991) for example provides a comprehensive discussion, Judith Allen (1990) problematizes the political theorists' concepts of public and private spheres, and others have explored the gendered concept of citizenship (Heater 1990; Walby 1994; Arnot 1997) and analysed the discourse and concept of equality (Pateman 1986; Brine 1995a). Yet others have critiqued the construction of the nation and nationalism (Yuval-Davis 1993, 1997), considered the relationship between the state and sexuality (Cooper 1995) and the role of feminists within it (Franzway *et al.* 1989; Eisenstein 1990; Yeatman 1990, 1993).

Sophie Watson (1990) identifies and introduces four feminist paradigms of the state: first, Marxist feminists' grafting feminism onto existing analyses of the capitalist state; second, radical feminist analyses of the patriarchal power of the state; third, liberal feminist attempts to influence the plurality of the state; and, fourth, the 'post' analyses in which the state is a category of abstraction, where attention is focused on the linkages between various parts of the state. To Watson's overview should be added feminist theory such as that of Folbre (1992) and Harcourt (1994) that focuses on what Zygmunt Bauman (1992: 60–1), referred to as the 'social space between the nation states' and the work leading to feminist neocolonial theory, for example Hoogvelt (1997). It is also important to remember that feminist theories of the state have rejected the essentialist concept of 'woman'. Rather, as in the work of Nira Yuval-Davis (1993, 1997) they have focused on the differences and power relations between women, for example of ethnicity, race and class and between all of these and men.

Franzway *et al.* (1989) provide a succinct appraisal of the state–gender relationship, pointing particularly to its historic (and positional) specificity. They see the state as the central institutionalization of social power, one that not only embodies a masculinized hierarchy, but that also sets limits to the use of violence, criminalizes aspects of sexuality and constitutes a gendered division of labour – domestic and paid employment. Yet the state is not simply a regulatory, managing agency maintaining the gender order, but is an active constituitive force producing and reproducing gendered power structures. Three further observations are relevant to an understanding of the regionalized state. First, the state both creates and obliterates historical possibilities. Second, the actions of the state are complex because the structures and the interests involved are complex, and third, the (democratic) state and its actions must be legitimated by the electorate.

A major strand of the feminist debate on 'the state' has taken place between the radical analyses of the patriarchal power of the state (Pateman 1980, 1986; Franzway *et al.* 1989; MacKinnon 1989) and the poststructural (and to a lesser extent, postmodern) analyses of the arenas where the mechanisms of power are played out (Allen 1990; Watson 1990). It is these poststructural analyses that have been most useful in exploring the effects of globalization on working-class women within the arena of education and training. Watson (1990: 7) focuses on the diffusion of power and power-knowledges throughout society and points out that 'recognising that the state is not a unity implies a series of arenas that constitute the state both discursively and through shifting interlocking connections and practices'. This interest in 'power at its extremities, in its ultimate destinations', at the 'points where it becomes capillary' (Foucault 1980a: 96) has helped frame my study of three local training projects for unemployed working-class women (reported in Chapter 7).

However, such approaches as that of Watson do not see the regionalized state as a site where economically determined policies can be enacted, but composed of culturally, geographically and historically located arenas where groups and individuals are not passive receivers of state policy, but where, in numerous ways, they struggle to find or make the spaces and gaps where they can exercise agency. As I will show later (in Chapter 6), such gaps can be found between the education and training policy of the regionalized state and the nation state, and in Chapter 7, between the policy of the nation state and that of implementing institutions, feminist activists, femocrats and individual unemployed women. Missing, however, from Watson's feminist poststructuralist approach, are the understandings of neocolonialism such as those previously discussed.

Nationalism

Benedict Anderson (1983) pointed out that a necessary part of the construction of the state is that it becomes an 'imagined community'. In the early 1990s the general lack of *European* identity led the European Commission, supported by its newly created symbols of flag, anthem, passport and citizenship, to actively construct 'Europeanness'.

In its adoption of the insignia of state and supported by the 'European dimension in education' (see Chapter 5), the European Commission is 'imagining' the European 'state'. This active construction of a European identity could, to borrow from Michael Billig (1995), also be termed as 'banal Europeanness'. Billig shows the importance of 'banal nationalism', such as flags and anthems, in the construction and reconstruction of the nation state. Pointing to the eighteenth century constructions of France and Italy, he also shows that the active construction of a state is nothing new. Similarly, the importance of education in the construction of the state is not new and as Andy Green (1990, 1997) argues, the periods of greatest activity in the reform of the state actually coincide with periods of intensive educational development. Of particular relevance to the construction of the European state is Billig's identification of language as crucial as there is frequently the adoption of an official language and the suppression of others. Billig points again here to the nineteenth century, and to the British ban on Welsh and Lowland Scottish being spoken within schools. The European Commission's official languages are English, French and German, yet as mentioned in Chapter 2, language is a contentious issue within the EU, particularly with the expansion to the north to include Scandinavian countries, and the expected expansion to the east and south to include, for example, the Czech Republic, Slovenia and Cyprus.

Globalization may, as Giddens (1990) points out, reduce some features of nationalism, but it can also contribute to its growth in two main ways. It can operate *between* nation states, for instance between those included and those excluded from a particular regionalized bloc. This is especially noticeable with those states that share a frontier with the bloc. It can also lead to a nationalism that operates, as racism, xenophobia, anti-Semitism and subordinated inclusion, *within and across* nation states.

Julia Kristeva (1993: 2) refers to the significance of the increasing 'cult of origins'. This claim of national identity is, she argues, not only a glorification of one's own origins but has a matching opposite in the 'hatred of those others who do not share my origins and who affront me personally, economically, and culturally'. She adds that national identity is confirmed and legitimated by notions and understandings of citizenship.

Citizenship

While migrants, immigrants and 'guestworkers', especially women, are frequently denied the national identity of citizenship, the citizenship of the 'included' is not, as Arendt (1958) has argued, itself static and unproblematic. Similarly, Catherine Hall (1992: 240) shows in her study of gender and ethnicity in England during the nineteenth century that national identity is continually contested, 'discursively constructed and reconstructed in conditions of historical specificity'. Thus the construction of citizenship and non-citizenship is, within the context of globalization, one of the key features that links the economic discourse to the social.

Studies of citizenship commonly take Marshall (1950) as the starting point. He defines three dimensions of citizenship: civil, political and social. Inherent in his account is the concept of 'progress', hence legal–civil rights became prominent in the eighteenth century, political rights in the nineteenth and social citizenship throughout the twentieth. This is clearly a gender-blind account since, within western states, women did not gain political rights until the twentieth century and the gendered nature of social citizenship remains an area of some dispute. Second, as Gøsta Esping-Andersen (1996: 1) points out, 'the newly emerging industrial democracies do not appear set to converge along the Western welfare state path'. Also, within some ASEAN states, the highly gendered philosophy of Confucianism provides a further obstacle to women's citizenship.

It is clear that the construction of citizenship includes the exclusion of the non-citizen – the 'other'. Hannah Arendt (1958) suggests that early twenti-eth-century constructions of European nation states produced two excluded groups: the minorities within a state and the stateless. Both groups have con-tinued as a dominant feature of European history. Arendt pays close atten-tion to their construction, their subsequent interpretations, and their harrowing manifestation in the Second World War. She maintains that it is impossible to define human rights as separate from citizenship rights; that the rights of individuals to belong to humanity simply because of their humanity are by no means guaranteed, and in fact, conversely, such lack of protection within the state can lead the individual (or the social group) to be seen as non-human, as 'savage', and hence place them in grave danger. Look-ing to the future of governments beyond the nation state, her work antici-pates the growing numbers of peoples excluded (socially and by citizenship) within nation states, and excluded (physically and economically) by the 'fortresses' around the wealthier regionalized blocs. Arendt writes (1958: 302):

> The danger is that a global universally interrelated civilization may pro-duce barbarians from its own midst by forcing millions of people into conditions which, despite all appearances, are the conditions of sav-ages.

Within the regionalized 'state' of the European Union the Treaty of the Union (EC 1992a) heralded the European citizen. This is a 'regionalized' citizenship, additional to that of the nation state. As will be shown in Chap-ter 5, the EU's foray into compulsory education policy is intricately linked with this concept of citizenship (see Coulby and Jones 1995). Madeleine Arnot (1997) identifies four feminist perspectives on education and citizen-ship, and in her critical overview of these argues that the concept of citizen-ship is a highly gendered one. She highlights the importance of education in women's struggle for citizenship, and also considers its relationship to the economy, pointing to the contradiction between the discourse of citizenship and the 'continued difficulty in improving women's participation in the labour market and in economic and political decision-making' (Arnot 1997: 291).

Urbanization and migration

Urbanization and migration appear as the inevitable consequence of global regionalization. Migration between states is, for newly industrializing coun-tries, compounded by urbanization–migration within the state as people move to the already overcrowded cities in the search for work and a 'better life'.

Urbanization–migration is a major feature within ASEAN. Aline Wong and Paul Cheung (1987) describe three main areas of concern: first, un- and underemployment – there are not enough jobs, and a very high percentage of those jobs that do exist are in the informal sector; second, the deteriorating quality of life in the cities with 'housing shortages, snarled traffic, pollution, [and] sprawling squatter settlements' (Wong and Cheung 1987: 24); and third, the forcing of women migrants into prostitution. Swasti Mitter (1986) describes women working in the free trade zones as being physically and sexually assaulted by their employers. The average working life of a woman working in a free trade zone is three to four years, and on being discarded in their mid-20s for being too old, or because of failing health (particularly sight), many women find their only option is prostitution.

The EU, NAFTA, APEC and ASEAN all see migrating labour as a problem. The EU faces migration from outside of the EU – hence one aspect of the concept of 'Fortress Europe', fortified against North Africa and the eastern European postcommunist states. Floya Anthias and Nira Yuval-Davis (1992) point to the gendering of these 'fortification' policies, arguing that 'Fortress Europe' has restricted the movement of 15 million minority women. Migration to the US and Europe, and migration between member states, are problems of ASEAN. In 1983 there were 380,000 migrant workers, mainly women, from the Philippines. The world recession at that time led many of these people to be repatriated, and according to Wong and Cheung (1987), posing employment and other problems to the 'home' country. Similarly, in 1998, the financial crisis in south-east Asia was seen to lead to the forced repatriation of migrant workers – more than 2.5 million from Thailand and Malaysia, and 270,000 from South Korea (Cumming-Bruce 1998). The majority of these workers are migrants from other ASEAN countries. Mitter (1986) points out that, during the mid-1980s, there were, in Britain, an estimated 20,000 Filipino migrants, again mainly women, working as domestics, hotel and hospital workers for low wages. These wages were, nevertheless, sent 'home' as highly valued foreign currency.

The migration of working-class women is seen as a necessary means of bringing foreign currency into the 'home country'; nevertheless there is national concern surrounding the migration of educated men and women. The receiving country is seen to benefit from the source country's investment in their education and training (Martin 1987). ASEAN's proposed common training programme is, like that of the EU, an attempt to address this problem of the 'home country's' lost investment in the migrating educated middle classes, by sharing across the regionalized bloc the costs of education and training.

Mexican migration was, as shown in Chapter 1, a key aspect in the formation of NAFTA; in fact Hufbauer and Schott (1993) argue that it formed part of the rationale for its existence. Although improvement of the border infrastructure does not include the physical construction of barriers, the US nevertheless police themselves not only the north Mexican border, but also its *south* border, restricting the flow of Central Americans into Mexico, and then into the US; 'Fortress North America' is thereby protected from immi-grants from poorer Central and South America.

Given the key involvement of the US in APEC, and given the inherent wealth and power differentials between the countries of APEC, it is likely that APEC's policies towards migration will mirror those of the US–Mexico relationship. Edward English and Murray Smith (1993) see this as the model for future regionalized blocs that include countries with 'different income levels'. Such agreements enable the free trade of goods, services and tech-nology, but do not make financial agreements nor provide for freedom of mobility. The sovereignty of each country remains intact and the barriers to migration and to the general free movement of non-key people are strength-ened.

The regionalized 'state' and social policy

Regionalized blocs such as ASEAN, NAFTA, APEC and the EU are, as detailed in Chapter 1, constructs: groupings of nation states that transfer some powers to a regionalized 'state'. Within the EU major nation state roles are currently being transferred to the European Commission. They include military powers related to joint external security; financial powers related to monetary union and a single European currency; and social powers related to the increased Commission competency in areas of social and education policy. Although Giddens (1985: 120) sees the 'direct control of the means of internal and external violence' as central to the nation state, it is mone-tary union and social policy that have provoked the most reaction from member states.

Interlinked then, with both the economic and the cultural aspects of globalization, is the social policy of both the nation and the regionalized state. The central question, as expressed by Halsey *et al.* (1997: 2) is, 'How, in a capitalist society based on inequalities of reward and status, are social cohesion and order to be maintained?' This dilemma lies at the heart of the social policy of the European Union and is also of concern to ASEAN (ASEAN 1967). The welfare state plays a key role in addressing the social inequalities of economic globalization, providing financial aid to those 'in need': the sick, the young, the elderly and the unemployed. The common argument is that demographic and technological changes have placed immense pressure on welfare state systems, which can be further increased by the demands of the IMF, for example on South Korea (Higgins 1998). Yet, to the extent that the state is not totally passive to economic globaliz-ation, it is faced with choices to make (albeit these can be difficult) and it does, generally, choose to reduce welfare provision and then chooses the way in which it will be reduced. Esping-Andersen (1996) sees, primarily rooted in globalization, a 'seemingly universal trade-off between equality and employment' where within even the most wealthy of western states there has been a trimming of state welfare benefits. For example globalization has led both Australia and Sweden to cut back on their relatively secure high employment, high waged, model, which could only operate within a protected labour market. The welfare state is then being reduced by both right and left-wing governments. Within the EU a further 'legitimating' discourse for this reduction is provided by the 'convergence' requirement on member states in the move towards a common currency.

The welfare state

Gøsta Esping-Andersen (1990) provides an understanding of the role of women in three main constructions of the welfare state. His work on capitalist welfare states show all three models existing within the EU. They are: the continental model of Germany, Italy, Netherlands, France and Spain; the Scandinavian model of Denmark, Sweden and Norway; and finally, the neoliberal model of the UK (shared also by the US and New Zealand, and to a lesser degree Australia and Canada).

The continental model is highly gendered: 'there is an implicit conspiracy to safeguard the prime-age male worker even when this harms his wife's, sons' and daughters' employment prospects'(Esping-Andersen 1996: 19). A system of high social insurance reliant on unbroken full-time employment, combined with underdeveloped state social services is based on the assumption that 'family members can depend on the full-time male breadwinner, and that wives are generally responsible for social care within the household' (1996: 18). This model is a clear example of what Franzway *et al.* (1989) describe as the state functioning not only as the central institution of social power but as one that actually embodies (and maintains) a masculinized hierarchy.

Although the Scandinavian model attempts to sustain full employment, this too is a gendered model. Women are concentrated in part-time employment in the public sector and men in full-time employment in the private sector. This has led to greater gender inequality of pay and poverty, especially amongst lone parents.

The neoliberal model of social welfare is based on labour and wage flexibility and rising inequality and poverty is common. This too is a gendered model. Deregulated wages are affecting unskilled, non-unionized workers, of whom the majority are women. Within the UK, neoliberal policies have dismantled much of the original welfare state. The US system assumes, like the continental system, that the lean welfare state system will be supplemented by private schemes, generally based on full-time secure employment, which again leaves women and the unemployed out in the cold. The Australian and Canadian welfare state systems are less universal, and particularly in Australia, have targeted benefits on the most vulnerable groups, leading to a substantially lower incidence of poverty than that of the other neoliberal systems.

Following on from this identification of the three worlds of capitalist welfare states, Esping-Andersen (1996) considers the future of the welfare states in relation to globalization. He sees the possible emergence of many forms of welfare state that reflect the diversity with nation states and the changes to the traditional basis of welfare – the model family. He also sees women playing a significant role in present reconceptions of the welfare state, which had originally relied on women to supplement the state by working in the home caring for the family.

Within the Asian–Pacific states, Esping-Andersen sees 'embryonic welfare states', welfare states that threaten to undermine the traditions in which families themselves save for their future welfare needs, and which are closely linked with Confucian 'familialism'. Although he tends to treat the Asian–Pacific states as uniform, they no doubt, like the western states, include a range of welfare approaches. At the time of writing, Korea and Taiwan in particular are extending citizen rights and, as their economic growth is slowing and they look to industrial restructuration, they (like the US and EU) anticipate increased unemployment and 'a host of new welfare problems' (1996: 23). Similarly, in Japan, the system of lifelong employment linked to corporate welfare support is also weakening. Other than Japan, which also has a growing ageing population, many of the other Asian–Pacific states are faced with a different demographic problem: massive urban migration. Within three-generation households the financial responsibility lies with the man, and that for practical and emotional care with the woman. Increased male unemployment threatens the familial welfare system, limiting resources with which women are expected to care for their elderly relatives. Quoting Hashimoto (1992) and Choi (1992) Esping-Andersen recounts, for Japan and South Korea, the high percentage of elderly people who live with their children (65 and 76 per cent) and the growing trend towards either avoidance or inability of the younger generation to provide the necessary care for the older generation. In the absence of state provision, this is leading to increased poverty amongst the elderly. As the Confucian model of familial welfare breaks down so, Esping-Andersen says, Japan is attempting to reinvigorate it, while Korea and Taiwan move towards a more comprehensive state social policy, offering little more than non-universal subsistence level support. Such limited state welfare is based on the assumption that male workers will gain welfare cover through the private sector, leaving women to administer, and then themselves be dependent upon, familial welfare.

All these conceptions and examples of social welfare then are gendered. With the possible exception of the Scandinavian model they are all based on a heterosexual, gendered, age-dependent model in which the full-time male worker, generally within secure employment, is the norm. Social welfare is geared to his working life and his social needs. Not only are women frequently disadvantaged by this male norm, but they are also a vital part of the welfare system that supports the individual male, the dependent family and the state.

The concept of 'dependency'

At the heart of the welfare state lie 'the unemployed'. The chief means by which both the nation and regionalized state relate to 'the unemployed' is through postcompulsory education and training policies, increasingly linked to social and welfare policies, and based on a pathological discourse of unemployed people in which the problem of unemployment lies with the person rather than with the state or the global economic system. This discourse of dependency is also inevitably classed, gendered and racialized.

Nancy Fraser and Linda Gordon (1994) provide an insightful analysis of the US genealogy of dependency which shows it shifting in relation to changes in capitalism. Referring to four registers of dependency: economic, sociolegal, political and moral/psychological, they show a discursive shift from an original preindustrial description of the relationship of workers (men and women) towards their masters (and to a lesser extent vice versa), to a current attachment to particular 'groups considered deviant and superfluous', and who are excluded from paid employment and dependency upon the state (1994: 312). The first step in this discursive shift began with western industrialization and the construct of 'paupers', who were not only poor, unemployed and reliant on charity but were also 'degraded, their character corrupted and their will sapped through reliance on charity' (1994: 316). The second step came with the construction of the 'colonial native' and 'the slave'. Their labour was crucial to the development of capital and industry, yet, because they were conquered they were seen as dependent, an initial reading that changed later to one in which they were conquered because they were dependent, their essential dependency thereby justifying their colonization and enslavement. The third step was the industrial era's invention of the 'housewife', a construction in which women's sociolegal and political dependency enforced their new economic dependency, and where, until the late nineteenth century, even married, wage-earning women had no legal rights over their own wages. This construction of the housewife was both classed and racialized, as the majority of white and black working-class women had little choice but to sell their labour.

The effect of this third step was 'to feminize – and stigmatize – socio-legal and political dependency' (Fraser and Gordon 1994: 318). The concept of dependency is then seen to slip from its original economic meaning to its current moral and psychological reading, firmly linked to a dual concept, first of the deserving poor: for example, household dependency such as that of 'wives' and children; and second, the undeserving poor: for example, dependency on charity or state benefit, such as that of lone mothers. This genealogy leads to a concept of dependency in which the 'undeserving' poor are stigmatized and watched to make sure they do not promote themselves as deserving. As will be discussed in Chapter 8, surveillance is a key aspect of the current pathologization of unemployed women and men. In the industrializing period of the nineteenth century, the genealogy of dependency was essentially gendered; however Fraser and Gordon (1994: 312) argue that in its postindustrial usage certain groups of women are more stigmatized than others:

> Growing numbers of relatively prosperous women claim the same kind of independence that men do while a more stigmatized but still feminized sense of dependency attaches to groups considered deviant and superfluous. Not just gender but also racializing practices play a major role in these shifts, as do changes in the organization and meaning of labor.

Un- or undereducated unemployed working-class women within this world of economic and cultural globalization and economic regionalization are either stigmatized, labelled as dependent on the state and left in poverty, or enticed into low paid, insecure and part-time employment (still impoverished) and subsequently blamed for the feminization of the labour market. They may also be employed in the informal or illegal economy (with all its associated social, economic and physical risks), or recruited onto education and training schemes intended to increase their (re-)entry into paid employment.

Education, training and equality policies

As has already been mentioned, education and training policies are at the interface of the economic and social policies of the regionalized state. They serve three key functions. First, they are linked to the discourse of economic growth – training and retraining workers for the labour market. Second, they are linked to the discourse of peace – provision for unemployed people is increasingly linked to the social effects of economic growth, to social exclusion and the fear of social unrest. Third, they are linked to the construction of the regionalized 'state', to the identity of the 'state' and, as in the case of the EU, to the concept of citizenship.

Training was incorporated into the founding Treaty of the EEC (EC 1957) with the explicit intention of training and retraining workers, women and men, for the labour market. Thirty-five years later, the Treaty of the Union (EC 1992a) provided the European Commission with the, albeit still narrowly defined, legal competency in the field of education, and introduced the Social Chapter which legally extended the Commission's range of social policy actions.[1] The EU's education and training policy is the focus of Chapter 5, therefore this section concentrates specifically on the policies of ASEAN and APEC.

The ASEAN Bangkok Declaration (1967) included the aim of providing 'assistance to each other in the form of training and research facilities in the educational, professional, technical and administrative spheres'. However, it was the social and cultural sections of the Bali Summit of 1976 that made education and training more generally available. This introduced 'the study of ASEAN, its member states, and their national languages as part of the curricula of schools and other institutions of learning in the member states' and it provides for the 'support of ASEAN scholars, writers, artists, and mass media representatives to enable them to play an active role in fostering a sense of regional identity and fellowship'(Palmer and Reckford 1987: 52).

Wong and Cheung (1987) point out that education has been a significant feature of ASEAN development where, allowing for national and ethnic diversity, there has been a trend towards providing broad-based and longer formal education in all member countries. Such policies also inscribe considerable gendered inequality of access, particularly in Indonesia, Malaysia and the Philippines, where there is still a tendency for poorer working-class families to restrict girls' access to education.

Despite the dominant discourse of economic growth and the lack of general social policy within APEC, education and training was placed on the agenda at the first meeting of APEC leaders in 1991. Education and training would, it was hoped, raise literacy rates, provide the skills necessary for maintaining economic growth, and contribute to the arts and sciences. In 1990 the Human Resources Development Working Group set up the Education Forum (EDFOR) with three principal concerns: to develop ways of monitoring the performance of education systems; to provide high quality instruction in key subjects like mathematics and science; and to facilitate the mobility of students, trainees, teachers, professionals and information. As in the EU, 'lifelong learning' has been a strong theme and 'gender issues' was one of the five key themes within it. Echoing the EU, the Osaka Action Agenda (APEC 1995) asserts: 'the people of the Asia–Pacific region are its most important asset' and education and training are the means of developing these 'human resources'. Five of the eight priority actions listed in the Agenda are thus concerned with education and training.

Education and training is, in ASEAN, APEC and the EU, an early item on the agenda of meetings and has tended, over time, to increase in importance. Moreover, it is often explicitly stated that education and training is for both women and men. There is an emphasis on postcompulsory provision that is clearly linked, through the discourse of economic growth, to the labour market, but there is also a concern with the more general 'liberal' aspects of compulsory education, especially in relation to cultural difference, and shared history (and often shared conflict) between the member states. Stress is placed on learning languages, encouraging racial, cultural and ethnic tolerance, and sharing intellectual ideas and creativity. All of these 'educational' aims are directly linked to the discourse of peace and the construction of the regionalized 'state'.

Equality

Unlike education and training, 'equality' is not part of each bloc's discourse. Within the discourse of the regionalized bloc, equality tends to relate most directly to the labour market, to pay, and to education and training opportunities. It is not a feature of APEC, other than as the exceptional mention of gender as an issue within lifelong learning. Neither does equality feature in the social section of the key Declaration of ASEAN Concord (1976).

Apparently, unique amongst regionalized blocs, the Treaty of the EEC included an Article on 'equal pay between men and women'. This legitimated the EC's involvement in the area of equal opportunities and placed a legal requirement on member state governments to enact appropriate legislation. This Article has remained the legal basis for all subsequent gender equality legislation. Significantly, this early equality statement was clearly linked to the discourse of economic growth, for its initial aim was that no member state should gain unfair economic advantage over another by employing cheap labour – women. However, despite the resulting Equal Pay Acts of the member states, the earnings of women across the EU, in all occupations from the most well-paid to the least well-paid, is, on average, two-thirds that of male earnings (van Doorne-Huiskes *et al.* 1995). The discourse of equality, although as we have seen is fairly weak in some blocs, will be picked up as a key theme throughout the remaining chapters of this book.

Conclusion

To summarize, regionalized blocs are actively being constructed, and as regionalized 'states' they are all involved in social, education and training policy. The transfer of powers from the nation state to the regionalized state is accompanied by the construction of an imagined community. This regionalized state, like the nation state, leads to constructs of nationalism and citizenship, and in including some states and persons, excludes and constructs 'others'. Migration appears as an unavoidable consequence of the regionalized state.

Focusing on the policies of the regionalized state, the welfare state emerges in many different forms. The particular model of welfare state policy is not only linked to demography and economy, but also to the underlying philosophy of the nation state or regionalized bloc. Yet, significantly, all the models and examples of social welfare are gendered. Women are an assumed and vital part of the welfare system that offers its strongest support to the individual male, the dependent family and the state.

Within the framework of the welfare state 'the unemployed' are targeted through postcompulsory education and training policies that are increasingly linked to social and welfare policies. These policies reflect a pathological discourse of unemployed people in which the problem of unemployment is seen as lying with the person rather than with the state or the global economic system. Undereducated unemployed working-class women are stigmatized, pathologized and blamed for their unemployment, poverty and 'dependence' on the state.

Within the regionalized state, education and training tends to be an early item on the policy agenda and is strongly linked to both the discourse of economic growth and the discourse of peace. Education and training policy trains 'workers' for the labour market and also attempts to mitigate the social effects of economic growth: social exclusion and social unrest. Education and training policy is linked to the construction of a new state – to the construct of a new identity, and in the EU, to a new level of citizenship. Although education and training policy is an early feature of the regionalized bloc, the discourse and policy of equality, especially gendered equality, is not – with the EU, so far, being the only exception.

Note

1 The Social Chapter is one of the most contentious aspects of European policy, rejected by the previous UK Conservative government, but accepted within the first few days of the new Labour administration and finally included in the Treaty of Amsterdam (EC 1997c).

4 Educating unemployed women: the EU 'state', its discourses and competencies

In this and the next chapter I use the European Union as a context for considering the themes and concepts introduced in the previous chapters. This chapter and Chapter 5 represent the first steps in a trajectory analysis of policy that continues through the focus of Chapter 6 on the UK government, on to the case studies of training projects referred to in Chapter 7. Throughout these chapters I refer frequently to the European Commission. By this I mean both the body of 20 senior political figures (the Commissioners) who provide the political leadership for the Commission and to the whole structure of the Commission – the EU's 'civil service'.[1]

This analysis draws on the discourses of economic growth and peace to explore the ways in which education and training policies are used in the construction of the EU 'state'. I then introduce four areas of legal competency that have a direct impact on education and training policies for under-educated unemployed women. These are the competencies for education and training and for the main funded training programme, the European Social Fund (ESF). The fourth competency covers gendered equal opportunities. This particular competency leads to an exploration of the discourse of equality in which I consider the difference between formal and material equality; the debate surrounding equality based on similarity or difference, and the relationship between unemployment and the shifting equality discourse.

Discourse and ideology

The literature relating to the poststructuralist use of discourse and Michel Foucault (1980b) is my starting point for the analysis. Irene Diamond and Lee Quinby (1988) and several contributors to Caroline Ramazanoglu (1993) suggest that within Foucault's texts women are marginalized, and gendered power ignored. He nevertheless provides useful concepts of normalization, power, power-knowledge and discourse. Particularly relevant to this book is his concern with the way in which discourses and practices transform people into subjects of a particular kind (Foucault 1970). Importantly, he also points out that discourses not only constitute subjectivity but *power-relations* also. Discourses are the linguistic and textual expression of ideas which, together with politics and social practice, constitute our subjective understandings of the world and our existence within it. Building on Foucault's work, John Fiske (1995: 3) defines discourse as follows:

> Discourse, then, is language in social use; language accented with its history of domination, subordination, and resistance; language marked by the social conditions of its use and its users: it is politicized, power-bearing language employed to extend or defend the interests of its discursive community ... [Furthermore] Discourse can never be abstracted from the conditions of its production and circulation in the way that language can.

Discourses are not static but capable of change over time, and as such, reflect, and are of that time; most importantly discourses contain the potential to be, at any time, constructed or produced differently. This flexibility is particularly true of dominant discourses, those that serve dominant power-related social and economic interests. Reflective of their time and their source of power, they are also capable of considerable discursive change and flexibility, often absorbing and acting on competing and reverse discourses, while at the same time continuing to maintain their main power-related interests.

Foucault's point (1980b) that some discourses are 'dominant' and some 'reverse' is relevant to the 'dominant/reverse' status of discourses involved in the construction of the European Union (the construction discourse). For example, within certain settings this construction discourse is clearly dominant, yet in relation to a particular member state, it can be seen as reverse. Some aspects of the discourses of the EU and the member states overlap each other and some conflict. Where they overlap, as in their shared perspective on economic growth, they form an extremely strong dominant discourse, but where they conflict, as for example in their approach to social policy, then the EU discourse is in a reverse relationship to that of the member state – or vice versa.

Also relevant to this analysis of European discourses and competencies is the work of Trevor Purvis and Alan Hunt (1993). They consider the relationship between discourse and ideology and argue that the 'intentionality' of ideology theory (that is, that ideology always works to favour some and to disadvantage others) actually relates to the *effects* of discursive practice. The power of discourse to construct social subjectivities maintains ideologically determined power differentials. Both the EU and the member state discourses are linked to a liberal–democratic ideological intentionality that maintains a classed, gendered and racialized power and privilege relationship.[2]

A key difference between discourse and ideology that is relevant to this chapter is that discourse is more than simply the vehicle for maintaining ideological power relations. Discourse is fluid and messy, with a diverse range of interested parties contributing to its construction, frequently as a reverse discourse to the dominant discourse's ideological intentionality. Neither, according to Foucault, is the dominant discourse static; it adapts to, and even absorbs, certain (threatening) reverse discourses. Two important aspects of this concept of the organic discourse are that first, it allows for the concept of agency within its construction, that is for the part played by actors with differing, even conflicting, interests (see for example, the European Equal Opportunities Unit considered in Chapter 5). The second key aspect is that although the discourse may be messy and fluid it is nevertheless firmly anchored to its ideological intentionality.

As will be shown later, this relationship of the EU dominant discourses to liberal–democratic ideology is particularly relevant to the discourse of equality, and to the education and training policies for unemployed working-class women.

The discourses of economic growth and peace

As shown in Chapter 1, both the discourse of economic growth and the discourse of peace were, from the beginning, evident in the construction of the European Union (EC 1957). In the immediate post-World War II period, the economic need to rebuild the European economy and provide employment was linked with the need to construct and maintain peace between the previously warring nations, and with constructing cohesion against east communist states. The original members of the EU had been devastated, socially and economically, by Nazism and war. Since this immediate postwar period, a shift in the discourse of peace indicates the concern with 'internal' peace, that is, peace *within and across* the member states. This discourse of internal peace does not appear to be part of the original discourse but a response to the social consequences of geopolitical changes, economic growth and globalization.

In its early years, EU legislation was driven primarily by the discourse of economic growth, which included for example, equal pay for women and men. Shifts in the dominant discourse are reflected in the name given to this regionalized bloc. The discourse of economic growth is evident in the first name: the European Economic Community. With the construction of the discourse of internal peace the legislation broadened to include political and social concerns and the EEC became the EC – the European Community. With further deepening of the social policy, the construction of a European identity and citizenship, it became in 1992 the European Union. The latter half of the 1980s was a period of transition and struggle between the two discourses of economic growth and internal peace, and resulted in a discursive shift that is reflected in the Social Chapter of the Treaty of the Union (EC 1992a), commonly known as the Maastricht Treaty. As mentioned in the previous chapter, this increased social policy role is perceived by some member states as a threat to nation state sovereignty.[3] By the mid-1990s the hitherto implicit relationship between training policy and the discourse of internal peace was made explicit (EC 1993a, 1994a, 1995a).

While responding to the discourse of internal peace, the Maastricht Treaty of the Union (EC 1992a) and the later Amsterdam Treaty (EC 1997c) also continue to reflect the discourse of economic growth. It is not, therefore, that the discourse of economic growth has declined in importance, but that the discourse of internal peace has increased, reflecting the Commission's fear of a 'dual society' emerging *within* the European Union, of a society of included and excluded people.

A key feature of the EU discourse of internal peace is the concept of social exclusion, a multideprivational model of inequality and disadvantage (apparently) based on social groups rather than pathologized individuals.

> It is clear that contemporary economic and social conditions tend to exclude some groups from the cycle of opportunities . . . At present, with more than 52 million people in the Union living below the poverty line, social exclusion is an endemic phenomenon, stemming from the structural changes affecting our economies and societies.
>
> (EC 1994a: 49)

The actual experience of social exclusion is variable and cushioned or compounded by numerous factors including those of gender, race, class, sexuality, disability and age.

The perceived threat from postcommunist states also remains a central part of the discourse of peace that is fearful of postcommunist instability and of the rise of Fascist political organizations which might join forces with neo-Nazi and other right-wing groups within the European Union. In his account of the rise of the Right in postcommunist Eastern Europe Paul Hockenos (1993: 314) concludes

> The problem of the right is not one of a couple of thousand Skinheads, but of the latent prejudices and sentiments that they express in their most extreme forms, and that right-wing parties have shown themselves deft at exploiting. Today, the political and economic crises affecting Western Europe also open it to far right forces . . . The West cannot afford to take forty years of stability for granted . . .

Such fears were instrumental in the EC's decision to make 1997 the 'European Year Against Racism' in order 'to highlight the way that racism, xenophobia and anti-Semitism threaten the respect of fundamental rights and the economic and social cohesion of the European Union' (EC 1996c). This statement, located within both the discourse of economic growth and the discourse of internal peace, echoes the post-1945 fears of resurgent Fascism, anti-Semitism and another European or global war.

The two dominant discourses of economic growth and peace survive in a state of tension; the economic and social needs of the Union are interlinked and the stability and well-being of each is dependent on the other. Any conflict between these discourses reflects both their basis in western liberal–democratic democracy, and the tension existing between the European Commission and the individual member states.

The tension within liberal–democracy surrounds its two key subdiscourses: that of economic growth and equality – or rather, capitalism and democracy. The discourse of equality is thus an integral part of the western discourse of internal peace.

There is nevertheless a conflict in liberal–democracy that is generated by its commitment to economic growth. This relies on a labour force segmented by a matrix of inequality reflecting both power-relations and distinctions based on constructs of citizenship (EC 1993a, 1993b, 1994a). Not only does this rely on the maintenance of economic and social inequality, but also on its construction – to the benefit of some and the detriment of others. The emphasis on internal peace demands that such inequalities be masked, deflected and distanced from that of economic growth. This is the ideological intentionality most affecting the discourse of equality.

The tension between the European Commission and individual member states has focused mainly on social policy and monetary union – both central functions of the nation state. These tensions were epitomized in the 1997 Amsterdam summit (EC 1997c).

While it was hoped that the Amsterdam summit of June 1997 would result in another major Treaty of the Union, the immediate political and media reaction was that its achievements have been slight (Palmer 1997; Smart and Coman 1997). The Amsterdam Treaty incorporated both the Social Chapter from Maastricht and the Schengen Agreement (removing border controls from all member states except Britain and Ireland, and to a lesser extent Denmark). It gave the EU foreign negotiating rights, and included a contentious (some say toothless) Employment Chapter, which aimed to coordinate economic policies and to focus on economic growth and job creation. It also included a Charter of Human Rights, which aims to banish discrimination based on the explicitly stated differences of gender, race, religion, sexual orientation, age or disability. Finally, it provided for freedom of information by granting European citizens the right of access to the Council of Ministers' documents.

The major disagreement during the Amsterdam summit between France and Germany echoes the tensions surrounding the discourses of economic growth and internal peace. The French support of economic growth linked to job creation, and the German for fiscal and monetary discipline linked to monetary union has simply resulted, it is argued, in a compromise.[4] The Amsterdam summit thus epitomizes the three levels of tension inherent within the EU: first between the discourse of internal peace and economic growth; second between the EC and the individual member state; and third, between the member states themselves. These tensions have, in different ways, been both calmed and exacerbated by the 1997 French and British governments, for although the UK Labour administration's rapid signing of the Social Chapter was a significant gesture towards the EC, there are, even amongst the left-wing governments of France, the Netherlands and the UK, quite different approaches to the problems of unemployment and monetary union.

The Amsterdam Treaty (EC 1997c) included few of the anticipated major advances associated with monetary and military union or expansion of the EU. Nevertheless it did make advances in social policy. The first of these was the Employment Chapter, which, even though no funds are attached to it, was nevertheless an important aspect of the legislation because it granted the Commission legal competency within the area. It is an example of the way in which the European Commission has slowly but steadily expanded its areas of legal competency, often content simply to get a toe in the door of national legal frameworks. The second advance was through the Amsterdam Treaty's consolidation of the earlier Maastricht policy, for example in regard to the Schengen Agreement and the Social Chapter. However, although the consolidated Schengen Agreement allowed freer movement around much of the Union, it was unlikely to be backed up by freer access to welfare state provision – an example of the restricted concept of mobility discussed in Chapter 3. The third advance of the Amsterdam Treaty related to citizens' rights and access to information. At the time of writing it was not possible to assess the impact of this, but for countries such as Britain, which did not have legally enshrined citizens' rights, the EU Charter of Human Rights would in all likelihood, based on previous appeals to the European Court of Justice, prove a significant piece of legislation.

The Amsterdam summit highlights the Commission–member state tension surrounding the discourses of economic growth and peace and, through the German-led discourse relating to the control of the EU's capital, points also to shifts within the dominant discourse of economic growth itself.

The legal competencies of the European Commission

In Chapter 3 we saw education and training policy as an early concern of ASEAN, APEC and the EU; nevertheless an interest in equality, especially gendered equality, was visible only in the EU. The legal basis for education and training and equality are located in the founding Treaty of Rome (EC 1957). The intention in this section is to provide a detailed context for the analysis of these policies, which will be investigated in the following chapters.

Training

The Treaty of Rome provided the EU with the legal competency for vocational training. However, it was the Decision of 1963 that first opened the door to training for women.[5] This Decision, located exclusively in the discourse of economic growth, saw vocational training as the means of developing 'human resources' and 'increasing the competitiveness of the European economy' (EC 1963).[6] The Decision stated that every person should receive adequate training. Significantly for women, it added that 'special measures may be taken in respect of special problems concerning special sectors of activity or specific categories of persons' (EC 1963). Nevertheless, throughout the 1960s and 1970s, training tended to focus almost exclusively on men and it was a further eight years before the EC, through the ESF, made an explicit reference to women and training (EC 1971). In the European Seminar on the Vocational Guidance and Training for Women Workers, women's right to vocational training and guidance and the need for special efforts to ensure their unhindered access was stressed (EC 1976a). Following this European Seminar, the Commission issued a Directive reiterating the demand that women should have equal access to vocational training (EC 1976b). Despite the legal requirement on member states to comply with this Directive, the general response remained slow and a further Recommendation required them to meet their training obligations and to report on their actions (EC 1987b). From the mid-1970s the European Social Fund and the Action Programmes for Equal Opportunities between Women and Men became the main focus for gendered training policy. These will be considered in more detail in the next chapter.

Education

Unlike the competency for training, that for compulsory education was not provided until the Treaty of the Union (EC 1992a).[7] Before this, the compulsory education of member states could only be indirectly influenced by being piggy-backed onto other policies such as training, employment or equal opportunities.

Education is an example of the European Commission's slow approach to increased areas of legal competency. Competency for education has so far focused simply on 'a European dimension'. This began with the Declarations of 1983 and 1984 in which the concept of European citizenship and the idea of a 'European dimension in education' was introduced (EC 1983a, 1984a). A few years later a Resolution (EC 1988) specified the economic and the social role of education policy and the European 'values' that should be included within the curriculum. Later again competency was included in the Treaty of the Union (EC 1992a) – nine years after the first Declaration.

In the fraught negotiations for the Treaty of the Union (EC 1992a), the then British Prime Minister, John Major, successfully argued against the proposed goal of federalism. It was agreed instead to endorse a goal defined as 'an ever closer union of the peoples of Europe where decisions are taken as close as possible to the people' (Palmer 1991). Thus the concept of subsidiarity entered the European discourse. In relation to education and training policy, subsidiarity recognizes that the member state is responsible for the curriculum content and organization of education and training systems, and the cultural and linguistic diversity within the curriculum. Subsidiarity allows member states greater freedom within the overall context of European policy to interpret and implement policy in their own way with the agency of the member state government built into the Treaty. Thus Chapter 6 focuses on the agency of the British government and considers the impact of subsidiarity on the education and training policies for unemployed working-class women.

The European Social Fund

The Treaty of Rome also provides the legal basis for the European Social Fund (ESF).[8] Becoming operational in 1960, the ESF is the oldest and arguably the most influential of the EU's training funding structures, providing the financial weight for the Commission's interpretation of primary legislation. The original aim of the ESF was to fund the training and retraining of workers. The Treaty of European Union (1992) reflected the later, more complex, global labour market such as that described in the previous chapters. With its aim of making it easier to employ people by training a geographically and occupationally flexible labour force, it is able to adapt to labour market changes in industry and production. Training and retraining are seen as the main methods of achieving this. Although the Amsterdam Treaty makes no explicit changes to the ESF, the adoption of an Employment Chapter will undoubtedly have a major impact.

There have been five major changes to the ESF: the Reforms of 1971, 1977 and 1988 (EC 1971, 1977, 1987c), the adopted Decision of 1983 (EC 1983b) and the Regulation of 1993 (EC 1993b). Each of these ESF changes specifically refer to unemployed women. The significance of these reforms are explored in the next chapter.

Equal opportunities between women and men

The legal basis for European equal opportunities policy is also found in the Treaty of Rome, Article 119. This states that there should be 'equal pay between men and women'. The Treaty of the Union and the Amsterdam Treaty have both maintained the focus of Article 119 on equal pay for equal work, while the European Women's Lobby has called, as it has done since the beginning, for the more radical demand of 'equal pay for work of equal value'.

As previously argued, European gendered equality is framed by the discourse of economic growth. Its immediate impact was that it required member states to implement it in their national legislation (Meehan 1992; Prechal and Senden 1993). Progress was, to say the very least, slow, leading the Commission, 18 years later, to issue a Directive reinforcing the Article's demands (EC 1975). Britain's Equal Pay Act (1970) and Sex Discrimination Act (1975), while responding to the Directive, were, along with the legislation of five other member states, considered inadequate, leading the Commission to take action against them. The UK government resisted until 1981 when, taken by the Commission to the European Court of Justice, the EPA (1984) was amended to include 'equal pay for work of equal value'. Equally importantly, Article 119 has provided the legal basis for all subsequent Directives relating to equal opportunities. For example, Article 119 legally enabled the key Directive demanding that women be given access to vocational training (EC 1976b).

For the first 20 years or so the EU 'equality' discourse developed slowly, reliant initially on its legal influence, until during the late 1970s the Commission's Equal Opportunities Unit (EO Unit) was established and quickly became the key player within the gendered equality discourse. The EO Unit produced Action Programmes for equal opportunities between women and men, which despite merely providing Recommendations (see Appendix III) and despite minimal funding, are nevertheless a major site for, and influence upon, the discourse of equal opportunities. The Action Programmes convey the official equal opportunities discourse and increasingly (as shown in Chapter 5) influence other policies and programmes with a greater legal force. From within the bureaucracy of the European regionalized state the feminist bureaucrats of the Commission's EO Unit call on 'networks' of women's organizations and panels of 'experts'.[9] This discourse of equality is inevitably also part of the ever-shifting, and heavily contested ground between reverse and dominant discourse.

The discourse of equality

The European discourse of equal opportunities uses language such as 'access', 'individual choice' and 'opportunity'. This is the language of liberal democracy to which the late twentieth-century additions of gender, women, ethnic minorities, migrants, disabilities, gay, and under-representation may be added. 'Equal' is then appended to choice, opportunity and rights. The power of the equality discourse is that in focusing on individual freedom of choice it often masks the social and economic inequalities inherent in the discourse of economic growth. Whereas it is possible to identify two forms of equality, formal and material, I shall argue that western liberal democracy, exemplified in the EU recognizes only formal inequality.

Formal equality

Formal equality is based on the legal 'rights' of the individual to compete on an equal basis for the opportunities within a society. This formal notion of equality can be traced back to the Enlightenment, to for example, Thomas Paine's *The Rights of Man* (1791/2), J.S. Mill's *On Liberty* (1859) and *The Subjection of Women* (1869), and Mary Wollstonecraft's *Vindication of the Rights of Women* (1792). The argument is that each individual, irrespective of class or sex (and later, race, disability and sexuality), has the same basic 'natural' rights, and that there is, therefore, no justification for any legislation that blocks or removes those rights. The legal and practical recognition of these 'natural rights' allow women access to the same chances as men and to compete on an equal basis. This is the underlying argument of theorists and activists who can be identified as 'liberal feminists' (for example Byrne 1978) and is an argument based on 'similarity'.

Similarity or difference

Many feminist theorists continue to question this Enlightenment argument of similarity, arguing instead for a recognition of difference and the social and economic consequences and manifestations of that difference.[10] Merle Thornton (1986) gives a summarized version of the two approaches. Accordingly, equality based on similarity is framed by the fundamental assumption that men and women have equal natures, so therefore, if women are given equal treatment through legislation and action then the outcome will be equality. Equality based on difference, in contrast, is framed by the assumption that men and women are gendered by nature, so that if women and men are equally enabled to develop their divergent capabilities they will perform differently, but will be mutually complementary and have comparable value. Hence again, equality will be achieved.

The argument against equality based on similarity is that it operates within a normative framework. This framework assumes that everyone can be treated alike and from within the same parameters in what may be described as a 'male' framework. Carole Pateman (1988) argues that citizenship itself, although notionally based on individuals, is in fact based on a male individual. Joni Lovenduski (1986) points to the gender blindness of EU policy and highlights the equality legislation that, by focusing primarily on the labour market, has ignored social and material gender equality issues such as those relating to women's health and reproduction. Similarly, Tuija Parvikko (1991) asserts that equality based on similarity actually obscures differences, which in turn obscures material inequality caused by gender difference.

Equality based on similarity, Meehan and Sevenhuijsen (1991) further argue, defines difference as inequality. To be 'different' means you are not the same as 'us' – the norm and therefore that you are not entitled to equality. Within British law, for example, the perceived 'difference' of gay men, lesbians and people with disabilities is such that they are denied full equality legislation.[11]

The argument in favour of equality based on difference is no longer based on the biological essentialism of some early radical feminism, but on the

> personal, emotional and psychological consequences of societal structures . . . the particular nature of the female experience, female identities and female subjectivities to be found in modern capitalist economies.
>
> (Arnot 1994: 7–8)

Sylvia Hewlett (1986) praises 'difference' as the basis of what she sees as the more successful European approach. In contrast Sylvia Walby (1994) has provided a critique of European feminists who, in working to influence equality legislation, have adopted the strategy of 'similarity'. However, despite the theoretical differences in their approach, both arguments of similarity and difference demand 'rights' and both are firmly located in the discourse of formal equality. From both sides of the sameness/difference debate one has 'rights' to formal equality (even though in some cases they are denied), but only 'opportunities' to material equality. In arguing from a position of 'sameness' all people are supposedly given the same opportunities. In arguing from a position of difference, different people can be provided with different opportunities. It is at this interface of equal rights and equal opportunities and of similarity and difference, that the equality discourse shifts from formal to material.

It is not the intention to minimize the importance of the struggle for formal political equality based on arguments of human similarity and the rights and responsibilities of citizenship, for lack of these can result in exclusion. As discussed in Chapter 3, such effects can range from the restricted rights of British gays, lesbians and disabled people to the extreme danger of exclusion, the 'savage other' described by Arendt (1958), as, for example, in the complex emergence of ethnic hatred within the 'Bosnian conflict'. As will be shown in subsequent chapters, this approach leads to the concept of 'equal opportunities', a discourse that can maintain material inequalities as well as reduce them. Equal opportunities can be seen as an example of a liberal well-meaning practice through which power is exercised but which has indeterminate outcomes (Foucault 1977).

From the other perspective, those who argue for equality based on difference demand different opportunities but not equal ones. They relate to the discourse of material as well as formal equality. The argument of difference can appear attractive primarily because the similarity argument has proved so very limited and because it points to women's strengths rather than weaknesses.

Yet misgivings still remain about this perspective. My fear is that our biology and our assumed strengths have consistently been used against us: 'women are good at nurturing, or good with their fingers, so therefore they should stay at home and look after the children, or work as machinists or manufacture circuit boards'. The argument of difference can so easily slip over into the narrow restrictions of 'it's only natural', the biological and psychological ground that has been in the past so easily commandeered by the right. The other misgiving is that in focusing so intently on *gender* the difference argument can resemble the similarity approach in its assumption of a non-problematic stance towards the category of women – apparently ignoring other inequalities such as class. Finally, although the issues raised by the similarity and difference debate are fundamental to the question of equality, 'women' are still considered primarily in relation to 'men'. Other power relationships within and across gender tend to be ignored or considered secondary. Such arguments, established on difference or similarity, and based solely on gender, can lead to sweeping generalizations that simply reconstruct new forms of inequality. My argument, threaded throughout the following chapters, is for a concept of equality that is based on an understanding of the complexities by which material inequalities are maintained.

Material equality

Material equality would require a redistribution of the wealth and success of society, from those with privileged access to its material *outcomes*, to those without such access. Unlike formal equality, which promises (with some notable exceptions) the same political and legal rights to each individual, only select groups can have material, that is *economic* power. However, the European Union, dominated by the discourse of economic growth, *necessarily* creates inequalities based on differences of class, race and gender (Larrain 1979; Holden 1988). The European discourse of equality is therefore positioned between the democratic legal concessions and rights of formal equality and the capitalist perpetuation of material inequality that together forms the apex of liberal democracy.

(Dis)-Belief and social exclusion

The formal 'rights' of the discourse of equality are reliant on popular belief. From within this discourse of equality, individual rights are allegedly sacrosanct and success is viewed as individualistic. The discourse of equality rhetorically embraces *all* people, yet in practice, the concepts of disadvantage and dependency direct policies and actions towards groups of people identified as being in an inferior position within society.

Within the overall European discourse of equality, this is a point at which equal opportunities merges within the concept of social exclusion discussed above. The discourse of equal opportunities refers to individual access, choice and opportunity, yet in practice targets particular 'disadvantaged' groups such as long-term unemployed people, low qualified women, migrants or people with physical disabilities. Conversely, the discourse of social exclusion talks of multiple disadvantaged groups and stresses its intention of targeting policies towards them aimed at inclusion.

However, despite this apparently quite sharp shift in the discourse of equality, from individualized equal opportunities to group-based social exclusion, the outcomes of equality policies remain the same – that is only exceptional or fortunate individuals from the ranks of the long-term unemployed will gain access to (relatively secure, full-time) employment and become part of the socially included.

Michael Apple's metaphor of equality defined as everyone having 'the right to climb the north face of the Eiger or scale Mount Everest' is pertinent here (1996: 30). One might imagine masses of long-term unemployed women and men gathered at the bottom of the Eiger: the young unemployed and the 'early retired', those with few educational qualifications and those with physical or learning disabilities, women and migrants, the poor – the socially excluded. Women and men of the working classes might be viewed as struggling to find the necessary equipment and clothing, and trying to gain the necessary knowledge, experience, training and skill to begin their ascent, while watching those already equipped making their way up, and they watch as some (generally white educated men already armed with cultural capital) are simply helicoptered onto the summit. A few, originally excluded, will climb, some even higher than many of those originally ahead of them but many (probably the majority) will not get far for they are in numerous ways ill-equipped and ill-prepared; indeed some may no longer see the significance of attempting the climb in the first place. This image could, of course, be extended further, to allow for people being pushed off, some carrying others on their backs, or due to the effects of reduced state welfare, some people being simply too impoverished and hungry to climb, or even no longer wanting to climb.

As will be seen in the European, British and local examples discussed in the next chapters, education, training and social policies are increasingly targeting funds onto 'deprived' areas of cities in an attempt to address issues of poor housing, inadequate healthcare, poor environment, high crime, physical isolation from social and leisure facilities, and persistent generational unemployment. Such funded schemes include 'job creation', 'work experience', a plethora of training schemes and more recently, 'second chance' education. However, the realities of the macroeconomic and social context means that while some individuals will undoubtedly benefit, the fact remains that none of these approaches, policies or training programmes will or can, in themselves, address the underlying fundamental economic poverty of 'deprived' areas and 'disadvantaged' groups. Nicaise *et al.* (1995) concludes that even well designed and accurately targeted active labour policies can only redistribute the *probability* of employment. A similar finding resulted from my earlier British research (Brine 1992).

That is, even if all those waiting at the bottom of the Eiger were equally equipped, they would still not all reach the summit. However this is not intended as a version of social Darwinism, for it needs to embrace the power-structures that influence the ease or difficulty in climbing. As Iris Marion Young (1990a) argues, 'opportunity' is related to more than simple 'equal distribution'. She suggests that even *if* material resources were distributed equally within education, social groups would still be adversely affected by the dominant social and economic structures of liberal 'oppression'. She defines her concept of 'oppression' as structural, and less an expression of the tyranny of a ruling group than the result of 'the everyday practices of a well-intentioned liberal society' (Young 1990a: 41), for example, the EU's equal opportunities programmes. She argues that her identification of five faces of oppression (exploitation, marginalization, powerlessness, cultural imperialism and violence) enable the recognition of material differences of groups and individuals.

The image of the north face of the Eiger is, it seems, a more appropriate image for considering social justice and equality than the so-called 'level playing field'. Alternatives to the mythical formal equality of the level playing field or the material inequality represented by the Eiger metaphor would demand changes to globalization. Nevertheless, localized, and more limited alternatives, are, and will continue to be, constructed out of the possibilities for agency and resistance. As suggested within Chapters 6 and 7, such alternatives may, to varying extents and in numerous ways, be constructed by member state governments, by government agencies, by educational institutions and providers, teachers, learners, unemployed people, community groups and other voluntary organizations.

The movement in the equality discourse from equal opportunities to social exclusion reflects the effects of globalization and regionalization on employment (Levitas 1996). It appears to indicate a point where the demands and needs of a critical mass of unemployed people has been, or is about to be, reached. The intense concentrations of unemployed people within particular regions and in particular areas of cities poses a threat to the individuality of equal opportunities. Within these 'disadvantaged' groups and deprived areas, the credibility in equal opportunities is at the very least, questionable, if not quite yet totally dismissable. The discourse of equal opportunities is then reliant on a belief in its possibilities and the visibility of its policies in action, including sufficient results to maintain that belief (Brine 1995a). The discourse of social exclusion appears to move away from individual blame towards identifying the individual as a member of a 'disadvantaged' group. This seems to be a necessary shift in the discourse of equality, as in the face of mass long-term unemployment, the individual deficit model is a suspect concept. When individuals are surrounded by other people all experiencing similar poverty and other aspects of exclusion, fault simply cannot be ascribed to the individual. The *belief* in equal opportunities breaks down.

Conclusion

In the first part of this chapter I focused on the discursive construction of the European Union. I was particularly interested in the shifting relationship of dominant and reverse discourse and their relationship to ideology. This analysis allowed for the identification of the concepts of agency and conflict, and while possibly messy and fluid, the flexibility of discourse was seen to maintain the power-relations of the ideological intentionality.

In returning to the discourses of economic growth and internal peace and considering their relationship to each other and to the development of European policy, I argued that the discourse of equality is an integral part of the EU's discourse of internal peace and furthermore is directly linked to the inherent conflict within liberal-democracy. This conflict is one in which the demand for a segmented labour force constructs material inequalities that must then be masked, deflected and distanced from the discourse of economic growth. This is the ideological intentionality of the discourse of equality.

The middle section of the chapter focused on the European Commission's legal competencies in training, education, the European Social Fund and equal opportunities between women and men. The intention here was to provide a detailed context for the analysis of the related policies that will be pursued in the following chapters.

The final section contains the first stage of analysis of the discourse of equality that will continue through the rest of the book. It is argued that the power of the equality discourse is that it attempts to mask the social and economic inequalities inherent in the discourse of economic growth by focusing attention on the individual's freedom of choice and opportunity. The similarity/difference equality debate was applied to formal and material concepts of equality, and an argument was put forward for a concept of equality based on an understanding of the complexities by which material inequalities are maintained. Finally, I considered the discursive shift between equal opportunities and social exclusion and again related this to the concept of formal and material equality, arguing here that such a shift has been a necessary response to the increased unemployment resulting from globalization – a response that attempts to maintain the vital popular belief in the discourse of equality.

Notes

1 Although there are many interesting and complex issues to be explored between these two aspects of the Commission, this definition is sufficient for the understanding developed in this book.

2 For analyses of liberal–democracy see Miliband (1973), Larrain (1979) and Holden (1988).

3 The British Conservative government's refusal to sign the Social Chapter of the Maastricht Treaty restricted the development of European social policy, not only within Britain, but across the EU. One of the first actions of the incoming Labour government (May 1997) was to sign this Social Chapter and to quickly adopt the concept of social exclusion (see Lister 1998). The social chapter was subsequently integrated into the Treaty of Amsterdam (EC 1997c). Social policy remains one of the contentious issues, along with monetary union, that divide Eurosceptics from Europhiles – most notably, although not exclusively, within the British Conservative party.

4 The French position at the Amsterdam summit echoes the earlier position of Jacques Delors, the previous French president of the European Union, in his key policy document, the *White Paper: Growth, competitiveness, employment* (EC 1993a).

5 Articles 57, 118 and 128 of the Treaty of Rome (EC 1957) provide the legal basis for the Commission's vocational training policy. These are superseded by the Treaty of the Union (EC 1992a) and the Amsterdam Treaty (EC 1997c) in which Article 127 enables the Commission to implement training policies to support and supplement the action of the member states in order to adapt to industrial changes and enable the vocational integration and reintegration of people into the labour market.

   Appendix III clarifies the distinctions within EC legislation and documentation.

6 Funnell and Müller (1991), Neave (1991) and Brine (1995b) provide overviews of the development of European training policy.

7 Article 126 of the Treaty of the Union (EC 1992a) and the Amsterdam Treaty (EC 1997c) covers the development of 'the European dimension in education, particularly through the teaching and dissemination of the languages of the Member States'.

8 The European Social Fund (ESF) is established through Article 123 of the Treaty of Rome (EC 1957).

9 I develop my ideas on feminists working within bureaucracies (femocrats) from the work of Franzway *et al.* (1989), Eisenstein (1990) and Yeatman (1990, 1993).

10 Feminists arguing for equality based on difference include Pateman (1988), Heater (1990), Young (1990a, 1990b), Parvikko (1991), Meehan (1992) and Arnot (1994).

11 There are early indications from the new British Labour government that some aspects of such formal legal inequality may (through the European Court of Justice) be addressed.

5 Education, training and gender equality in the EU

The aim of this chapter is to provide a gendered/classed analysis of European policy during the latter half of the twentieth century. The aim of this account is not to present an unproblematic historic progression but to identify a series of changes that reflect many, often conflicting, interests full of contest and compromise. For example, the previous chapter explored some of the areas of tension that exist between the European Commission (EC) and the member states, as well as some of those between member states themselves. Moreover, the European Commission itself appears riddled with bureaucrats' individual and departmental power positionings and struggles – as is also the case with individual member state governments, albeit on a somewhat smaller scale.

This chapter begins by focusing on the 'femocrats' who work within the European bureaucracy – particularly those of the Equal Opportunities Unit (EO Unit). It highlights the way in which each shift in the discourse and policy represents a highly contested site. Yet, at these sites, the struggles for opportunity and resistance point to both the agency of people and the shadow image of policy constraints. The focus is then turned onto the European Social Fund which is the main source of funding for training unemployed women. An historic overview is provided of the development of European education and training policy interlinked with an analysis of the impact of the equality discourse.

Feminist discourses and the EU

The EO Unit, introduced in the last chapter, provides a site for feminist involvement within the Commission and furthermore legitimates feminist actions and interventions. Feminist activities include various groups: 'femocrats' working within the bureaucracy of the Commission, feminist Members of the European Parliament, feminists' interests represented in non-governmental organizations (NGOs) and networks, and individual feminists who act as experts and consultants. Yet even here within explicit feminist intervention in state policy, there is no one identifiable feminist discourse, but numerous shifting discourses which as Hester Eisenstein (1990) found in her work in the US and Australia, reflect national differences, differences of politics, differences within the women's movements and differences in national dominant feminist theory. Furthermore, the development of second-wave feminism differs considerably from one member state to another, as Gisela Kaplan (1992: 21), in her exploration of feminism across Europe, states:

> in one western European society it may be regarded as 'wrong' for anyone to be considered a feminist but entirely acceptable to belong to the local/national women's movement. In another it may be approved that women attain equal status but frowned upon if this is meant to be achieved via a women's movement.

Moreover, laid upon these 'national' variations are differences that reflect the diversity of feminist perspectives – in theory and in practice (for instance, liberal, socialist, radical, lesbian, black, revolutionary). These perspectives disagree over the extent of compromise and definition of aims and objectives, tactics and strategies.[1]

The European Commission is an example of what Anna Yeatman (1993: 141) describes as a 'corporatist "new" welfare state'. She suggests that feminist claims on the state need to fit with the state's prevailing economic (and I would add, political) strategy. It is this apparent necessity for compromise that leads to tension between internal femocrats and external activists and academics. Eisenstein describes a continual calculation of degrees of (partial) trust negotiated between feminists inside and outside state organizations: those on the outside mistrusting the pull of loyalties (and job insecurities) of those on the inside, and critical of their slow, reformist strategy for change. Eisenstein offers support to the femocrats and their struggle with the male bureaucratic structure and the individual men with bureaucratic power. She argues that the 'struggle was always to extend the areas within which one's gender experience and expertise was recognized by the men who continued, overall, to set the agenda' (Eisenstein 1990: 102).

The EO Unit appears to exemplify such an area of tension and possibility, and the attempt to broaden the gendered agenda is particularly relevant to the 'mainstreaming' of equal opportunities, which is considered in this and the following chapter. However, this chapter focuses on the EO Unit's Action Programmes and their impact on education and training policy. It is argued that the EO Unit operates as 'discursive guerrillas' in the political and cultural struggle for gender equality.

The First Action Programme for equal opportunities between women and men ran from 1982 to 1985; the Second from 1986 to 1990; the Third from

1991 to 1995, and the Fourth from 1996 to 2000. These Programmes provide a 'mission statement' of priorities for action and funding that acted as an interpretative filter within the implementing process. As Recommendations that carry no legal force, they nevertheless indicate the EC/EO Unit's position at a particular time. They also focus attention on the Commission's commitment to equal opportunities on gender, generating questions of tokenism, containment and femocratization within the EO Unit, and also questions relating to member state interpretations of Commission policy. Despite this critique, which will be examined throughout future chapters, the Action Programmes do nevertheless play a positive role, influencing a range of EU social policy such as workers' rights, social security entitlements and pensions. They have also ensured (at least legally) that women have access to funded training provision.

Researching policy

In an analysis of European policy, each shift in the discourse and the policy can represent a highly contested site. Moreover, in locating this analysis within a state-centred framework such as that described by Jenny Ozga (1990), her concern with the role played by the state in education policy making is pertinent. Yet at the same time, it is necessary to be wary of confusing policy, White Papers or legislation with actual outcomes.

The research into European education and training policy on which this book is based contains several interlinking aspects: first, the analysis of policy texts. A fine textual historical analysis of Commission policy documents is followed by a similar analysis of those of the member states. A documentary trace of the process of policy interpretation is the next step: from the Commission to the member state governments, and from there, on to the internal structures such as those explored in Chapter 6.

Second, the research is concerned with the agency of policy makers, administrators, educators and students. Moving away from the Commission and member state policy makers, the focus in Chapter 6 turns to these people who participate in the *interpretative* process. The intention is to go beyond the public pronouncements of policy makers while at the same time bearing in mind warnings against the personalization of policy (Ball 1994a). This policy network analysis focuses on groups who are directly involved with the state in the policy process (Raab 1994). Finally, this engagement with the interpretation of policy leads, in Chapter 7, to the providers and receivers of training. The overall intention is to engage in what Whitty *et al.* (1993) have described as trajectory analysis; an analysis that traces policy from its political inception, through interpretation and implementation, onto a consideration of its effects on social justice and inequality.

This consideration of effects centres on the ways in which, in various arenas, we find spaces and gaps to create opportunities, to resist, adapt, struggle and even to take differing forms of ownership of policy. The vast range of sites of discourse and action within the process of implementing school education policy (Raab 1994) is also true of education and training policy for unemployed people. The links of the chain here correspond to the member state, the region, a sector of administration, a training scheme or college, an individual course, a practitioner or learner – none of these, politically or educationally, are an exact reproduction of the other. Yet while not clones, they all operate within a shared political and economic context, albeit affected by sector and region/country. In Britain, for example, elements of differentiation in ESF policy interpretation have been found between Scotland, Wales and England (Brine 1996a). At all levels of the interpretation and implementation process, the constraining structures and processes of European education and training policy are evident, but equally so are the struggles for opportunity and resistance – the impact of agency of all involved in the interpretation and implementation process.

The Commission's crumbs

The major source of funding for training unemployed women and men in Britain is the European Social Fund (ESF).[2] Until 1994 the ESF carried a separate budget for training women, which will be considered in relation to the overall ESF budget.

Within the EC budget for 1990–92, 239 million ecu (mecu), were allocated to 'specific schemes to assist women encountering difficulties on the labour market'. At the rate of exchange of 1.38 ecu to the pound, 239 mecu may be calculated as £173 million.[3] Although this appears a large sum of money, this 239 mecu was only 5.8 per cent of the total 4,020 mecu allocated to training unemployed people (EC 1990a: 38–9).[4] The total allocation to the entire ESF for this period was 60,315 mecu (EC 1990a: 13).[5] The 239 mecu allocated to women was therefore just under 0.4 per cent of the total funding allocation available. This means that European women are only gaining specifically gendered access to a very small portion of the total funding available. Of the cake, or perhaps more accurately, the bakery, unemployed, undereducated women get the crumbs. Moreover, the entire ESF budget is a mere 7 per cent (approximately) of all Commission funding (EC 1990a) meaning the specific allocation for training women is an extremely small part of that 7 per cent. Within the overriding economic concern of the European Union the budget allocated to training unemployed, undereducated women appears tokenistic, yet conversely, within the UK for example, ESF funded training for women has provided relatively well-funded provision with built-in allocations for child-care and travel expenses.

Historic overview of policy

Building on the earlier work of Neave (1991), four periods within European education and training policy are identifiable, with the first three concerned almost exclusively with training policy (Brine 1998). The first period began with the establishment of the EEC in 1957. The second and shorter period covers the late 1970s to the mid-1980s. Both these periods were concerned exclusively with training policy, training that should lead to training-related employment. The third period covers the mid-1980s to the early 90s with the most recent fourth period covering most of the 1990s. The Reforms of the ESF, introduced in the previous chapter, are significant markers in the identification of these periods.

This framework based on periods of training policy has been chosen because the analysis of education and training policy predates the EO Unit. It shows the shifting influence of the dominant discourses of economic growth and peace, and second how the Action Programmes impact on the education and training policy, not vice versa. The Action Programmes do not, therefore, exactly match the defined periods of the policy framework.

This chosen framework enhances the analysis of three main themes: first, the early concerns of this book, that is the relationship of policy to the dominant discourses of economic growth and peace; second, the debate surrounding the relationship between the nation and regionalized state; and third, the impact of the equality discourse.

The first period: late 1950s to late 1970s

This first period was firmly located in the discourse of economic growth. The first two major Reforms of the ESF fell within this period (EC 1971, 1977). Although the oil crisis of 1973 also fell in this first period, its impact on policy was not felt until the late 1970s. The main concern at this time was cyclical youth unemployment.

The 1971 Reform of the ESF

The first Reform of the ESF introduced a system of 'Priorities and Guide-lines' through which funding for certain social groups was to be prioritized. Although 'women' constituted such a 'group' this development actually generated very little attention for women and resulted in even less direct practical impact.

The second period: late 1970s to mid-1980s

This was a key period primarily because it introduced five major policy changes which subsequently had a considerable impact on later periods. First, the discourse of peace began, slowly, to influence policy. Second, there was a related realization that unemployment was neither cyclical nor confined to youth, but was *structural* and involved adult unemployment as well. Third, decentralization of control enabled member state governments to incorporate European funds into their national training programmes. Fourth, while continuing to emphasize the 'group' of women as needing attention, the particular needs of undereducated working class women were highlighted. Finally, stress was placed on training related to (traditional) occupational underrepresentation.

The 1977 Reform of the ESF

The second Reform shifted the administration of the ESF onto the member state government. Within Britain, management was given to the Department of Employment (DE). This enabled the member state government to incorporate European-funded training into its own national employment and training policy. Furthermore, as will be seen in Chapter 6, the now renamed Department for Education and Employment (DfEE) is itself a major recipient of ESF funds.

The 1977 (EC 1977) Reform identified two separate priorities for women:

i. schemes promoting women's participation in new jobs and in jobs where they are under-represented;
ii. schemes concerning traditional female jobs . . . enabling them to get a job more highly qualified than their previous one.

(Morgan-Gerard 1980: 65)

Despite these twin priorities, full funding was only allocated to the first priority: occupational under-representation and participation in new jobs.[6] The Reform stated that to receive European funding women needed to 'be aged over 25; have lost jobs, never worked, or wish to return to work after a break; have no or inadequate qualifications – that is, are unskilled or semi-skilled' (EC 1981: 2). A later analysis (EC 1987d) of the Priority system identified three choices open to training providers: putting together a programme that fully corresponds with the funding criteria; adapting a programme to meet the funding criteria; or not applying. The Report (EC 1987d) concluded that providers, focusing on the funding criteria of the programmes, tended to ignore the needs of working-class women that differed from those specified.

The equality discourse

For the first 20 years or so following the Treaty of Rome (1957), the equality discourse developed slowly, reliant mainly on its legal basis. The Commission's Women's Information Service (EC 1981: 2) provided an interpretation of the 1977 Reform:

> The highest priority is given to programmes that train women for occupations that have been traditionally reserved for men or for programmes that train them for new jobs open to both sexes. When first priority applications have been met, second priority is given to programmes that concern traditional female employment but (i) are for women involved in mass dismissals; (ii) *or* facilitate women to reach a higher level of employment than their previous employment.

While this interpretation gave equally high priority to both training in traditional male occupations and to new jobs, training related to hierarchical under-representation was far down the list. The overriding significance of this interpretation was its introduction of the concept of *traditional* occupational under-representation – a key feature of all subsequent policy. The Women's Information Service was shortly subsumed within the EO Unit, established in 1976.

The first Equal Opportunities Action Programme (1982–85) which began towards the end of the second period of training policy, had little impact. This Action Programme was in fact generally ignored until the EC's demand for women's training was reinforced by the policies of 1983 and 1984, as discussed below.

The third period: mid-1980s to early 1990s

This crucial period of policy coincided with aspects of globalization discussed earlier. Although located primarily in the discourse of economic growth, the period became increasingly influenced by the discourse of peace, which led to significant changes in the discourse. The initial concern with peace *between* member states was evidenced by the concentration of Funds onto those member states and regions most economically disadvantaged, for example, Spain, Portugal, Greece and Ireland. During the 1980s, the discourse shifted to include peace *within and across* the member states. This discursive shift reflected several key European factors of change, for example, the collapse of the eastern European communist states, the reunification of Germany, the rise of Fascist organizations within the EU and the postcommunist states, as well as the continuing increase in long-term unemployment and the demands made on state welfare systems by unemployed and elderly people. It was also influenced by the social and political consequences of the constructed European Single Market (Social Europe 1988) and the social welfare reforms demanded by European Monetary Union.

Most of the major developments throughout the 1980s were linked to the crucial shifts between the discourses of economic growth and peace. These shifts reflected the Commission's growing concern with long-term unemployment and social exclusion. The development of 'human resources' were the main concern, but despite the underlying belief that no state should benefit by cheap (women's) labour, the average pay of women, from the lowest to the highest paid, remained, across the EU, at 60–70 per cent of equivalent male workers (EC 1994b; van Doorne-Huiskes *et al.* 1995).

Education policy

It was not surprising, given the Commission's increased concerns with unemployment and social unrest, that the discourse of peace became more dominant and there was an emergent concern with compulsory education that prepared the ground for the further development of education policy during the 1990s. Linked in the first instance to the Single European Act (EC 1986), the EU discourse of education began with two Declarations (EC 1983a, 1984a) introducing the concept of European citizenship and the idea of a European 'dimension' in education. A few years later the 1988 Resolution stressed the economic and social role of education policy and specified the European values that should be included within the curriculum (EC 1988). It was this Resolution that fed directly into Article 126 of the Treaty of the Union (EC 1992a, 1997c).

The 1988 Reform of the ESF

This Reform reflected both the discourses of economic growth and of peace. It signalled the growing importance of training policy in the construction of the EU for it recognized the ESF as a key instrument of economic and social cohesion. While women continued as a designated priority group, they were now more tightly defined as 'unemployed women with few qualifications or marketable skills' – and even more narrowly focused on women of the working classes. Significantly, neither the terms 'under-representation' nor 'traditional' were mentioned in this Reform. As previously, neither 'race' nor ethnicity was a recognized category for special attention.

As part of the overall process of subsidiarity, the Reform continued to devolve decision-making and managerial power away from the Commission and onto the member state governments. As part of this devolution of power, a new and highly significant procedure was introduced whereby all member states agreed to a general framework for funding priorities and allocations.[7] The framework specified the parameters within which individual member states negotiate their priorities to reflect their national training and employment policies.

There were four reasons why the 1988 Reform was a key policy. It included a number of major innovations: concentration of effort, increased partnership, strategic planning, and clarification of 'additionality'.[8] Second, it emphasized compatibility and synergy with other policies and programmes. Third, it demanded greater accountability throughout the implementing process. Finally, it stressed its direct relationship with social cohesion and economic growth.

The equality discourse

It was during the third period of policy that the influence of the EO Unit and the equality discourse could be clearly identified. The lack of response to the 1977 Reform provoked the Commission's Decision of 1983 (EC 1983b). This reinforced the Reform's intention that unemployed women be targeted for training. It equally significantly reiterated the 1981 interpretation (EC 1981) linking *traditional* to occupational under-representation. The ESF was to:

> Support programmes specifically to help women aged over 25 to find new jobs, especially in the fields of computers, electronics and office work. It also helps women to find jobs in industries where they are traditionally under-represented, or more qualified jobs in industries where women are frequently employed.
>
> (EC 1984b: 9)

The 1977 Reform was further reinforced by the 1984 Recommendation on 'positive action for women' (EC 1984c) which recommended that member states:

1b) . . . encourage the participation of women in various occupations in those sectors of working life where they are at present under-represented, particularly in the sectors of the future, and at higher levels of responsibility in order to achieve better use of all human resources . . .

4) . . . diversification of vocational choice, and more relevant vocational skills, particularly through appropriate vocational training . . . encouraging women candidates and the recruitment and promotion of women in sectors and professions and at levels where they are under-represented, particularly as regards positions of responsibility . . .

8) To make efforts also in the public sector ... particularly in those fields where new information technologies are being used or developed.

(EC 1984c: 34, 35)

This Recommendation was again concerned with under-representation, but this time made no reference to 'traditional', emphasizing instead future sectors of employment, that is those relating to the growth and impact of new technologies and also equally concerned – at this stage – with hierarchical under-representation.

The Second Action Programme (1986–90) continued to focus on occupational rather than hierarchical under-representation. Despite the earlier references (EC 1983b, 1987b) to the growing concern with 'new technologies' and 'sectors of the future' in which women are 'encouraged towards an equal level of participation in employment linked with new technology (EC 1985: 9) the second Programme simply appended 'new technology' to the general descriptor of occupational under-representation.

Consequently, during the early 1980s there were within Britain many training projects for women established, and many of these appended basic word-processing to the equally basic training in areas of traditional under-representation, such as plumbing or bricklaying (Brine 1992). This emphasis on new technology and the future sectors of employment was, it turned out, short-lived and, as we have seen, has disappeared from subsequent Programmes dominated by traditional occupational under-representation (Brine 1995a).

The fourth period: the 1990s

It was in the fourth period that the discourse of internal peace engaged most directly with the discourse of economic growth, as exemplified by the Amsterdam Treaty (EC 1997c) discussed in Chapter 4. During the 1990s, the discourse of internal peace became increasingly evident in the Commission's policy documents and funding programmes. Long-term mass unemployment caused disunity within each member state and led to social exclusion and the fear of a 'dual society'. This increased dominance by the discourse of peace was reflected in the training policy. Until the late 1980s training was supposed to relate to the needs of the labour market and result in training-related employment.[9] By the 1990s the discourse had changed, reflecting the new understanding of the global labour market and its location of responsibility on the individual. Documents no longer referred to vocational skills or training related employment but of improved chances and opportunities, guidance and counselling, and increased self-confidence. In the mid-1990s there was evidence of a fear that social exclusion and the dual society would threaten both economic growth and peace and, with the rise of the Right within the EU and the postcommunist states, eventually threaten external peace as well (Brine 1997a).

This fear highlights a crucial underlying tension within advanced capitalist societies, between the creation (and need) of an unemployed reserve labour force and the potential threat from the unemployed towards existing power-relations and structures, a threat that ranges from non-violent protest and the presentation of alternatives to social unrest and riot. This shift to concerns about social exclusion creates the major interface between the discourses of economic growth and internal peace. It is also, as was argued in Chapter 4, a major area of tension between the European Commission and particular member states.

Currently at the heart of the discourse of internal peace, and consequently underpinning much of European policy, is the question, 'What do we do with the young unemployed and the long-term unemployed?' The complexities behind this apparently simple question are uncovered by an understanding, such as that developed within this book, of the power-relations operating towards 'the unemployed'. Furthermore, 'the unemployed' are not a homogeneous group, and (another list must be produced in order to emphasize this) these power-relations differ according to gender, class, race, age, and (dis)ability, reflected for example, in the constructs of the 'deserving' and 'undeserving' poor discussed in Chapter 3. Across Europe the social or state benefits of unemployed people are increasingly linked to training programmes. For instance, in the UK, state Unemployment and Income Support benefits are replaced by the Job Seeker Allowance, Project Work and Welfare to Work. These are seen as accelerated moves towards a compulsory US-style 'workfare' system, introducing powers that will force claimants to take low-paid jobs.[10]

The process of subsidiarity and devolution of control from the regionalized state to the nation state has continued throughout the 1990s. The ongoing trend of targeting funds and policies onto priority groups and regions has continued with member states required to address education and training issues related to unemployment and social exclusion.

The White Papers

From the beginning of the EU there has been a direct relationship between training policy, the European Social Fund, and the European labour market. Between 1993 and 1995 three key policy documents were published, all of which stressed the crucial role to be played by education and training in maintaining economic growth and social stability.

The White Paper on Growth is the linchpin of post-1994 economic, social, education and training policy. Although it relates primarily to globalization and to the economic growth of the EU, it also addresses the resultant problems of mass unemployment and social exclusion, arguing that economic growth and social policy must be linked. Highlighting the importance of education and training, it points to the clear linkage between low-skill, low educational attainment and subsequent unemployment and social exclusion. In particular, it identifies 'educational failure' as 'a particularly important and widespread factor of marginalization and economic and social exclusion' (EC 1993a: 188).

This concept of social exclusion is developed in the White Paper on Social Policy (EC 1994a) where the strong connection between social exclusion, low educational attainment and long-term unemployment is reiterated. Finally the *White Paper: Education and Training* (EC 1995a: 9) reaffirms the connection between education and exclusion:

> There is a risk of a rift in society between those that can interpret and those who can only use; and those who are pushed out of mainstream society and rely upon social support: in other words between those who know and those who do not know.

The first White Paper was concerned primarily with economic growth and unemployment, the second with unemployment and social exclusion and the third with the impact of both on European education and training policy. In the process of policy impacting on practice, it is clear that the agency of nation states, organizations, education and training providers, and unemployed women will also have an impact on policy.

Education policy

The Treaty of the Union (EC 1992a) extended the Commission's interest in education beyond vocational and postcompulsory education into schools, albeit, as described in Chapter 4, only in relation to the European dimension. Unquestionably, this period marks a significant discursive shift as the importance of education is stressed in all three key White Papers of this time (EC 1993a, 1994a, 1995a). Furthermore, the Commission's central 'Framework' research programme includes for the first time social and educational research (EC 1995b).[11] These White Papers point to the intertwined relationship of education and training policy within the discourses of economic growth and internal peace.

This education and training White Paper (EC 1995a) defines the EU's three essential requirements as: social integration, enhanced employability and personal fulfilment. These three requirements are not seen as incompatible. It states that its main concerns are with first, unemployment – hence education, training and lifelong learning; second, social exclusion – hence the importance of education; and third, the free movement of people – hence the importance of languages and the European dimension. The White Paper recommends a dual approach: first, to improve the broad base of knowledge and second, to increase abilities for employment and economic activity.

The *White Paper: Education and Training* thus provides a powerful analysis of the role of education and training but with weaker action guidelines. Yet in recommending 'second chance' education, in critiquing the present systems of education, and in advocating an education where students, pupils and teachers are all critical, analytical and creative, it may also be seen as a controversial document – or simply political rhetoric. The problem is clearly and powerfully stated, but despite reiterating the White Paper on Growth's clear recognition of global factors (EC 1993a), and despite reiterating the White Paper on Social Policy's elaboration of the group based, multideprivational concept of social exclusion (EC 1994a), the solution remains located on the individual. The Paper stresses the development of the individual's own abilities, knowledge base, transferable skills and 'learning culture'. While the White Papers on growth and social policy identify 'disadvantaged' groups of social exclusion, *Education and Training* continues to focus primarily, but not unproblematically, on the individual (EC 1995a).

The ESF Regulation of 1993

This Regulation (EC 1993b) maintains, strengthens and reinforces the four major innovatory principles of the 1988 Reform: concentration of effort, partnership, programming, and additionality.[12] It further highlights the relationship between the ESF and the labour market and stresses two key themes: 'mainstreaming' equal opportunities and unemployment. Accordingly, member states need to agree with the Commission a strategic plan covering their intended use of ESF. These plans need to describe the national labour market and the position of women within it. They need also to show the contribution of ESF towards the promotion of equal opportunities for men and women in the labour market.

Training policy is currently more sharply focused than before on those considered to be 'most vulnerable' to exclusion: the long-term, poorly educated, low-skilled, unemployed; the young unemployed; and, for the first time, those who are in work of a 'vulnerable' nature, that is, in those occupations most at risk from industrial change or changes in production systems.[13]

The Regulation has a significant impact on training for unemployed working-class women primarily through its stress on compatibility and synergy with 'the principle of equality of opportunity between men and women' (EC 1993b: 29). Coming between the Third and Fourth Action Programmes it legitimated the EO Unit's demand for 'mainstreaming'. By including it in the Regulation it became a policy in which the compliance of the member state could be legally demanded. While 'mainstreaming' gender-based equal opportunities, the ESF also continued to provide for 'women-only' training:

> equal opportunities for men and women on the labour market especially in areas of work in which women are under-represented and particularly for women not possessing vocational qualifications or returning to the labour market after a period of absence.
>
> (EC 1993c: 40)

This is an important statement because it clearly refers to *women*. The next chapter shows that this specification has been ignored by the UK government, which interprets the Regulation to mean men as well as women. It is also important because it specifies the women targeted by ESF as those women 'not possessing vocational qualifications, or returning to the labour market after a period of absence' (EC 1993c: 40). ESF provision is targeted on a *particular* group of women: low- and undereducated women, those women most at risk of unemployment and social exclusion (Council of Europe 1992; OECD 1992).

The equality discourse

The Third and the Fourth Action Programmes, both highly significant, took place during the fourth period of training.

The Third Action Programme

Referring back to the previous (Second) Programme this Third Programme (1991–95) (EC 1990b) reiterated the need to encourage more women towards occupations of under-representation and to increase women's hierarchical representation within those occupations. Yet hierarchical under-representation within traditional female occupations continued to be ignored. More significant is the absence of any explicit reference to new or information technology. Whereas the Second Action Programme had emphasized under-representation and new technology, new technology was missing in the new Programme, and the omission made it easier for member states to make broader interpretations of the policy. Moreover, the Commission Reports made progressively less mention of women – in some cases vaporizing them away altogether in the continued reference to the male worker (EC 1990c). This has happened despite the Commission's own Recommendation of November 1987 (Social Europe 1989a) and the findings of the European Toledo Seminar of 1989 where the need for training in the 'occupations of the future' such as new technology was stressed (Social Europe 1989b).

Finally, this Third Action Programme is an example of the struggle of the femocrats described by Eisenstein (1990) to extend the scope of the gendered agenda, in this case through the integration of gender-based equal opportunities into all European policies and activities – in other words, 'mainstreaming'. Several years later the ESF Regulation (EC 1993b) and then the White Paper on Social Policy (EC 1994a) both reiterated this mainstreaming theme. Furthermore there is an apparent synergy between the demand for 'mainstreaming', the other key White Papers of this time (EC 1993a, 1995a) and other major education and training programmes such as Leonardo, Socrates and Media. Nevertheless, while gender mainstreaming is introduced in the Third Programme, it is the Fourth that provides consolidation.

The Fourth Action Programme
The Fourth Action Programme (1996–2000) (EC 1995c) extends the concept of mainstreaming in its main aim, which is to integrate gender equality into Community, national, regional and local policies, including those relating to training and the labour market. The Fourth Programme continues the earlier Second Programme's emphasis on those 'occupations and sectors of activity where women are traditionally under-represented'(EC 1995c: 8). Despite this explicit reference, the Fourth Programme's first objective is mainstreaming: 'to promote the integration of equal opportunities for the male and female dimension in all policies and activities', and its third objective: 'to promote equal opportunities for men and women in a changing economy, especially in the fields of education, vocational training and the labour market' (EC 1995c: 39). There is in the Fourth Programme a dual approach to training. Although mainstreaming is undoubtedly the prime objective, some discreet 'women-only' provision is also maintained. The next chapter considers the effects of this Programme within the UK and consider its implications for working-class women.

Conclusion

This chapter has concentrated on the relationship between education, training and equality policies. In telling a tale of more than 40 years of policy it is unavoidable to adopt a narrative tone. Nevertheless, to reiterate the important point made at the beginning of this chapter, such a tale unavoidably masks the many shifting conflicts, alliances and compromises behind these changes in policy.

The historic framework of this chapter enables an analysis of the three main themes that are woven throughout each period. The first theme, linked to Chapters 1 and 3, explores the relationship between education and training policy and the discourses of economic growth and peace. The second theme continues to explore the relationship between the nation and regionalized state. The final theme, and the main concern of this chapter, focuses on the relationship between education and training policy and the discourse of equality.

First, it is important to emphasize that the discursive shift from economic growth in the first period to the emergent discourse of peace in the second and third, to the discursive struggles of the fourth, are not separate from education, training or even equality policies. They are the interface, the membrane between on one side the various aspects of globalization (Chapter 2), and on the other side the construction of the regionalized bloc (Chapter 1), and its policies (Chapter 3). The image of the membrane is deliberately chosen for its porosity and flexibility – the membrane could, if necessary, turn itself inside out.

Second, and in apparent contradiction to Chapter 3, from the 1977 Reform there is a devolution of ESF power and control from the Commission to the member state government. It is 'apparent' because while this devolved power allows considerable member state interpretation of policy, the Commission has not simply retained but increased its demands for member state accountability (especially financial) and has on several occasions reinforced its demands for gender equality – forcing the compliance of member states.[14]

Third, despite the slow start of the equality discourse, it has exerted a definite influence on education and training policy for women, especially during the 1980s and 1990s. The 1981 interpretation of the 1977 Reform (EC 1981) introduced the concept of *traditional* occupational under-representation, which was reiterated by the 1983 Decision (EC 1983b). While both the 1984 Recommendation (EC 1984c) and the Second Action Programme emphasize training related to new technologies, this concern is omitted from the Third Action Programme.

Fourth, although the Fourth Action Programme's overwhelming concern is with mainstreaming gendered equal opportunities across all EU policies and programmes, it nevertheless continues to refer to *traditional* occupational under-representation. The significance of this is explored in the next chapter. However, within the actual education and training policy itself, the only explicit reference to traditional occupational under-representation is in the 1983 Decision; it is not mentioned in the 1984 Recommendation, the 1977 Reform, the 1988 Reform or the 1993 Regulation. This emphasis on the traditional originates in, and is maintained by, the EO Unit's discourse of equality.

Finally, within the European equality discourse, this subdiscourse of gender equal opportunities is an exclusively gendered discourse, women, as an apparently unproblematic category are seen as needing equal opportunities with men, who are also seen as an equally unproblematic category. This seemingly class–race blind discourse is in fact based on numerous class–race assumptions and prejudices, which, as I will show in the next two chapters, maintain class and race-based power structures between women as well as those with men.

Notes

1 An account of differing feminisms can be found in Alison Jagger (1983) and Judith Evans (1995), and specifically in relation to education, Gaby Weiner (1994).
2 Training for unemployed people is catered for under Objective 3 of the ESF.
3 This sum represents, at the rate of exchange of 1.135 ecu to the US dollar, US$ 210.5 million.
4 At this time Objective 3 provided funds for unemployed people aged over 25 and Objective 4 for those aged under 25.
5 The ESF is one of the EU's four Structural Funds. The others are the European Regional Development Fund (ERDF), European Agricultural Guidance and Guarantee Fund (EAGGF), and the Financial Instrument for Fisheries Guidance (FIFG).
6 New jobs tended to mean those connected with setting up cooperative businesses. This type of training is included as one of the case studies of Chapter 7. Janet Hannah (1989) has written a useful critique of cooperative training.
7 This is the Community Support Framework (CSF).
8 The European concept of additionality has always been a difficult one. This Reform defined it to mean that any increases in EC funds received by a member state must be matched by an equivalent increase in their nation state expenditure; European funds could not simply be used to replace member state expenditure. Additionality was now defined solely in terms of financial contribution and no longer in terms of additional provision, either through its targeting or its curriculum.
9 Although as both Nicaise *et al.* (1995) and Brine (1992) have shown, there are few positive training-related employment outcomes.
10 The Job Seeker Allowance (JSA) came into effect in October 1996, and Project Work a month later. I return to this linkage of training with state benefits in Chapter 6. The new Labour government's Welfare to Work programme maintains this 'earn your benefit' approach.
11 Admittedly this Fourth Framework Programme makes the smallest allocation of funding to the Targeted Socio-Economic Research (TSER) strand (0.275 per cent of the total Framework budget). The implications of TSER funding for social justice research are explored in Brine (1997b).
12 To prevent EC funds simply replacing member state funds, the Commission provides a further definition of 'additionality' in which the member state is obliged to maintain 'its public structural or comparable expenditure at least at the same level as in the previous programming period' (EC 1993b: 25).
    See Appendix III for clarification of a Regulation.
13 The UK Conservative government refused to adopt ESF Objective 4 which provided training for those in work of a vulnerable nature.

14 The first example of enforced compliance with the Commission's demands for gender equality related to equal pay. The 1977 demands for women's training were reinforced by the 1983 and 1984 Declaration and Recommendation. The Fourth Action Programme's demand for mainstreaming is legitimated by the 1993 Regulation.

6 The 'agency' of the nation state: training policy for British working-class women

The trajectory analysis of policy continues in this chapter, which considers the involvement of the UK government in European education and training policy. The UK provides an example of the neoliberal state involved in the construction of a regionalized 'state'. At the time of writing, with the exception of the US it has the most deregulated and unprotected labour market of any of the OECD economies (Avis *et al.* 1996). Since the late 1970s the differences between the wealthy and the poor in the UK have increased markedly (Rowntree Trust 1995). Furthermore, the numerous redefinitions of 'unemployment' have made it difficult to compare one year with another, or the UK with other countries (Levitas 1996).

The chapter is structured using the same four periods defined in Chapter 5 and each section concludes with an analysis of the implications of the policy for working-class women. It concludes by considering the possible impact of policy up to 2000. The next chapter provides a case study of the UK implementation of policy in 1996. This relates directly to the Third and Fourth Action Programme's concept of mainstreaming introduced in the previous chapter.

Through its Department for Education and Employment (DfEE) the British government produces two quite different sets of policy documents regarding EU regulations.[1] The first are the annual *Guidelines* on Objective 3 of the ESF (ESF/3).[2] They are produced in response to the 1977 Reform of the ESF which, as detailed in Chapter 5, began the process of decentralizing control of the ESF onto the member state governments. The guidelines are for use by ESF administrators, sector managers and providers of training within the UK. The second set of documents began to appear in the early 1990s and are the required response to the ESF Regulations of 1993 (EC 1993b). These are strategic plans, called the Single Programming Documents (SPD), which need to be presented to the Commission for approval.

An analysis of the *Guidelines* produced annually since the 1988 Reform of the ESF, shows that, year by year, there have been significant discursive shifts in British policy, first in relation to ESF/3 policy, and second in the then Conservative government's explicit understanding of unemployed people.[3] Moreover, and of significance to the earlier considerations of the relationship between the nation and the regionalized state, an analysis of both the *Guidelines* and the Single Programming Documents show significant discrepancies between the nation state discourse constructed for the European Commission and that constructed for the UK audience.

The first period: late 1950s to late 1970s

During this period the ESF was administered directly by the Commission with no direct involvement from member state governments. This means there is then no evidence available for an analysis of the UK government during this time, and the legislation of 1983 and 1984 (discussed below) suggest that across the EU, there was very little take-up of opportunities to train unemployed women.

The second period: late 1970s to mid-1980s

Despite the 1977 Reform's significant devolution of ESF power to the member state, and despite its emphasis on women as a targeted group for training, there appeared to be a general lack of interest in or involvement with training for unemployed working-class women.

Policy implications for working-class women

Because of this lack of member state interest in training unemployed working-class women, the full impact of the 1977 Reform was not felt until after the reinforcement legislation of 1983 and 1984 (EC 1983b, 1984c); that is not until the third period. What is crucial about this second period is the long-standing influence of the policy introduced by the Reform. Two major themes introduced then not only continue into the late 1990s but were considerably strengthened along the way. The first theme was that ESF training should be focused on undereducated (generally working-class) women. The second theme was the almost exclusive emphasis placed on occupational under-representation, and equally importantly, on occupations of *traditional* under-representation, as mentioned previously. Although equally high priority was given to training in traditional male occupations as to training for 'new' jobs, training related to hierarchical under-representation was not accorded the same priority and therefore, as the Report on Priorities found (EC 1987d), applications in this area stood very little chance of successful funding.

The third period: mid-1980s to early 1990s

Immediately following the Decision and Recommendation (EC 1983b, 1984c) there were several ESF-funded projects set up throughout the UK for training unemployed women. The majority of these were developed either by local authorities such as city and county councils or by organizations within the voluntary sector. For example, the Industrial Common Owner-ship Movement (ICOM) ran several projects training women to set up worker cooperatives. However, the involvement of the UK government was still negligible and it remained possible in 1983–84 to negotiate directly with the ESF administration in Brussels.

Yet once involved, the influence and control of the UK government rapidly increased, so that by the end of this period this was the major determinant of ESF policy in the UK. The process of decentralization has enabled greater member state agency, an agency with a potentially important impact on training for unemployed undereducated working-class women.

To reiterate an important point made in Chapter 5: neither 'under-representation' nor 'traditional' were mentioned in either the 1988 Reform or the UK's required framework agreement. Yet, despite this, the UK *European Social Fund: Guidance on Applications for 1991* (DE 1990) opens by actively encouraging training projects for women entering non-traditional areas of employment. It adds that claims to train 'women' can only be for areas of traditional under-representation. Other than in the extracted Sex Discrimination Act's example of 'plumbing or construction' the main text does not further qualify 'traditional under-representation'. The *Guidelines* make no mention at all of new technology training for women. Between the agreement of framework priorities with the Commission and the publication of British *Guidelines*, a decision was made to emphasise traditional under-representation and not to mention new technology.

This reference to 'traditional under-representation' was a persistent fea-ture of guidance documents throughout the 1980s and continued to be reiterated and reinforced throughout the 1990s. Moreover, the *Guidelines* (erroneously) state that it is the framework agreement that specifies 'tra-ditional under-representation' and that this criterion is:

> based on the Community Support Framework for Great Britain and other established practices under the ESF. . . Therefore applications, must facilitate the integration of women into occupations where they are traditionally under-represented.
>
> (DE 1990: 33, 35)

Interestingly, inserted into the above preamble is the phrase, 'other estab-lished practices under the ESF'. This implies that previous practice, priorities and guidelines can continue to operate, even if they have not been specific-ally covered in the agreed framework. The British government, more in line with the equality discourse than the training policy, continued to prioritize training unemployed women in areas of 'traditional under-representation' at the expense of providing them with training for either new technology or advancement in traditional areas of work. This may be an example of what Foucault (1977) referred to as the exercise of power through what appears to be a liberal well-meaning discourse.

Policy implications for working-class women

From the 1977 Reform onwards, both the equality policy and the UK interpretations of training policy have continued to prioritize training for traditional occupations of under-representation. This policy frequently translates into training for occupations such as plumbing, bricklaying and other occupations related to the building renovation and construction industries. Simultaneously, the lack of priority given in policy to hierarchical under-representation has meant that there has been very little training in this area (Brine 1992).

The analysis begins by returning to the discourse of equality introduced in Chapter 4 where it was argued that this discourse can only recognize gender inequality. This is because it is possible to address gender inequality through formal, legal, measures that supposedly give women the same rights of access and opportunity as men. Conversely, recognizing and addressing class and race inequalities would demand the recognition of material inequality and significant changes in the current capitalist discourse of economic growth. The continuation of material inequalities based on gender, class, race and ethnicity is then sustained. This inability to recognize material inequality results in the gender exclusivity of the discourse. It is a discourse that lacks class or race analysis yet, at the same time, it is actually reflecting strong class and race assumptions. In short, this gender exclusive discourse means that black and white working-class women are trained for black and white working class men's jobs.

As well as being confined in this way by the restrictions of a *formal* equality discourse, the EO Unit's own discourse reflects both an essentialist and a class-based perception of the category of women that might be thought reminiscent of the theory and discourse of the 1970s and 1980s. This reflects the classed and racialized assumptions, and middle-class, predominantly white, interests of the femocrats themselves.

In addition to a class analysis of the concept of 'traditional' pursued throughout this chapter, a classed assumption may be identified behind the relegated concern of *hierarchical* under-representation. This relegation assumes that hierarchical under-representation is of concern only to middle-class educated women who have adopted the constructed concept of the glass ceiling. It ignores the numerous degrees of hierarchy within traditional (male and female) working-class occupations, largely favouring men.

The basic gender exclusivity of the equality discourse is subsequently compounded by the UK government in its interpretation of policy. As shown in Chapter 5, the first reference to 'traditional' under-representation was made in the 1981 interpretation of the 1977 Reform (EC 1981). This was reiterated in the Commission Decision of 1983 (EC 1983b) but omitted from the Recommendation of 1984 (EC 1984c). Moreover, neither the 1988 Reform (EC 1987c) nor the 1993 Regulation (EC 1993b) mentioned the terms underrepresentation or traditional. Nevertheless, later the Fourth Action Programme for 1996–2000 (EC 1995c) continued the equality discourse's focus on traditional occupational under-representation.

This concept of 'traditional' under-representation frames the UK government's interpretation of policy, and has been annually reinforced by the *Guidelines* documents. The combination of this concept of traditionality and the gender exclusivity of the discourse means that only occupational under-representation is recognized, and only in those most visible, most traditional occupations of working-class men. Changes in these, it is believed, will provide the greatest evidence of 'equal opportunities' in practice (Brine 1995a). Working-class women are then as disadvantaged by their class – educationally, environmentally and economically – as they are by their gender, and black working-class women, living in a white-dominated, racialized (and frequently racist) society, by their race and colour also.[4] This discourse of equal opportunities then does not recognize any differences, diversity or power relations existing between women.

This has meant that throughout this third period from the mid-1980s to the early 1990s (and beyond), working-class, unemployed, undereducated women have been 'encouraged' out of training for advancement in traditional occupational areas, for instance, textiles or clerical work, where they might have re-entered the labour market at a 'higher' position – with correspondingly higher pay and status and possible influence. Instead they have been directed towards occupations of traditional under-representation (often in stages of decline), such as those of the construction industry, or towards the creation of new jobs by setting up cooperatives and other enterprises.[5]

Traditional male occupations have not been offered to women as a 'choice' but frequently as the only ESF-funded option available. Although the Second Action Programme for 1986–90 (EC 1985) stressed the underrepresentation of women in occupations of new technology, the British interpretation metamorphosed this into traditional under-representation, as we have seen. At a time during which information and computer technology affected most occupations, the European focus on new technology training was, within Britain, intentionally marginalized.

There are two problems with this concentration of training in areas of traditional under-representation. The first is, that the training was given in traditional male skills such as bricklaying or plumbing. The second problem is that the training was not given in new and information technologies or other new areas of work, or in training for advancement in traditional female occupational areas. Throughout this period, until the recession of the early 1990s, the main growth area of employment in Britain were those of professionals, technicians, managers and administrators (Hamnett *et al.* 1989; McDowell 1989; Sarre 1989). Despite such trends the British government interpreted the Commission framework agreement more conservatively, as we have seen. Yet not only was this not an occupational area of growth, it was actually in continual decline (UN 1986; EC 1987a). This was part of a general decline in skilled manual jobs (Sarre 1989). Moreover, construction and renovation work itself is often physically hard and it is an industry from which men themselves retire early.

Furthermore, where women were trained in traditional male occupational skills, the qualification gained was often merely that of a certificate confirming completion of the course rather than an established qualification with transferable currency (Seeland 1980; Brine 1992). Cynthia Cockburn (1987) studied young women engaged in manual skills training and observed that they were encouraged to look for things that 'girls could do', such as in engineering, wrought ironwork; in carpentry, wooden toy making. This took them out of direct competition with boys and meant that the hierarchy of male power was maintained in those areas of traditional male skills into which women were being encouraged. At the same time, the lack of training for higher qualifications in women's own traditional skills areas (the second priority area of the 1977 Reform) equally effectively maintained the hierarchy of male power in these areas of work.

The British interpretation of policy thus ensured that across the relevant class and ethnic groups men were able to retain their economic power over women. Throughout the 1980s the discourse of equality encouraged working-class women into manual skills, and middle-class women into science and engineering. Using pay as the indicator, the UK's *New Earnings Survey* (DE 1992b) shows that women have been unable to disrupt the hierarchies of entrenched male power existing at either the highest paid or lowest paid sectors of the labour market.

The gendering of new technology

It is argued in this book that women should be given every chance to choose, and encouragement to succeed in any traditional male manual skill – if they so wish; undoubtedly the door to such skills has been shut to women for a very long time. Yet while appearing to give access to a wider range of possible jobs, the discourse of equality directs women of the working classes to the door labelled 'traditional inequality', behind which are numerous obstacles hindering their employment: declining labour market, male exclusivity and physical hardship. At the same time, other doors are poorly signed or closed, particularly those directed at the future.

This is a crucial point, particularly for this third period of EU legislation, when the labour market of new technology was expanding rapidly (McDowell 1989) and when very few people (women or men) had appropriate previous skills or experience. Yet during this period of technological expansion in what was, for a brief period, an ungendered occupational area, working-class women were being kept away from the power of development, control, knowledge and understanding of new technology and electronics. Felix Rauner (1985: 69) found that although training for computerized office work predominated amongst EC-funded projects at this time, women's experience of computer technology was 'only on the surface' for they were denied the opportunity of investigating the insides of computers or of experimenting with other applications or software. Similarly Karen Mahoney and Brett van Toen (1990: 322) found that where women were generally engaged in work with new technology they were often restricted to spending most of their working day working with wordprocessing, database and spreadsheet packages 'which keeps them away from the power of the how and why and whether of the technology'.

There are two basic levels for understanding the mechanics of computer technology: the electronics that make it work and the potential of the software – how to write it and how to creatively engage with software. Not all the new and information technology centred jobs held by men depend upon knowledge of the interior electronics. The crucial difference in 'end-user' technology training, such as that experienced by women on these ESF-funded projects, is between active creative engagement and relatively passive manual keyboarding (Brine 1996b). This is as important an area of gendering as that of the more obvious area of electronic engineering itself. Furthermore, within this globalized technology, impacting directly on most industries, occupations and areas of daily life, there has been a relative decline internationally in the number of professionally or technically involved women. For example, in the UK, despite all the various EC and UK government policies and legislation and other public-body initiatives concerned with equal opportunities, there was a 50 per cent decrease in women's professional and technical involvement during the latter half of the 1980s (Mahoney and van Toen 1990). Behind the equal opportunities facade of attempts to revive traditionally under-represented skills, by the end of the 1990s computer and information technology was effectively gendered male. Thus the beneficiaries of new technology development are men, the losers, women. In this gendering of new technology women are excluded from the development and research of new technology hardware and software, and equally importantly women are excluded from the creativity of new technology. The exceptions to this general exclusion are, ironically, those women of the working classes, who are the prime 'end users' in offices and supermarket checkouts and are, from South Wales to Taiwan, recruited as workers for the electronics assembly-lines.[6]

Particularly throughout the 1980s new technology, information technology and the electronics industry in general represented *the* main growth area within both the European and the global economy. Cockburn (1986: 82) points out that during this period new technology not only enabled capital to regain control from skilled workers and their union organizations, and to increase productivity and profits, but also within this 'men as men appropriate and sequester the technological sphere, extending their *tenure* (not control – that remains with capital) over each new phase, at the expense of women' (original emphasis). Despite the technological emphasis of the ESF Recommendation (EC 1984c) this was, across the European Union, the gendering process of the 1980s.

The fourth period: the 1990s

Chapter 5 described how the Third Action Programme for 1991 to 1995 introduced the concept of mainstreaming, which subsequently became the main demand of the Fourth Programme (1996–2000). This demand was included in the 1993 ESF Regulation (EC 1993b) and in this way became a policy in which the compliance of the member state could be legally demanded. Despite the introduction of mainstreaming in 1991, no mention whatsoever of equal opportunities is made in the UK *Guidelines* from 1991 to 1993 (DE 1990, 1991, 1992a). Within Britain, gendered equal opportunities have not been mainstreamed; training provision for women has instead been consistently marginalized (Brine 1996a, in press).

So far, the focus has been mainly on the UK's annual *Guidelines* documents. I now turn to the strategic plans demanded by the ESF Regulation of 1993, and shall consider the Single Programming Document (SPD) for 1994 to 1999 (DE 1993a), and then the renewed SPD for the 1997 to 1999 (DfEE 1996a).

Following the 1993 ESF Regulation, training policy for unemployed people has been divided into four priorities or pathways. The first pathway is to employment; the second, a good start in working life; the third, integration, and fourth, the equal opportunities pathway for men and women (the EO-pathway). A crucial conception was that long-term unemployed women were 'eligible beneficiaries' under all four of these pathways.

In the first SPD, the UK Conservative government made numerous gender-based equal opportunities statements, referring often to the *principle* of equal opportunities and, presumably in order to meet the Regulation's demand for mainstreaming, at the end of each pathway was a statement outlining the possibility of single-sex provision.[7] Relevant to later developments of policy was the specification of lone parents (pathway three). The SPD informs us that 'there are around 1.3 million single parent families in Britain – of which 90 per cent are headed by women' (DE 1993a: 22). The focus on lone parents will be revisited in Chapter 9.

A significant discursive shift is discernible between the SPD for the Commission (DE 1993a) and the 1994 *Guidelines* (DE 1993b) for the UK administrative sectors and providers. The SPD's concern with the economic and social cohesion of the European Union, its apparent understanding of the labour market and women's position in it, and the principle of equal opportunities were, within the 1994 *Guidelines*, either marginalized or simply excluded. It was the 1994 *Guidelines* and not the SPD that were subsequently continued and reinforced by the 1995, 1996 and 1997 *Guidelines* (DE 1994; DfEE 1995, 1996b).

In its specific references to equal opportunities, the 1994 *Guidelines* differed in three significant ways from the SPD and the ESF Regulation. First, a general selection criterion was inserted requiring applicants to show

> good practice in equality of access and equal opportunities and applicant organizations should have an equal opportunities policy with regard to its own staff and recruitment, and it should be monitored.
> (DE 1993b: 54)

The equal opportunities *policy* demanded here relates to the training *organization*, not training practice. Second, the possibility of single-sex training across all four pathways was removed, leaving only the EO-pathway with this explicit opportunity. Third, the single-sex provision of the EO-pathway was broadened to include provision for men-only training, and, moreover, was also interpreted to mean training for women *and men* in sectors or occupations where they have been traditionally under-represented. The importance of this is further strengthened by the apparent neutrality of the other pathways. Other than the few references to 'ethnic minorities' the language of the other pathways is gender and race neutral. While this 'neutrality' does not explicitly prohibit access to any of the pathways of specific groups, explicit references within the EO-pathway has led, as will be seen in the case study of Chapter 7, to a marginalization of provision for unemployed women.

From 1993 to 1996, the chameleon-like discourse constructed by the UK Conservative government looked one way to the European Commission (DE 1993a), and the other way to the UK ESF sector managers and training providers, speaking, as just shown, in a different voice to each (DE 1993b, 1994; DfEE 1995).

Up to 2000

The SPD for 1997–99 (DfEE 1996a) is the second of the key UK documents submitted to the Commission during the 1990s. The SPD relates to the second half of the 1994–99 period covered by the Commission Regulation of the Structural Funds (EC 1993b).

It has been shown, immediately following the SPD for 1994–99 (DE 1993a) and its compliance with the 1993 Regulation, that the UK *Guidelines* for 1994 were constructed by a quite different discourse. The *Guidelines* also represent a move away from the earlier training outcomes measurable in terms of training-related employment, towards less quantifiable, broader outcomes with an emphasis on motivation, confidence, informed choice and vocational guidance (DE 1994; DfEE 1995). Looking towards 2000, the second SPD consolidates the earlier trend towards what might be viewed as the pathologization of unemployed people.

To explain, the SPD is built upon two fundamental assumptions: that all the social groups targeted within ESF/3 lack recent or relevant work experience, making employers reluctant to employ them, and that long-term unemployed people are overdependent on state benefits and need 'encouragement' into work. The SPD has thus proposed an 'improved benefits system which offers both strong encouragement to make efforts to find work and improved incentives to work' (DfEE 1996a: 24). Although the document made only one further mention of the benefit system, declaring its intention to overcome the 'disincentives to look for work caused by dependency on benefits' (DfEE 1996a: 24), this 'improvement in the system' and 'encouragement to find work' provided clear indications of government policy that was subsequently enacted in late 1996. The second SPD (1997–99) (DfEE 1996a), the responsibility of Gillian Shepherd, the last education minister of the 18 years of British Conservative government, pointed to an increased use of the EO-pathway within the government's own training programme and to a widening to include the promotion of equal opportunities to employers.

Produced towards the end of the British Conservative government, the SPD's intentions related directly to the Job Seeker Allowance and Project Work which, like other neoliberal states such as Australia (Dean 1995) were inspired by the US workfare scheme of linking state benefit directly to compulsory work experience. Under the Conservative government the Job Seeker Allowance (JSA) came into effect in October 1996. The JSA paid unemployed people seeking full-time work non-means tested benefit for six months (as against the previous 12 months). The punitive measures of the JSA included reducing the hours that long-term unemployed people could study from 21 to 16 a week; ending the link between unemployment benefit and inflation; lengthening the time before payments are made; and reducing the availability of hardship payments. Draconian powers were assumed to force claimants to take low-paid jobs and, as such, the JSA was part of the accelerated move towards a compulsory workfare system. The combined package consisted of job search skills, guidance and counselling and compulsory work experience. The SPD, the Job Seeker's Allowance and Project

Work were all framed by, and have in turn constructed, the discourse of the pathologized unemployed. The new Labour government did not rescind or soften the JSA in any way, and simply replaced Project Work with their own flagship programme, Welfare to Work, which, targeted initially on young unemployed people and lone mothers, was later extended to include people with disabilities and long-term unemployed people aged over 25. Although within the first year of the Labour government it was possible to identify a philosophical difference between Project Work and Welfare to Work the difference in reality, especially for unemployed people, was questionable, particularly given similar degrees of compulsion with threatened loss of benefit.

The ESF-funded training programme detailed in this SPD (DfEE 1996a) by the British Conservative government bore little resemblance to the Commission's Regulation (EC 1993b) for this period, and unlike the Commission White Papers (EC 1993a, 1994a, 1995a) discussed in Chapter 5, appeared to be oblivious to the impact of globalization on structural unemployment and the consequences of technological and demographic change – in short, oblivious to all those changes influencing the European discourse of economic growth. Equally important, it appeared ignorant of the concept of social exclusion and the possibility of grave social unrest contained with the European discourse of internal peace.[8]

Policy implications for working-class women

Although the second SPD continued to make occasional reference to the 1993 Regulation on the Structural Funds (EC 1993b), it addressed it less directly than previously. The SPD was now more targeted and more prescriptive, making several significant changes to the earlier version. Although the four pathways remained unchanged, the actual marginalization of equal opportunities into the EO-pathway described in the case study of Chapter 7 was strengthened further. Moreover, the SPD increasingly referred to the 'special needs' of men, especially the EO-pathway, stating that 'men find it difficult to break into employment areas which have been predominately female' (DfEE 1996a: 36). Similarly, while recognizing 'the vital and growing contribution of women to the labour force', the SPD showed a consistent concern for the position of men:

> Men are disproportionately affected by long-term unemployment as the industries in which they were traditionally employed are declining, and those sectors which are increasing are taking on part-time employees, an area of employment which is dominated by women.
>
> (DfEE 1996a: 36)

Despite references to equal opportunities and the 'occupational growth area of high skilled white collar occupations, especially amongst women'

(DfEE 1996a: 6), the SPD implicitly portrayed the labour market as one in which long-term unemployed women, often with no or few educational or vocational qualifications, will, if lucky, become part-time workers located in the low-skilled, low-paid, occupations within the service sector.

The mainstreamed 'essential' criteria of 'equal opportunities', expressed in the *Guidelines* for 1994, 1995 and 1996, were redefined in the first draft of the SPD (DfEE 1996c: 42) as 'improving awareness and application of equal opportunities'. By the final version of the second SPD (DfEE 1996a: 37), it is stated that the priority for equal opportunities should 'be concerned with *complementary* actions' (original emphasis) aimed primarily at improving awareness of (and developing training towards) 'employment opportunities in occupations dominated by men or women'. At the same time the Commission-approved UK SPD redefined equal opportunities as no longer gender-specific but concerned with race, disability, age and religion as well as gender and 'women's rights more generally' (DfEE 1996a: 25). However, the meaning of 'women's rights' was not clarified. Whereas the European discourse of equal opportunities was exclusively related to gender, ironically the UK discourse was more generally inclusive. This redefinition shows the discursive shift between the European and the British concepts of equal opportunities during this period. At the same time UK policy in this area further diluted the EU attempt to mainstream gender equal opportunities and to provide unemployed women with access to the full range of funded training opportunities within ESF/3.

The aim of this analysis is to show that while continuing to declare compliance with the principle of equal opportunities for men and women, this discursive shift in UK policy-making has continued and strengthened the process of marginalization and evaporation that occurred throughout the annual *Guidelines* of 1994–96. It did this in four ways. First, it explicitly stated that equal opportunities covers race, religion and disability as well as gender. Second, it attached no explicit 'equal opportunities' statements to the other pathways, and made no reference to the possibility of single-sex training. Third, it confined gender-based equal opportunities to the EO-pathway. Finally, while it might be possible to argue that there has been some evidence of mainstreaming in the *UK-defined* equal opportunities, there has been no evidence of mainstreaming the EC-defined *gender-based* equal opportunities – as defined in the Third and Fourth Equal Opportunities Action Programme and included and legally required by the ESF Regulation of 1993.

As shown in the previous chapter, the ESF Regulation detailed the Commission's policy for mainstreaming gender-based equal opportunities while at the same time maintaining some specific provision for women. The UK Conservative government's interpretation contained in the SPD 1997–99 (DfEE 1996a) highlights their scant regard for the spirit of these intentions.

The tension between mainstreaming and specific provision has been a central theme throughout the 1990s, for it is this tension that has created the spaces and flexibility in which the discourse of gendered marginalization can be constructed. The discourse has changed through the second SPD (1997–99) (DfEE 1996a), with the inclusion of the pathologization of 'the unemployed' and the direct linkage of training with state unemployment benefits. The implications of this marginalization are explored further in the case study of the next chapter.

The emphasis on work experience within the second SPD could represent yet another step away from 'women-only' provision along with a probable reduction in the opportunities offered to them. It is likely to lead to training programmes where the emphasis is on confidence-gaining and ESF-subsidized 'work experience'. Earlier this chapter critiqued the ESF for concentrating too rigidly on training women for occupations of traditional under-representation and for ignoring occupations of hierarchical under-representation and under-representation within new occupations such as those linked with new and information technology. However, the SPD for 1997–99 radically reframes the UK's use of ESF, provoking different sets of questions concerning training for unemployed working-class women – one of which relates attention to lone parents who are almost exclusively lone working-class mothers.

The equality discourse

Of particular interest at this point is the concept of 'traditional'. To reiterate an important point, within the Reforms of EC training policy, traditional is mentioned only in the 1983 Decision (EC 1983b) – it is not mentioned in the 1971 or 1977 Reforms (EC 1971, 1977), the 1984 Recommendation (EC 1984c), the 1988 Reform (EC 1987c), or in the 1993 Regulation (EC 1993b).

There are two separate roots of origin for this concept of 'traditional'. It can be traced to the discourse of equality constructed by the EO Unit which first appeared in the 1981 interpretation of the 1977 Reform (EC 1981), and it can also be traced to the UK's Sex Discrimination Act (Home Office 1975). Chapter 4 only partially explained the importance of 'traditional'. It is a central discursive feature of both the EO Unit and the UK government, yet it is not identical in each case. Nevertheless, there are three key features that are common to both. The EO Unit and the UK government both address inequalities of *past* practice, focusing attention to the past rather than the future; they both unproblematically adopt an essentialist understanding of gender inequality; and they both express an understanding of equality that is based on 'similarity' and not difference, which means that women must be treated the same as men.[9]

Conclusion

This chapter has focused on the UK government whose active involvement in European training policy began in the mid-1980s (the third period of training policy) and, reflecting the process of subsidiarity, increased considerably throughout the 1990s.

The analysis of the fourth period of training showed the Conservative government's disregard for the spirit of mainstreaming gendered equal opportunities across all EU policies and programmes.

Although the Conservative government's discourse was neither the only discourse nor an uncontested one, for the last 18 years it has, in the UK, been the dominant one, in which the EU discourse has been constructed as 'reverse' to it. However, following the May 1997 election of a new Labour government, this dominant UK discourse is changing, as was immediately evident in the speedy adoption of the Treaty of the Union's Social Chapter (EC 1992a). This change in government poses an interesting dilemma because the second SPD (DfEE 1996a) presented by the Conservative government was approved by the Commission and therefore defines UK training policy up to 1999. The extent to which the Labour government will (or can) change this policy is questionable, particularly given its flagship Welfare to Work policy.[10] Interestingly, neither the Conservative government nor, so far, the Labour government have publicly acknowledged the extent to which European funding sustains UK training programmes, let alone the degree to which such programmes have been influenced by European policy. The next chapter considers the interpretation of policy by UK administrative sectors, and will show their construction of reverse discourses to both the dominant discourse of the government and to that of the European Commission.

In discussing the relationship between the regionalized and nation state, Chapter 2 showed the regionalized 'state's' early concern with social policy – a traditional concern of the nation state. Beginning with the 1997 Reform there was a steady devolution of decision-making powers to the nation state, yet at the same time the Commission retained ultimate control – the devolved powers of subsidiarity are a delegated power. The Commission has not only retained but also strengthened its demand for member state accountability, for example, the submission of member state strategic plans (SPDs) for Commission approval and agreed frameworks for European-funded training programmes.

The construction of the EU is a long-term project. This is not to imply the existence of either one overall director or a group-led modernist progression to a predetermined federal state, for at any time its construction is full of contest, struggle and compromise, not only between the member states themselves, but between individual politicians and bureaucrats; between administrative departments and of course between different individual interests and interest groups. Despite this complexity, delays, diversions, stop-overs and even breakdowns do seem to be an accepted part of the development of EU policy. In the contested struggle between the regionalized 'state' and the nation state, as we have seen, the concept of subsidiarity has devolved some powers to the member states. Yet as Chapter 3 showed, this long-term approach has meant that the Commission has been quite content to gain a toe-hold in the door of a new area of competency such as compulsory education, and then gradually extend its area of influence.

Notes

1 The DfEE was known as the Department of Employment (DE) up to 1995. For ease of reading I shall refer to both as the DfEE.
2 Objective 3 of the ESF (ESF/3) is the ESF's Objective for funding unemployed people.
3 As the Conservatives were in government from 1979 until 1997 it can be assumed that, unless otherwise stated, the analysis in this chapter relates to their administration.
4 I use the problematic concept of race in order to refer to the socially constructed basis upon which groups of people, based primarily on skin colour, experience structural inequalities and discrimination.
5 Worker cooperatives are businesses that are collectively owned and controlled by the workers in it, for as long as they are in it. They are generally non-profit making, and while each member has a shared legal responsibility for the business, they do not take any capital with them when they leave. The financial (and emotional) risk involved in these businesses is considerable, and success is rare (Hannah 1989).
6 Throughout the 1990s even this office-based 'end-user' involvement with technology is weakened as computers, networked and connected to the internet, proliferate across desk tops, and more people become less reliant on secretaries and other office support staff.
7 The Sex Discrimination Act (SDA) (1975, amended 1986), legitimates single sex training related to occupations of traditional under-representation. However, the SDA itself acts as a restraint on the opportunities, allowing single sex training only within tightly defined terms.
8 These issues are explored in greater depth in Brine 1996a.
9 See my analysis of the equality discourse in Chapter 4 in which I considered the debate on similarity or difference.
10 Given the considerable differences between the first SPD for the entire 1994–99 period (DE 1993a) and the second SPD for the last two years (1997–99), and the general lack of relevance to the EC's 1993 Regulation, the Labour government could presumably redefine this policy – if they wished.

7 Marginalizing women's training

This chapter is based on Commission-funded research (Brine 1996a) and it provides a case study of the UK implementation of policy in 1996. Although it related directly to the Third and Fourth Action Programme's concept of mainstreaming introduced in Chapter 5, the interpretations and implementation of European Social Fund, Objective 3 (ESF/3) policy by the administrative sectors of the UK were based not on European policy but on the UK government's interpretation provided by the annual *Guidelines* already considered in Chapter 6. Some of the administrative sectors were seen to construct reverse discourses to both the dominant discourse of the UK government and to that of the European Commission. The degree to which the reverse discourse was constructed varied from one sector to another, and was further influenced by individual 'key people'. It is from within these reverse discourses that the sector managers and other individuals exerted their agency, and found the spaces and the flexibility for their own interpretations of ESF policy. Yet at the same time as some sectors constructed reverse discourses, other sectors, and individuals across all sectors, continued the general discursive drift towards the marginalization of women's training. This chapter is structured to address the five specific UK sectors involved in the implementation of ESF/3 that were included within this case study. Interviews that were conducted with 'key people' within these sectors are analysed for their understanding of ESF/3 training for women in general, and in relation to mainstreaming in particular.

The five UK sectors

The first sector was the government's Department of Education and Employment (DfEE).[1] Sixty per cent of the UK ESF/3 allocation has been top-sliced to fund the government's own youth and adult unemployment training programmes.[2] Contracts for the delivery of these programmes were negotiated between the DfEE and the Training and Enterprise Councils.

The Training and Enterprise Councils (TEC) were the second sector, and it was these employer-led quango organizations that administered the government's own training programme (McGinty and Fish 1993). They have been organized into national, regional and local chains of communication and decision-making.[3]

Third was the postcompulsory sector of further education. Since 1992 the Further Education Funding Councils (FEFC) have replaced the local authorities in funding the colleges of England, Wales and Scotland. They have also been responsible for interpreting and providing guidance on ESF/3 funding.

Fourth was the voluntary sector, including charitable and other non-profit organizations not in the public sector. Although England, Scotland and Wales each had an organization to represent its own voluntary sector, the British government has preferred to treat the English organization, the National Council for Voluntary Organizations (NCVO) as representing all three countries. The NCVO similarly described the voluntary sector as 'a network of six regional offices in England, plus one in Scotland and one in Wales' (NCVO interviewee).

The final, fifth sector was the Women's Training Network. From the mid-1980s this operated as a voluntary network for women trainers, and by 1991 was established as the specialized administrative centre within the broader voluntary sector. It has existed solely to promote ESF/3-funded women's training. Although this might be viewed as the only sector to be deemed explicitly feminist, the next section will show that its approach to ESF/3 has not been unproblematic, and at a regional and local level, others have also pursued a gender perspective.

The administrative structure of the sectors varied from the highly centralized further education sector to the well-developed regional structure of the TECs and voluntary sector. The DfEE has continued to operate nationally, as has the Women's Training Network, although the latter's general lack of financial and staff resources has effectively restricted the network to England.

Interviews with the sectors

This analysis is based on 21 semi-structured interviews, conducted in 1996, with key people from five ESF administrative sectors within the UK (Brine 1996a). The term 'key people' refers to those who were, nationally or locally, in charge of their sector's ESF or ESF/3 provision.

Interviews were conducted at the national level in England, Scotland and Wales, and were further supported by a regional case study where local representatives from each sector were interviewed.[4] Although the analysis is concentrated primarily on the sectoral interpretation of policy, any significant national differences will be highlighted.

The interviews all began with a discussion of organizational structure, relationship of organization to government policymakers, internal decision-making procedures and their own understanding of ESF/3 policy. The interviewees were then asked for their opinion of the training needs of women. Despite having responded easily and knowingly to all the preceding general policy questions, the interviewees from the DfEE, the Training and Enterprise Council and the further education sector responded to this question about women by saying they were not the right person to be asked. Those from the voluntary sector and the Women's Training Network however, responded relatively easily to this gender question. Despite their key positions within the organization, and their clear policy roles in relation to the ESF/3, this general initial response of 'I'm not the right person to talk to' was closely linked with a second statement of the following kind: 'This is a training question and I'm to do with policy'. While at another time it may be fruitful to question the extent to which the culture of these institutional settings encouraged such responses, the fact remains that all the interviewees were 'key people'. Their response implied that training for women was first, not a policy issue, and second, not an issue of concern to the 'top' personnel, but at best a delegated responsibility.

The 'equal opportunities' selection criteria

Responding to a subsequent question regarding their understanding of equal opportunities within ESF/3, the majority of interviewees referred to the DfEE's 'equal opportunities' selection criteria. The general feeling across the TEC, further education and voluntary sectors was that the equal opportunities criteria were concerned with general policy of the provider and not actual training provision. Sometimes this feeling was expressed critically, but more often uncritically. With the exception of the Women's Training Network, there was varying degrees of confusion regarding the concept of equal opportunities. One national further education interviewee thought equal opportunities actually prohibited single-sex training; another understood equal opportunities to refer to men as well as women, and another was not even sure that it was an essential selection criterion in the first place. The demand of the Fourth Action Programme (EC 1995c) and the 1993 Regulation (EC 1993b) to mainstream equal opportunities, it seems, has been metamorphosed into the DfEE's equal opportunities selection criteria, and the weighting, if any, each sector awards to it.

The EO-pathway is the pathway for women

Most interviewees interpreted the question concerning the training needs of women as, in effect, a question relating to the EO-pathway. There was, with the exception of the voluntary sector, an overwhelming belief that the EO-pathway was in fact 'the pathway for women'.

The DfEE use a national database to assign ESF/3 funds to unemployed individuals. Its representative interviewee assumed that *all* provision for women would be included under the EO-pathway, particularly the subsection relating to traditional underrepresentation. It was also pointed out that there were no ESF/3 or equal opportunities guidelines actually defining under-representation and so an 'arbitrary figure of 40 per cent' was used (as contrasted to the TEC figure of 10 per cent of the occupational workforce). The arbitrariness of the DfEE figure appeared to be directly linked to their own set of ESF 'targets':

> We arbitrarily agree on the cut-off point for under-representation. If at the trial database we didn't have sufficient training weeks to meet our ESF target, we would increase that 40 per cent to say 45. We'd trawl the database again. As long as we use the cut-off point at 49 per cent, one can argue that 49 per cent is under-represented, even though it's only marginally. We would probably argue with that if we needed 49 per cent to meet our ESF targets.
>
> (DfEE interviewee)

This theoretical and pragmatic interpretation of the EO-pathway represents a disregard for the spirit of the pathway and the Commission's explicit demand that equal opportunities be mainstreamed. The combined use of a computerized database and shifting definitions of under-representation will enable the DfEE to quantitatively show the Commission that equal opportunities are being mainstreamed, while qualitatively the actual provision for women (especially the more radical types of provision discussed in the following two chapters) will decline.

Within the TEC sector there appeared to be confusion and contradiction in understanding both specific and mainstreamed provision. This TEC interviewee first argued that the whole of ESF/3 unemployment training should be available for women, but later went on to link women exclusively with the EO-pathway, and men with the other three pathways:

> If there is high male unemployment then basically you can do projects for them under the pathway to employment, the long-term unemployed, or the pathway to integration, under inner cities or something like that.

Although the Further Education Funding Council has constructed an apparent 'neutrality' within the ESF, its representative interviewee did not link women's training specifically with any one pathway. Such lack of direction thus leads to the marginalization of women into the EO-pathway or to the absence of training for women. An English regional interviewee thought that individual colleges would decide for themselves whether 'they might identify that particular niche market [i.e. women] as an area where there was a demand.'

Although approaching the issue from a completely different 'feminist' perspective, the Women's Training Network (WTN) took up a similar position to that of the government's DfEE: training for women as located in the EO-pathway, especially the subsection for traditional under-representation. This interpretation of training for women as identical to the EO-pathway reflects the rationale for establishing WTN as a sector manager in the first place. Perhaps even more so than the other sectors the Women's Training Network's relationship to the ESF has been influenced by the Sex Discrimination Act (SDA) which, as suggested previously, can, despite its apparently liberal intentions, actually restrict opportunities for women.

The majority of interviewees responded to the question concerning the training needs of women either by interpreting it to mean single-sex provision for women (seen as only available under the EO-pathway), or by interpreting it to mean the EO-pathway (single-sex provision). Either way, there was an unquestionable automatic relationship assumed between women, single-sex provision and the EO-pathway. This had the effect of marginalizing training for women into this particular pathway and, as I will show, restricting access to the funded provision available through the other three pathways.

The EO-pathway is for men as well as for women

At the same time as generally locating the training of women within the EO-pathway, there was within the TEC and further education sector a belief that the EO-pathway was for men as well as women.

> There are not actually that many 'women-only' projects for women returning to the labour market. It also includes men returning or men going into sectors where they're traditionally under-represented, because the equal opportunities pathway isn't just about women returning to the labour markets, it's also about men returning and the promotion of men and women into sectors where they are traditionally underrepresented.
>
> (English TEC interviewee)

Similarly, a Welsh national further education interviewee pointed out that the 'returners' programmes within the EO-pathway were open to men as well as women, saying:

> They are obviously women-oriented courses, but they couldn't prevent a man from going on it – and neither could they prevent that man from getting funding. And quite often there are a couple of men on these courses.

In Scotland a college was running, under the EO-pathway, a 'men-only' training course in childcare. Ironically, the perceived market need for this course came as a result of other ESF/3 provision for women. The colleges in the region insisted on using registered childminders, and subsequently discovered both a general shortage and a gender (male) under-representation. Although the 'official' rationale was that it was safer to use registered childminders, the interviewee added, 'It is really to avoid students benefiting members of their family, by using ESF funds'. In the explicit interest of 'safety', and the covert interest of fund allocation, men were in this instance, being trained under the EO-pathway to become registered childminders, while it was simultaneously acknowledged that the policy to pay only registered childminders and not family or friends, actually 'presents a problem for a lot of students – finding a registered childminder.' This concern with the traditional under-representation of men, and with men-only training, contributes to the mainstreaming of the EO-pathway rather than the mainstreaming of gender-based equal opportunities. The question of whether, given concerns about abuse of children, women will be happy to leave their child with a male childminder, has not, it seems, been considered.

The other pathways are for men

Primarily, although not exclusively within the DfEE and TEC sectors, the assumption that the EO-pathway is the pathway for women has led to the marginalization of women into this pathway and their simultaneous exclusion from the others. The pathways to employment and integration have both been seen as being for unemployed *men*, not women. The Welsh TEC interviewee explained:

> The other three pathways are open competition for both male and female – but the number of females, looking at the statistics, that are actually fit to go on the schemes is limited.

Reflecting on why this might be so, the interviewee suggested it might be because of

> the structure of the courses and things like that. It might be full-time and they need to go to college and this might not fit in with their domestic circumstances and so on.

This interviewee assumes that women should 'fit in' with standard 'male' provision and implied that their lack of involvement across the pathways is a direct result of their 'domestic circumstances'. Within this regional Welsh TEC the provision under the other three pathways, while apparently gender-free, is nevertheless designed for men, with women being expected to 'fit in' when possible. Similarly, an English DfEE interviewee suggested that in some of the TEC-operated DfEE programmes, there would be nothing under the EO-pathway in a particular TEC because 'there's no need – there's no real need for that equality.'

Mainstreaming

The general UK understanding and interpretation of equal opportunities has, as we have seen, been focused on the EO-pathway. Mainstreaming has been 'unproblematically' addressed through the equal opportunities selection criteria, concentrating on the providers' own policies and their actual provision for women. The exception to this is the voluntary sector, which has made the greatest effort to mainstream gender-based equal opportunities across the whole of ESF/3. The English voluntary sector, uniquely, wanted to find out how many women are trained under *each* pathway, not just the EO-pathway (NCVO 1995). Furthermore, they prioritized and believed that they achieved 'a high preponderance of female participation rates' across all courses as well as for 'women-only' courses.

A Scottish interviewee from the further education sector referred to a rare example of mainstreamed gender provision, speaking of 'one project for women under the pathway for young people and one under the long-term [pathway to employment].' This interviewee displayed an unusual understanding of *European* as well as UK policy, and this understanding enabled the college to find, within the DfEE *Guidelines,* spaces in which to manoeuvre in order to fund more innovative courses. Their provision was not officially women-only but the interviewee asserted that they would in practice 'attract women only, but because of the Sex Discrimination and the equal opportunities ruling we can't advertise it as such'.

Further research is needed in this area, but research so far shows that there have been individuals, primarily in the further education and voluntary sectors, and more often in Scotland, and to a lesser extent (particularly in relation to women) Wales, who have found the spaces and gaps within the UK-interpreted European policy to use the ESF/3 funds to act in the interests of, amongst others, working-class women. Their degree of agency appears to have been linked to a knowledge of the underlying European policy. For example, Scotland has developed a consortium of colleges, Local Authorities, Local Enterprise Councils and the voluntary sector that has supported an office close to the Commission in Brussels. Until recently, the English voluntary sector also had its own 'European Officer'.

Although the Women's Training Network suggests that, in theory, provision for women was possible across the whole of ESF/3, in practice they have continued to focus on under-representation and single-sex training for 'returners' – the exclusive concerns of the EO-pathway. With the exception of the voluntary sector, all sectors saw training for women as almost exclusively equated with the EO-pathway. Similarly, with rare individual exceptions, all sectors in Scotland, Wales and England commonly believed that single-sex training was only possible under the EO-pathway, and moreover that 'equal opportunities' meant this particular pathway and no other. Only the voluntary sector and one Scottish interviewee were concerned with mainstreaming equal opportunities across the whole of ESF/3. However, in terms of informing future policy and influencing change, these rare individuals appear to have had only minimal influence. Crucially, however, in implementing the policy at a regional or local level, they have indicated the importance of the agency of individuals and social groups within policy-imposed structures.

Marginalizing

Throughout the sectors there seems to have been very little resonance or synergy with the Commission's ESF Regulation (EC 1993b) or with the mainstreaming demands of the Fourth Action Programme (EC 1995c). Within the UK, mainstreaming has been reduced to a demand for an equal opportunities policy statement and a policy statement that relates primarily, and often exclusively, to the training organization itself and not the training provision. While this may provoke the training organization to review its equal opportunities practice and construct a policy, the focus has shifted away from the EC mainstreaming of *provision* for women across ESF/3.

There is an identifiable sequence in the assumptions made by the majority of interviewees: starting with the first, each assumption leads to the next. First, provision for women equals the EO-pathway. Second, single-sex provision equals the EO-pathway. Third, the EO-pathway comprises all of the 'equal opportunities' provision. Fourth, equal opportunities provision equates to single-sex training for men as well as women. In this way most of the sectors and key individuals have continued the discursive drift away from European mainstreaming policy. The sectors have continued to translate 'mainstreaming equal opportunities' to mean 'mainstreaming the EO-pathway'. This has marginalized training opportunities for women into the EO-pathway, and excluded women from the 'gender-neutral' provision of the other three pathways.

It is also significant that all the sectors except the DfEE expressed a very strong criticism of the bureaucracy of both the DfEE and the European Commission. There was particular anger over the constantly changing rules and regulations that made long-term planning impossible. The structures, processes and possibilities have changed yearly, and have meant that sector administrators and individual providers have frequently fumbled in the dark for information. They are caught between the Commission and the member state government, grasping at, and recirculating, rumours and snippets of changing information (Brine 1997b).

While the UK government has exerted its agency in relation to the European Commission, the UK administrative sectors have themselves operated primarily in relation to the dominant discourse of the UK government. Yet the reverse discourses that they have constructed are as Foucault (1980b) stated, automatically marginalized by the dominant discourse, as for example we have seen with the voluntary sector. Alternatively the dominant discourse may shift to subsume the reverse discourse. In several instances the sector managers exercised their agency by establishing their own relationship to the Commission, its bureaucrats and its policy.

The sectors differed considerably in their degree of active involvement in policy-making with, perhaps unsurprisingly, the DfEE and the TEC sectors showing the least agency, and the voluntary sector showing the most. However, the local providers of TECs and further education, in contrast to their national representatives, were far more active in exploiting the gaps and spaces in policy. There was also a tendency for Scottish interviewees to express a greater commitment to agency than the English. All of this suggests that the closer one is to the dominant discourse the less likely one is to construct a reverse discourse and the less one searches to exploit the gaps and spaces of policy. It is also highly pertinent that it has been those furthest away from the dominant UK discourse who have been most actively turning to the policy and interpretations of the European Union to enable them to express their autonomy in relation to the UK government.[5]

As well as showing these struggles for agency, this chapter has also highlighted the tendency to marginalize women's training – particularly by the DfEE, the national Training and Enterprise Council and the Further Education Funding Council. These national management bodies should however, be clearly distinguished from individual local TECs and colleges where individual institutions and people frequently struggled against their sectors' national interests and discourse.

This marginalization emerged when interviewees disavowed any knowledge or interest in women's training. It continued in their, what was to me astonishing, lack of clarity regarding equal opportunities – in general and specifically in relation to ESF. Several interviewees turned to the Sex Discrimination Act, sometimes correctly and sometimes erroneously, to legitimate their actions. Apart from the exceptional individual (such as the aforementioned Scottish further education interviewee), only the voluntary sector appeared to exploit the spaces in policy and administrative structures for the benefit of working-class women – to extend their opportunities for training across the whole of ESF/3. Ironically, all the other sectors found the spaces and gaps that enabled them not only to marginalize women into the EO-pathway but to open up this small pot of money to men as well.

Finally, the analysis of the differing 'official' expressions of agency within the UK leads me to the conclusion that the exercise of agency does not necessarily have positive outcomes. The original policy may be more radical and beneficial to women than subsequent interpretations.

Notes

1 The separate departments of Education and Employment were merged in 1995.
2 The UK Conservative government training programmes for unemployed people include Training for Work, Youth Credits, Modern Apprenticeships and Accelerated Modern Apprenticeships.
3 Known as the Training and Enterprise Council in England and Wales, they are known in Scotland as the Local Enterprise Council. For ease of discussion in this chapter I shall refer to them all as Training and Enterprise Councils (TECs).
4 Sue Kilminster, the project's research assistant, was the interviewer.
5 This research project accidentally coincided with an unexpected announcement from the DfEE outlining their proposed 'regionalization' of the UK administrative sector (Brine 1996a). Further information can be found in the *Guidelines* for 1998 (DfEE 1997). This 'regionalization' places greater control of ESF funds in the hands of the DfEE, TECs and FE sector, and removes it from the voluntary sector.

8 Gaps, spaces and complexities: educating feminists

Chapter 4 considered the perspectives of femocrats working within the EO Unit of the European Commission. This chapter turns now to women in Britain: to women providers of European-funded training and to unemployed women who are students on these projects. Women participated in these courses voluntarily. The funds provide financial support for childcare and travel costs. The chapter draws on three case studies: 'Bricks', 'Co-ops' and 'Office'. They fall within the period 1983 to 1993 – that is within the third and fourth periods of training policy (mid-1980s to late 1990s) and the second and third Action Programmes (1986–90, 1991–95). They represent arenas of education and training where the mechanisms of power are played out. They are, as Foucault (1980a: 96) said, 'those points where [power] becomes capillary', that is with the ultimate destination of power, manifested in its local forms and institutions such as those that will be seen in this chapter.

These case studies were put together in slightly different ways. 'Bricks' is based on semi-structured interviews with the workers of the project, 'Co-ops' on annual evaluation studies, and 'Office' on a group interview with workers and students.

The three case studies

The women targeted by each of these three training projects were long-term unemployed women – whether officially registered as unemployed or not. They were also women with no educational qualifications, although not all the women, nor even the majority, appeared to need basic education tuition. Within each project there were two implicit, sometimes explicit, educational intentions. Such intentions were often quite separate from the explicit training skills to be taught. As seen in previous chapters, the 'skill' training, for example, plumbing, was determined by the EU policy and UK interpretations.

Driven by a gender-based discourse of equal opportunities that lacked class and race analysis, this policy led to working-class women being trained in working-class men's traditional skill areas. The first educational aim centred on perceived basic education needs. The second aim appeared, superficially, to fall into the liberal adult education model, but actually represented a radical approach to adult education and was overtly political. This strand of the curriculum was adequately expressed by one of the projects as 'women's studies'.

The explicit aim of 'Co-ops' (1983–87) was to train women in the skills necessary for setting-up cooperative businesses. It originated from within the voluntary sector and was 'match-funded' and administered through the Economic Development Units of Local Authorities.[1] There were no qualifications to be gained through this project, no separate basic education provision, nor any discrete provision that could be called 'women's studies'. Both educational aims were nevertheless addressed, where relevant, through the explicit training curricula of business skills.

The aim of 'Bricks' (1985–90) was to train women in the traditional male manual skills of the construction and building renovation industry. A local woman politician was the driving force behind this second project. In the beginning it was administered, like the first project, through the Local Authority's Economic Development Unit, but was later transferred to the Local Authority's own newly formed Equal Opportunities Unit. Again, this project did not, during the time of the case study, offer any educational qualifications, although it did operate within a longer-term perspective, with arrangements made with local colleges to enable some trainees to continue training within the college and work towards qualifications which would be recognized by the industry. This project included both basic education provision and 'women's studies' as explicit and discrete weekly timetabled aspects of the course. Whereas basic education was an option for those who needed it, women's studies was, as far as possible, compulsory.

'Office' (1992–93) was set up by a further education college to train unemployed women in basic office skills. Although advertised as basic 'office skills' the course was firmly embedded within the college's basic education programme. Unlike the other two projects, educational qualifications were, from the start, linked to this course. Selection of applicants, like that in the other two projects, was made on the basis of previous low educational attainment. Additionally, this project also specifically recruited women needing basic education tuition; 'overqualified' applicants were directed towards other courses within the college. The project interpreted 'basic educational need' to include students for whom English was a second language, and also students with disability or chronic illness-related needs. This project, unlike the other two, made it very clear that this was a very basic, introductory course. It was not intended to result directly in related employment but would enable students to access more advanced 'office-related' training.

Feminist educators

Irrespective of its particular institutional framing, each project was set up and managed by women.[2] The curriculum content of each project resulted, as we have seen, from women finding spaces and gaps within the UK-interpreted European training policy. All the women employed on all three projects described themselves as feminists.

This section draws on the 'Bricks' project to explore the political agency of the *employed* women, the 'workers'. The workers of 'Bricks' were all aged in their mid to late 30s; all the interviewees were white: five English, one Irish. The three black workers on this project did not return my phone calls and cancelled our appointments.[3] I later discovered that this lack of cooperation was, as I discuss later, an early indication of the extremely tense situation that existed between the white and black workers. At the time of requesting interviews, I had no reason to anticipate such a response. The silence of black women was therefore immense and highly significant.

Of the white women interviewees, three were instructors, two were outreach workers and one the coordinator. The skill areas of the instructors were plumbing, mechanical engineering and bricklaying. The two outreach workers were two of the original three workers employed on the project. Two of the instructors were amongst those first appointed and the third had worked on the project for almost two years. The coordinator had been in post for 18 months. Five of the six women were, or had been, married; four had children; four described themselves as lesbian; all were able-bodied. Two described themselves as middle-class. Three had degrees, three were qualified social workers, one experienced in community work. Significantly, all the women saw their identity as being a determining factor in their work on the project. For example, one woman explicitly saw herself as a 'political change agent', and another said:

> Feminist for many years, socialist as well. Quite politically serious. At times in my life, active, although I'm not particularly now . . . My work has taken the place of it, in terms of doing things . . . My politics are a general indicator of how I should live. My work fits in with that. I wouldn't be happy doing a job which I didn't feel was putting my ideas into practice – and those are quite political ideas.

This following statement from a third woman points to the issue of class within feminist activism:

> Very politically active, but half the time not aware of it . . . In the early 70s I had a little flirtation with the women's movement – but I just felt alienated, dismissed, made to feel quite ignorant. I hadn't read the books, I didn't know the names. I was coming in because I was really interested in Women's Aid, partly because of what I'd seen with my

parents, and with my extended family, and, you know, you see women on the street, and they look so bloody miserable, hauling three or four children around.[4] Right, they might not be battered black and blue, but they look washed out, they look worn out. That's why, that's why I'm here.

While there were many differences between this small group of white women workers there was a shared feminist belief which permeated all of their responses: the importance of women's economic independence. A second shared feminist understanding was a strong critique of male violence (see Brine 1994).

The instructors who trained women in the skills of plumbing or bricklaying for example, expressed aspirations that tended to relate explicitly to their skill area. They wanted to pass on their own knowledge and skills, and they wanted to increase the number of women working in these occupations and reduce the isolation of those already there. Over time there was some dilution of this aspiration along with a move, by the instructors, towards sharing the aspirations of the management team – coordinator and outreach workers. This management team leaned more towards broader, educational aspirations within which the actual skill training was simply a hook. One management worker expressed this in the following way:

> To create an environment where women who perhaps had not had the best chances to start with, could come into a situation where things would be explained, where they could grow, and learn a skill that was going to enable them to motivate change in their own lives – that's what the basic ethos is about.

The concepts of both nurturing and motivating change were common themes throughout the interviews, from both the instructors and the management team. Yet there was also a consistent pragmatism to these nurturing intentions: eventual employment and economic independence:

> I wanted to give women economic independence because I actually do see that as being the nub of the whole thing. Whilst women and children are dependent on men they're never going to get anywhere.

Significantly, unlike the policy itself, the workers did not restrict this employment aim simply to training-related employment, that is to the trades of the construction and building renovation industry.

European-funded training policy actually provided an opportunity for these workers, within the overall context of adult education and training, to be paid feminist activists. Despite their strong ideological intentions and their belief in the possibility of instigating change, they were nevertheless also *constrained* by the European policy and by the funding structures. This generated a strong sense of cynicism and mistrust, which in many respects echoed that of the administrative sectors of the previous chapter. The strength of the women's disillusionment is evident in the following extracts. One woman thought the intentions of the European policy makers was simply 'cosmetic'. Another said:

> They continue to fund it enough so it can't really grow – it can't grow. But they won't shut it – yet . . . It's set up to fail. It wasn't resourced properly, never resourced properly . . . It's all minimal – less than tokenistic. We're marginalized, we're on the edge. It's a miracle actually that it got taken on. This is all on the edge. It's all outside of the main system. Outside of employers, outside of colleges. We're just tagged on the end, so we don't alter the main thing, and the main thing doesn't wish to alter. They'd have to give up some of their goodies and they don't wish to do that.

All the workers, including the instructors, also questioned the policy of *only* training women in construction and renovation skills, and in this way believed that 'failure' had been built into the project from the beginning. The exact focus of the workers' suspicions varied but their combined comments led to a strong questioning of three particular aspects of the training project: first the specific targeting of undereducated unemployed women aged over 25; second the particular skills being offered; and third, the mismatch between the training offered and the apparent needs of the local labour market. This worker covers the points commonly made:

> The situation was set up whereby we would actually get very few successes out of it in those terms [women working in the construction and renovation industries] because the scheme was combining the idea of 'women into non-traditional skills', with the idea of 'positive action for women who'd never had a chance before' . . . There's huge numbers of women whom life has treated so negatively that in one or two years, which is what we originally aimed to do, there is no way in which they can be successfully transformed into successful people in the employment market which is geared to youth, fitness, academic brain, all that – oh yeah, and ruthlessness as well.

Another woman concluded:

> Ultimately, it was about trying too hard to make things work, with the wrong ingredients: it was trying to make a pudding but using the wrong ingredients, and the only thing that could happen was that it would be a, a disaster.

In 1990, after five years of this project, less than one woman in 20 had gained *training-related* employment (Brine 1992). This figure relates solely to those women who gained employment as a result of the construction and building renovation skills taught. Similar poor training-related outcomes resulted from the cooperative business project, where four cooperatives were established in four years and only one survived for more than two years. This reflects the general difficulty experienced in this particular area of job creation (Hannah 1989). Significantly, turning away from the narrow confines of training-related employment, the broader success rate of these projects was much greater. Between 50 and 70 per cent of women either continued with further training, returned to education or gained non-training-related employment. Yet, this non-training-related employment was frequently simply a return to an earlier occupation – often below and rarely above the point of departure. Nevertheless, workers in all three projects were aware that they achieved greater outcomes from the education curriculum than from the skills training itself. As stated at the beginning of this chapter each of these projects maintained a strong educational curriculum as well as a training one: basic and radical education. Each project justified its success not by reference to the skill training but by pointing to the women who went on to alternative or more advanced training, and even more frequently by pointing to those women who returned to education.

Adult basic education

The differences between the basic educational provision within these ESF projects and that offered by mainstream adult basic education classes lay in their explicit *vocational* focus: numeracy, literacy and communication skills are vocationally driven. The need for such skills was vocationally based and practically useful within the overall goal of setting up a business, plumbing or bricklaying, or running an office; they are not abstract concepts divorced from reality. In what was a generally supportive rather than competitive environment, the students, as adults, brought practical experience of the world on which they then drew in their learning.

The women attending these projects were not representative of the adults (generally less literate and less numerate) who attend specific adult basic education classes. All three projects had a basic requirement that students be able to read and write and be basically numerate, but that was all; there was no requirement for more advanced skills. For example, the manager of the basic office skills project said:

> The students should benefit from this basic level of tuition; they should not be frustrated by it. They had to be able to read so that they could read instructions on the screen, but we didn't demand a higher level of literacy, necessarily than that.

Training projects that target undereducated working-class women tried to provide basic education to those women who would not otherwise attend either basic or general education classes. In a labour market seen as demanding increased literacy, numeracy and technological literacy skills it is important that undereducated working-class women receive this basic education along with any vocational skills training. Nevertheless, the place of basic education within the curriculum differed in the three projects.

'Co-ops'

Basic education was fully integrated into the cooperative business curriculum; there was no discrete provision. Bookkeeping, for example, required calculator and number skills; producing a business plan required literacy and written communication skills; cooperative working required verbal communication and negotiation skills. The greatest educational gain was seen in the area of numeracy, which was also the area of greatest difficulty for the students, and as such reflects much of the school-centred research on the low mathematical attainments of girls (Burton 1986). Unlike much of the teaching of mathematics in schools, the starting point of this project's basic bookkeeping course was the numerical and financial knowledge of the women themselves – their own experience of budgeting and of making numerous calculations based on known income and intended or expected expenditure. The women needing basic numeracy support were given additional extra-curricular individual tuition and, significantly, they also received support from the other women in their particular 'co-op' group. As the course progressed, all the women engaged in new areas of study, and to differing degrees, struggled with numeracy. This resulted in increased support and peer-teaching between the women.

There are four points to make regarding this process. The first is that there was a clear need for numerical skill; it was not an abstract requirement, as is often the case in school exercises. The second is the practical numerical experience that working-class women brought with them; they had all, throughout their adulthood, managed the intricate calculations involved in living on a restricted budget. The third is that each woman at some time struggled with an aspect of the course, and that each woman at some time was able to offer support to someone else. The final and perhaps most important point is that all the women had joined the project in order to learn how to set up a cooperative business. This seemed to provide a degree of status that is generally not provided by adult basic education classes. These women did not have to admit, at any time, that they had basic educational needs. Their need for additional support was seen as no different from their needs in the other more vocational areas of their training.

'Bricks'

Within this project, the discrete basic education provision was provided by 'bought-in' specialist further education tutors who gave weekly additional support sessions. Some students attended these classes regularly, and some occasionally, for specific needs. The basic education provision within this project approximated most closely to the adult basic education and mainstream student support model of colleges and schools. This meant that students wanting additional support first had to acknowledge to themselves, albeit within a supportive structure, that they actually had basic education needs. This was particularly so for regular attenders, even though to some extent this was diluted by the occasional attenders. The specific basic tuition was reinforced by its practical application in the vocational sections of the course. Plumbing for example, demanded quite complex calculations. As in the 'Co-op' project, all the trainees seemed at some time to struggle over a particular aspect of the course, and likewise at some time most women found themselves in a position to help someone else. A common feature within all three projects was that this cooperation and support was actively encouraged by the project leaders, tutors and instructors.

'Office'

The third project was one in which basic education was most fully integrated into the vocational provision. Half the weekly timetable was taken up by specific skills training which were team-taught by an office skills tutor and a basic education tutor. The particular basic education needs were addressed throughout the entire course, supporting the students in their office skills tasks. In addition to this integrated approach there were discrete basic education sessions that emerged from the office skills vocational work. For example, numeracy sessions grew out of the office skills sessions on wages; literacy work grew out of office skills sessions on filing or writing letters. From within the office skills curriculum the students worked towards basic accreditation in English language.[5] An introduction to information technology delivered by an Information Technology tutor formed the final major part of this project. The students studied the application of a word processing package, a database and a spreadsheet, and worked towards accreditation in Computer Literacy and Information Technology.[6]

Adult radical education

Each project appears to be permeated by the feminist perspectives of the workers. Echoing the findings of Jane Thompson (1983) in the Women's Education Centre in Southampton, all three project workers spoke of their wish to address women's experiences of gendered oppression. The following worker from 'Bricks' explains:

> I'm raising their consciousness, I'm trying to give them a different awareness of their life and their living situations. I suppose I'm trying to educate them about what choices they might have about the way they live their lives, about the effect of things all around them, about things

they've accepted, well, since they were born, that they've just accepted without question. I've asked them to question them . . . It's very slow. You know it's a very slow process.

This particular adult education model, with its feminist emphasis on consciousness-raising and empowerment, has much in common with the educational approach of Freire (1985: 83), who also stressed the importance of the educational 'empowering' process:

Each project constitutes an interacting totality of objectives, methods, procedures and techniques. The revolutionary project is distinguished from the rightist project not only by its objectives but also by its total reality. A project's methods cannot be dichotomized from its content and objectives, as if methods were neutral and equally appropriate for liberation or domination.

Policy intentions alone are not in themselves necessarily either empowering or politicizing, but rather, it is the *methods*, and crucially, the *intention*, the *aim*, or the *belief* behind the methods, which makes the process potentially revolutionary. A general lack of official interest in either the content or the process of the training effectively creates relatively well-funded spaces in which the political, feminist, intentions of the workers could be integrated into the general curriculum. Yet although radical education was a central part of each project, its actual curriculum context differed from project to project.

'Co-ops'

Of the three, the cooperative business project was the one with the least explicit approach to women's studies, although any concerns emerging from the explicit business curriculum were immediately followed up. For instance, the need for start-up finance and collateral provoked the question of why the working-class women on the course had neither capital nor collateral. Discussions on occupational gendering, and gender, race or class-based power-relations emerged through the work on bank managers and other financial support agencies. Other related issues included wage levels, childcare and the need for economic independence. Broader concerns of loneliness, fears and experiences of violence and struggles for personal freedom and fulfilment were raised by students, and were then discussed, if necessary, at the expense of the business curriculum.

'Bricks'

Taking a quite different approach, the construction and renovation project decided, as part of its initial structure, to include women's studies within the curriculum. Women's studies included a very wide range of topics, from filling in application forms and practising job interviews to sessions designed specifically to meet a particular cohort's needs (for example weight-training or self-defence) to the extremely contentious discussions around racism and sexual preference. There was some disagreement amongst the tutors and skill-instructors as to what to include in women's studies; some believed its role was to raise women's consciousness through addressing contentious subjects, and others believed it simply 'stirred up trouble and made matters worse'.

A further, and less contentious intention underlying women's studies related to work placements and future attendance at college. The project workers believed that the students would meet racism, sexism and homophobia in the next stages of their training, and they hoped the women's studies discussions would enable women to withstand and contest these prejudices. There was general agreement amongst the workers that the importance of women's studies lay in its ability to politicize and to 'empower', even though they disagreed as to the extent to which it could do so. Within this project the specific provision of basic education and women's studies expanded to demand more of the actual skills training time and more of the instructor's attention, particularly after a session on racism or homophobia (for more detail, see Brine 1994).

'Office'

In this third project, the issues covered by the concept of women's studies were discussed through a weekly session entitled 'Women at Work'. Topics included the occupational and hierarchical position of women within the labour market, equal opportunities, childcare, domestic responsibilities, women's rights, unions, job-search skills, health issues – physical and mental – 'anything, in fact, that affected women's experience of work'. This particular approach to women's studies falls midway between the other two; there is a particular time in which to address such issues; the curriculum can be defined by both tutor and student and not, as in 'Co-ops', left to chance; and yet, unlike that of 'Bricks', the topics were not so overtly contentious and tended to relate more directly to the training curriculum.

These brief accounts show three different approaches to the radical education of women's studies. Within 'Co-ops' women's studies did not explicitly exist and any discussion of political issues arose directly out of skills training. Within 'Office' women's studies went under the banner of 'Women at Work', and although students appeared to enjoy these sessions, and despite the general work focus, they nevertheless questioned their relevance. This was addressed by the project in two ways. It further stressed the work relevance of topics to work situations, and perhaps more effectively raised the status of the sessions by linking them to a qualification.[7] 'Bricks' was undoubtedly the most overtly political. An instructor with the project spoke of some of the conflicting issues surrounding this politicizing education:

> It's difficult for women to talk about themselves, especially to talk about the issues we want them to talk about. They see the training scheme as giving them a skill in non-traditional areas rather than in raising their consciousness about women's issues. Some of them enjoy it but they find it very difficult to cope with – all of them, no matter who they are. Some issues they're all right with, but other issues they find very difficult. It's important to keep it because it does raise their consciousness, and they need that to go out into the likes of the world and fight. What are they going to do when they come across sexism and racism and homophobia, out there, or maybe they'd be ignorant and not realize it's happening to them, maybe then they'd get along better, but, eventually, they'll need to know how to deal with it . . . After the women's studies, the trainees carry on talking about it – and it's left to the instructors to deal with the aftermath of women's studies. Sometimes this results in good discussions and sometimes it's really very difficult.

This somewhat lengthy quotation expresses several significant aspects of this project's women's studies programme. First, women's studies tended to spill over into the training curriculum. Second, it frequently addressed difficult and contentious issues. Third, it was intended to empower the students. Finally, there was, amongst the workers, a general attitude spanning a continuum from the evangelical to the patronizing. Barry Troyna's (1994) critique of the concept of empowerment within educational research is also relevant here (see also the work of Ellsworth 1989 and Gore 1993). He writes that:

> the targets of these research interventions begin as 'disempowered' (or powerless) and at the 'end' they either remain so or have achieved a state of empowerment. There is no room for manoeuvre, no shades of grey.
>
> (Troyna 1994: 12)

He also questions 'when and how researchers might know if their intention has empowered their subjects' (1994: 13). Both of these observations could be applied to the 'Bricks' project, for there was a clear tendency amongst the workers to see the students as needing their 'help'. They constructed the student as one who is passive, naïve, or even ignorant, of racialized and gendered oppression, who will subsequently leave the project with a 'raised consciousness', able to 'deal with' the world. This construction of their students, who were also unemployed working-class women, denies them any agency or possibility of manoeuvre, for example powers of decision making, and realities and struggles with different forms of oppression. While this construction is surprising given the strong feminist identities of the workers, it does point, yet again, to a pervasive gender exclusivity that is shot through with class and race assumptions.

Reverse discourse and localized power

So far the project workers have been portrayed as a clearly identifiable group. Yet they were not an homogeneous group and neither did they exist in a simple relationship to the students or to the state. This section explores the differences and power-relationships that existed between women. In doing this I return to the 'Bricks' project where, as I already mentioned, my attempts to contact black workers were unsuccessful. This lack of response reflected the racial tensions that existed within this particular training scheme and that only became clear as a result of the interviews. The responses of the white workers showed that fracturing based on race, class and sexuality, were defining features of their working lives.

The only shared characteristic, other than gender, was that all the students were working class. The majority of workers and students were in their 30s. The white workers believed they shared a racial identity with the white students, and believed that the black workers similarly shared an identity with black students. The extent of the shared black identity however could only be ascertained from the black women involved. The lesbian workers believed they shared a common identity with the lesbian students. The working-class-identified workers, while recognizing their employment and educational attainment status, nevertheless identified strongly with the working-class students. It is doubtful whether the students shared this mutual class identification.

In describing their own identities the workers explicitly positioned themselves, according to class, race and sexuality, in relation to other women; workers and students. Throughout the interviews these group identities emerged as a major area of concern that the workers referred to as the 'issues'. These 'issues' intersect any assumed commonality of women, generating constantly shifting positions and struggles for individual and group power. Foucault's work on the localization of power, discourse and reverse discourse provides a framework for considering the 'workers'' responses (Foucault 1980a, 1980b).

Reverse discourse

This chapter returns to Foucault's (1980b) argument that the construction of the dominant discourse is integral to the maintenance of power. Chapter 4 explored the relationship between discourse and ideology by focusing on the EU dominant discourses of economic growth and peace and their impact on education, training and equality policy. This chapter turns to the strength of the power of discourse in its *localized* manifestation. Although reverse discourses can, and are, constructed against the dominant one and represent clear sites of resistance to it, they are nevertheless automatically marginalized by the dominant discourse, and therefore any power they might have is necessarily precarious. It is this understanding, in particular the concept of the reverse discourse, that has proved useful in considering the differences, the 'issues' existing between the women within 'Bricks'.

The construction of a reverse discourse, and its strength, was linked to four identifiable factors. First, the presence of 'representative' women. For instance, the absence of women with disabilities meant that other than a general policy-awareness, as in ramps for wheelchair use, issues around able-bodied arrogance or ignorance were never aired. There were no women with disabilities to construct a reverse discourse to the dominant able-bodied discourse. In contrast to this, the presence of lesbians enabled a strong reverse discourse to be constructed.

> The stuff about lesbianism has only really been pushed because [now] there are two lesbian instructors . . . It's being dealt with now because it's being pushed, but it wouldn't have been.

The numbers of black and white women (workers and students) within the project were fairly equal. Yet, more important than simple numbers were the hierarchical positions occupied by the black and white women. The coordinator was white, and although there were two white and two black outreach workers, the black workers had been appointed six to 18 months after the first white workers, and whereas the white workers were on permanent contracts for the duration of the project, the black workers were on temporary contracts. All the instructors were white.

The second factor was the *number* of 'representative' women; the third, their project-status; and fourth, their broad political awareness and identity. For instance, the black reverse discourse increased considerably with the eventual appointment of the second black outreach worker as there was then a stronger black presence, particularly within the management group. Likewise, the lesbian reverse discourse increased after the appointment of a lesbian coordinator. The working-class reverse discourse inevitably in these circumstances, remained marginal.

The closed community

The projects provided a 'women only' space. In this 'closed community' women who generally (to differing degrees) did not have a voice in the wider white, male, heterosexually-dominated society seemed to shout at each other and jostle and push for new power positions and balances – both individual and group-based. The power-relations between white and black women, between lesbian and heterosexual, between able-bodied and disabled women and so on could be, as this worker explains, individually fought out:[8]

> It became one of the most painful working experiences of my life . . . Tied up with staff interactions, racism issues, classist issues, lesbian issues. If you like, what we tried to do in that building, we tried to tackle all the problems what are in the macrocosm in a microcosm – what we created was a vacuum where the staff group nearly blew up, really, in an emotional sense.

However, as a site where power became localized, it also became the site where resistance and struggle took place – not with the external structures of power, but with the power relations amongst the women themselves.

Within this project, the workers and trainees engaged with the divisive issues of race, class and sexuality. The expression of this, localized as it was within the project, focused on what were seen as individual 'representatives': the black woman, the white woman, the working-class or middle-class woman, the 'straight' woman, the lesbian. Such labelling was both confused and challenged by each individual woman's own identity, which constituted a combination of class, race and sexuality, as well as education, wealth, and role within the project: student or worker, and hierarchical job position. Meanwhile, the external institutionalized structures (for example, of racism, homophobia and patriarchy) through which all the women had been constructed, remained unchallenged.

Race

The white women's comments on race issues suggest a construction of a strong reverse discourse by the black women. The absence of the black workers' comments lies in stark contrast to the following quotations taken from the interviews with the white workers. The white women's perception was that the black women's 'black' identity, their experience of racism, and their need to combat it, overrode all other divides or subjectivities. The interviews suggested that although class and sexuality constantly cut across both black and white groups of women, they had a more divisive effect on the white women. Several white workers referred to their perception of the black workers' solidarity, not only with the black women in the project, but also with other women from the black community. In contrast to this white perception of black solidarity were the accounts of individual white workers' struggle with their own racism.

> I mean my social behaviour just changed completely, because it was highly highly stressful . . . and I was coming home at night and thinking, 'Am I a racist?' – and working through all these issues. . . And it was

like conflict, after conflict, after conflict. . . My personal life was actually totally affected by the conflicts which were within – because I had to take them home to sort them out. . . In the training scheme you didn't have the support to say 'Hang on a minute, I don't, I don't understand, I'm trying so hard not be racist'. . . It can become a very head-banging experience.

The point about this lack of white solidarity is not that the white women lacked a solid oppositional grouping to the black women, but that they lacked a forum for discussion and a means of support for understanding institutional racism and the personal roles and benefits, individually and collectively, they gained by it. The localized power of racism was resisted locally by the black women, and the effect of this resistance was felt individually by the white women.

Sexuality

The fractures between the women in the 'Bricks' project criss-crossed each other. For instance, sexuality cut across race, class and project-status. Like the black women, the lesbians (black and white) created an equally strong reverse discourse to the dominant, external, heterosexual one. The presence of lesbians was crucial to the confrontation of heterosexism. The strength of the reverse discourse reflected the number of lesbians involved and their project-status position. This became evident with the appointment of a new coordinator.

The new coordinator is more upfront about racism and being lesbian – these two issues have got more at the front – especially being a lesbian, because she's a lesbian herself. It's the first time lesbian issues have been right at the top there, hand in hand with race issues, whereas it never really got anywhere before.

Both the black and the lesbian reverse discourses were identifiable by their positioning against the dominant white and the dominant heterosexual discourses.

Class

From amongst the workers, class was not so clearly identifiable as a reverse discourse. A class-based reverse discourse would be that of the working class constructed against the dominant middle-class one. The class identity of the workers was fairly equally spread between middle-class, working-class now identified as middle-class; and those who remained strongly working-class-identified. This constituted, according to the white workers, a perceived class fragmentation that was not necessarily held by the students, black and white, and solidly working-class. Whereas the white workers perceived a strong degree of identification between black workers and black students, and between lesbian workers and lesbian students, there was little or no identification between working-class students and those workers who continued to identify themselves as such. Despite this apparent fuzziness, a weaker working-class reverse discourse nevertheless emerged, and further fractured the other stronger reverse discourses.

There was a particular class permeation of discourses about race that was emphasized by those white workers who remained working-class-identified. For instance, a white working-class worker contrasted herself – the daughter of a manual worker and self-educated through evening-classes – with a 'black politicized woman', the privately educated daughter of African professionals. Another white working-class-identified worker was told by a black worker that if she 'really cared about racism' she would resign or else she should be 'sacked':

> And this was in an open meeting where everybody was being awfully nice to each other, and I said, 'Don't you ever tell me I should be sacked'. And like, there was my class – upfront – and like 'you're not the only person who's had to struggle'.

The absence of the black workers' perceptions of class, job position, and the struggle with white women for power, or even simply 'equality', was clearly evident. Nevertheless, the concern here is with the intersections between class, race and sexual preference, the multisubjectivity of each woman, and the tensions resulting from the limited privileges and opportunities available to black women, 'out' lesbians and working-class women. The classed and racialized power relations of neocolonialism were as evident within a British localized site as they are globally between nation and regionalized states: between those included in its citizenship, those marginalized to its edges, and those excluded.

The agency of unemployed women

To conclude this trajectory analysis of policy, this section considers the unemployed working-class women students of the projects. First, it explores the workers' perceptions of their needs, and then it focuses on the understandings of unemployed women themselves.

The white workers of the 'Bricks' project were asked for their perceptions of the students. They saw some women as 'opportunistic', as seeing the project as 'an opening for women to go to, and so they go into it, regardless of what it's offering'. One worker explained:

When you've sat in a council house for five years with three kids, and suddenly you can get out and meet other women, and get £4 a week – you know it isn't very much, but you don't even have to tell the Social [state benefit]. You get your bus fares paid and your kids looked after. Come on, I mean, that's as good a reason as any.

This need to 'get out of the house and do something' was frequently linked by the workers to women's loneliness and isolation. The following short extracts from three of the workers show their perceptions not only of the loneliness and the isolation of unemployed women but also of their need for achievement and respect.

I think the trainees who came, the biggest majority of them came because they wanted the social contact with other women, and they wanted somewhere where they could get childcare paid for, and drop their kids off.

A lot of them come on [the project] because they're bored or because they want company. Some of them come on because they want to prove something, they want to show someone that they can do something. They want their kids to respect them. That's another big one, because they're sort of common and scum and not rated by anybody.

These observations that point sharply to the day-to-day lived reality of unemployed working-class women echo the concern for 'respectability' that Beverley Skeggs (1997) identified in her work with working-class 'care' students.

The workers saw some of the unemployed women as actively sharing their own enthusiasm about the specific skills offered by the project:

Some women came onto the scheme full of the same sort of enthusiasm as I was describing about the workforce, and they definitely perceived it as an opportunity to do some real training and to come out of it with some status and long-term job prospects.

Yet at the same time they also saw some women as naïve and unrealistic:

They want something totally unrealistic, I think – like 'oh, I can get qualified and earn a living very quickly. I'm going to earn a lot of money in the trades'.

A job. A job is the main thing in their mind. Lots of money and a job. And somebody to look after the kids. I think they're quite naïve about what to expect.

These were of course simply the perceptions of the white workers and not of the students themselves.

Students' voices

The students of the 'Office' project spoke overwhelmingly of needing work experience in order to increase their chances of getting a job. Several women also specifically wanted to learn about new technology. More so than the other two projects, women joined 'Office' specifically because of the training offered and because they hoped this would eventually lead to a training-related job. At the end of this course the majority of women continued with further education and training, with several women joining courses related to information technology.

The attraction of the 'Co-ops' project was that, unlike 'Bricks', it could be linked to women's existing knowledge, skills and expertise, and yet, unlike 'Office' it offered a dream of autonomy and freedom, of being one's own boss. All the students seemed to know someone who, without any educational qualifications, had set up a successful business. The fact that these entrepreneurs were generally men was seen as irrelevant. The business dreams of women students reflected specific everyday tasks which they were good at but for which they were not paid – food preparation, food provision, cleaning, dressmaking or childcare. While only a very small number of cooperative businesses emerged from this project, it did have a high success rate in non-training-related employment (60 per cent), and in continuing education or training (12 per cent). The following comments were made by students on this project:

> I wanted an idea for a co-op. A group of women to work on it, a start towards setting up. I now have a realistic idea of what I can manage in my present situation – certainly not setting up a co-op at the moment! A small measure of self-confidence – I am *not* just a cabbage.

> I really enjoyed the course. I'm going to miss it. I can't say I've an inspired idea for a co-op or feel confident enough to set one up. But, I have enjoyed two days to myself each week – totally for my own use without the worry of childcare or money . . . I have been doubtful in the past of needing 'women only' things but this proved that women work really well together without a mixed group influence.

> I have just started a job for one year but I'm interested in starting a co-op in the future. The best things I've got out of this course are a positive attitude towards my future and realizing I could gain skills in whatever I'm interested in and hopefully use them. I started the course with a panicky feeling that I must start something now but hadn't any skills that I could use. The other thing is making new friends and meeting women from all different backgrounds.

Two women from this project expanded a little further. Both these women identified themselves as working class: Cath was white and, as a child, lived in a rural village; Evelyn was black and has lived all her life in the city. Both women were educated during the late 1950s and early 1960s before the raising of the school leaving age to 16 and before the 11-plus system had given way to comprehensive schooling. Neither woman had any qualifications – both considered themselves to be 'failures'. The interviews explored their experiences of the project and of their schooling.

Both Evelyn and Cath were in low streams at school. Cath was arbitrarily placed in the B stream of her three-stream secondary modern school. Despite regularly being at the top of her class, especially in biology, there was never any question of her sitting exams. Cath left school at 15: 'We never had a choice'. Without her knowledge her father had found her a job on a poultry farm, and that is where she went to work. She was 'very unhappy' about this. In a tale reminiscent of the days of enforced working-class domestic labour, Cath was soon sent to live and work on another farm.

> I lived in. The bedroom was wet and damp and she didn't give me enough bedding. She didn't want to feed me, and I'll never forget one day, it'd been absolutely pouring with rain, and I'd been up at six in the morning. I was just coming up to 16. And I had to do all the milking. We had 20-odd cows to milk every morning, and fetch them in. Ever such a lot of work, and God knows what beside that. And then there was the poultry to feed and see to, and I was dying of hunger. And I mean hunger. I've never been so bloody hungry in my life. I didn't know what hunger was. I've never known it since then either. And she used to go to market on a Tuesday, market day. And, she'd leave me dinner on the table on a plate covered up in a tea towel. And this particular day she'd left me two rounds, like she'd cut it into four little squares, with just cheese. And I thought good grief, I'm never going to manage the day on that, and there was some more cheese in the fridge and I helped myself, and when she came home she hit me.

Cath had wanted to be a vet.

Evelyn went to a school that she described as a 'dunce's school', a school where black pupils were the 'dumbest'. Evelyn recalled having to tell the class about Africa even though she had lived in the same English city as they all her life. She said:

> I didn't feel like I got any encouragement at all. That they'd given up, basically, on me. That was when I was 13.

Evelyn, like Cath, left school at 15, thinking herself 'thick' and destined for the factory:

> That came over quite strongly from the teachers that that was what we were going to do. There wasn't anything positive at all: there wasn't anything positive. There wasn't. Nothing positive for us to move out of

that class thing if you like. Maybe we had a load of disillusioned teachers, I don't know.

After several other jobs, including laundry work and factory work, Evelyn became a state enrolled nurse. She was later married and then divorced and at the time of joining the project, was unemployed and had five children.

Both women compared their experience of school with that of the 'Co-ops' project. Cath saw participation as the defining feature of the project and passivity as that of school.

School was a different thing altogether really. You see, you could discuss things on that course, openly, where before, you more or less sat and listened. You could discuss things you know, you could bring up any subject – we talked about everything – and it was good, because everybody had their say about whatever they wanted to say about, and yet we still got the work done, whatever we were supposed to be doing.

Thinking about her experience of the project Evelyn concludes:

It was non-sexist. I don't know about non-racist – but well, sort of working on racism anyway. Definitely non-sexist, working on racism and sexuality . . . It was so different from school. All of it was like the opposite – but how do I get it over. Completely the opposite. But it was showing, it was showing a lot of things – but, because it was an all-women's course, taught by all women, all the tutors and everything were women, right, middle-class women, working-class women, black women, white women – there was all these different categories of women, right, in different roles whatever, but they all tried to sort of work along together and shared their skills, which was fabulous. There wasn't all that crap.

Despite this apparently positive account, Evelyn suggests an underlying experience of racism, which in the more open and contentious curriculum of 'Bricks', might have surfaced more forcibly.

Evelyn had joined the 'Co-ops' project because it was there, a supportive space that she saw as an opportunity that would hopefully lead to employment.

I hadn't done anything for a couple of years and I thought it would be a good idea to join. I joined that course mainly because it was for women over 25. It was all women, that was one of the priority things. And then there was like opportunities, you know, for employment, because I'd been unemployed so I thought there might be some possibility of getting a job, being self-employed.

Cath had joined because:

Well, I'd been out of work for quite a while. I had been self-employed prior to that. And then I went into hospital and then was off work for quite a while and I thought that it would give me an insight into how things sort of were now. And well, really, it did help with my outlook on a lot of things that were happening, you know, but unfortunately it didn't bring me a job.

Evelyn, Cath, and the other unemployed women decided to join these ESF-funded projects primarily because they wanted employment. They did not necessarily, or even generally, want employment in the specific area of training being offered, but they took the scant opportunities that were available. These ranged from taking advantage of the space provided by the project's funded childcare, to putting their feet on the ladder of further education and training, to actually getting paid employment. At the end of their 'Co-ops' course Cath was still unemployed but continuing to dream of returning to self-employment. Evelyn returned to college to join an access course; after several further setbacks, she is, at the time of writing, on a degree course.

Conclusion

The women of this chapter should be viewed against the global as well as the local. Struggling with and against each other in a shifting complex of identities and power-relations, taking whatever opportunities are offered, in many ways other than those envisaged by the policy makers and policy interpreters, women, workers and students, expressed their agency in finding the spaces and gaps in the policies and structures of the European and British state.

The workers found the space to construct feminist radical education ranging from the discrete provision of 'Bricks' to the completely integrated approach of the 'Co-ops' project. There was, however, a tendency to evangelize the unemployed working-class women which, despite the workers' undoubted best interests, nevertheless verged on the patronizing. This approach towards the 'needy' echoes nineteenth-century British philanthropy (Thompson 1968). In particular, some of the 'Bricks' workers tended to see themselves as 'empowering agents' in their students' lives. This 'empowerment', commonly linked to the concept of 'confidence gaining', was frequently given as a factor of success and justification for the training projects. Yet this avoided the unemployed women's main wish, which was for paid employment, and added to the general individualized and pathologized misconception of unemployed women. When a woman has 'gained confidence' she will become employed – conversely she is unemployed because she 'lacks confidence'. This is based on observations made of women participating in or finishing a course of training – there have been no follow-up studies of whether any increased confidence was retained. This raises the question of what happens to a woman's confidence when she returns to the isolation, to unsupported childcare and to the social and economic poverty of unemployment. Moreover, not all students increased their confidence, as one construction project worker pointed out:

> Some women, through trying something and failing, have less confidence at the end of the course than they did at the beginning.

Another worker blamed individual women's failure in the project on non-supportive partners, and their daily struggle against the gendered complexities of unemployment and poverty.

> I think some of them don't realize what they're up against and are disappointed, so they come in really excited and raring to go, sure that they can cope with this – and six months later they're defeated by circumstances. It's never usually anything to do with the course, it's nearly always either marital, health, or something to do with the kids. There's one woman at the moment – the DHS [state benefit] are messing her about so much, she's not getting any money, and that's just adding to everything else. Another one, her husband said, 'It's either me or the training, I'm not going to stand it any more.'

Although to some extent, increased confidence, continuation with education and training, and non-training-related employment may act as substitutes for the lack of training-related employment, the workers' high political investment and hope and enthusiasm for the project led to anger and frustration at their lack of success. This can be seen in their frustration and cynicism towards policy and government (EC and UK) such as that expressed by this worker:

> Well it does give women the space to do it, it does give women the opportunity to do it, but it helps some more than others, by virtue of what it is. If you were single or with a partner, and have got children, it's a huge help because it can pay costs, your childcare costs. The allowance is minimal, the bus fares, right, well you've got to pay them anyway. And, if you've got kids, and you're youngish, then you might be happy to work three or four years towards getting what you want. But I think, take some of the single women, which would include some of the lesbians, it's a very slow route. What does it actually achieve? It makes it possible, you see nothing else has changed. The women end up with a City and Guilds qualification and very little hands-on experience and it's worth bugger-all really.

Noticeably, the workers expressed more anger and frustration than the students themselves who seemed to take whatever opportunities were offered – especially when they were so relatively well-resourced as these projects.[9] Working-class women seemed to take from the projects what they wanted and left, or glided over, what they did not. With the exception of

'Office', most women did not want the training skills offered by 'Co-ops' or 'Bricks' – yet these were the specific focus of the policy and provision. These three projects suggest that unemployed working-class women want the opportunity to do something, anything, that will increase their chances of paid employment and, given the general lack of choice within ESF programmes, they seem to see their opportunities in broad adult educational terms rather than in relation to the specific skill training.

Notes

1 ESF funds have to be matched by other funds (45 per cent ESF, 55 per cent match-funds). Throughout the 1980s this match-funding had to be from public funds. This 'public fund' requirement has since relaxed slightly but the demand for match-funding continues.
2 With the exception of the 'Office' project within the further education college, the management committees of the other projects consisted solely of women: community representatives, local politicians and local authority officers.
3 As a white woman I experienced difficulties similar to those described by Rosalind Edwards (1990).
4 Women's Aid is a national organization of refuges for women wishing to escape from violent relationships. It grew, during the late 1970s and early 1980s, from within the British women's liberation movement. Many women involved with Women's Aid – either as paid workers, volunteers or management committee members, are women who were themselves in violent relationships.
5 The qualification Wordpower level 2, equates with the British National Vocational Qualification (NVQ) level 2.
6 This qualification was Computer Literacy and Information Technology level 1, equating to NVQ level 1.
7 The 'Women at Work' sessions were linked to the oral communications requirements of 'Wordpower'; see note 5.
8 Further exploration of the differences between women, especially the differences and struggles between feminist activists, can be found in Sarah Green's (1997) account of feminist activists in London during the 1980s.
9 All three projects were free, and in addition provided free childcare, free travel, free stationery and, on the 'Bricks' project, free tools and materials for the duration of the course. Furthermore, 'Bricks' also paid each student a small subsidy within the limits allowed by the state benefit system.

9 Globalization, education and unemployment

Introduction

This book has attempted to show that there is no simple, easy overall analysis of the forces of globalization, the formations of regionalized blocs or the gendered education of working-class women. Chapter 2 built on the work of theorists such as Hirst and Thompson (1996) and Pannu (1996) to reject the globalization argument that infers the demise of the nation state, and worked instead with an understanding of an unfettered internationalization of capital in which the nation state has a vital, albeit drastically changed, role to play. It is clear that global transfers of capital, geopolitical concerns, the transnational corporations' (TNCs) transfer of production, and the impacts of global technology on culture and movement are undoubtedly major factors that impinge in numerous ways (good, doubtful and bad) on our lives. Rather than immerse myself in debating the origins of globalization, geopolitical economics and politics, or postmodern notions of pluralism, ambivalence and consumerism, the intention has been to maintain a focus on the relationship between globalization, gender and education, in which it is argued that they should not lead us to a deterministic reading, for there are many conflicting and collaborative interests, along with possibilities for opportunity and change as well as resistance.

Several of these interests have been explored throughout this book. Beginning at the level of the global, I introduced a gendered analysis of the interweaving interests of the TNCs, the regionalized blocs and the nation states, and found theories of neocolonialism to be particularly useful. When the focus was narrowed down to the education and social policy of the regionalized bloc and nation state, I explored the intricate and complex relationship between the regionalized bureaucracy and the member state government. Moreover, within the nation state and across the regionalized bloc, other interest groups were evidently using, resisting and finding the spaces and gaps for collective and individual agency within the policy. These included differing government agencies, educational institutions and voluntary organizations. It included femocrats working on policy development within state institutions and feminist educational activists interpreting and implementing the policy. Finally it included individual unemployed women who engaged, for a variety of reasons, on these courses. These all interpreted and variously implemented the education and training policy of the regionalized bloc/state.

The regionalized blocs' discourses of economic growth and peace have been speckled with occasional references to concepts of social justice; even an occasional thread of equality policy was found woven into the dominant economic cloth. This equality policy was also seen as a complex and contradictory discourse, which as well as apparently providing opportunities for women to enter non-traditional skill training and employment, was also one in which sequential interpretations of 'mainstreaming' led to the marginalization of provision rather than expansion. Moreover, the actual gender exclusivity of the discourse was seen to mitigate against the interest of white and black working-class women.

This concluding chapter, rather than reiterate the main findings of the previous chapters, instead explores the key themes that have emerged from them – especially the relationship between them – and asks what this means for undereducated working-class women. This final theoretical exploration falls into four main sections: first, the global, in which the relationship between neoliberalism, neocolonialism and education is revisited; second, the regional, in which the space between the regionalized bloc and the nation state is re-entered in order to question the meaning of training and welfare policies directed towards unemployed people – especially women. This leads into the third section and a return to the discourse of equality. The chapter finally returns to the education and training policy of the nation state in order to explore the relationship of post- and neo-Fordism to gendered training provision.

Neoliberalism, neocolonialism and education

Despite the transnationalization of capital and the whittling away of many of the state's economic powers, the state (regionalized and nation) continues to play a key role within the global economy – and within the lives of its citizens. In Chapter 2 it was suggested that an understanding of neocolonialism provides a useful vantage point from which to view globalization. A subsequent focus on the policy of the EU highlighted the importance of neoliberalism as a further defining factor – particularly in the UK, North America, Australia and New Zealand.

Raj Pannu (1996) argues that the free market emphasis of neoliberalism not only promotes globalization but legitimates it, deflects criticism and enables capital to operate freely and without constraint. The state, it is argued, is being 'remantled' into a strong state with a central role to play within market forces. Yet as the state attempts to mitigate 'the worst personal and social effects of the deepening class and power cleavages and antagonisms that are exacerbated by the neoliberal economic development agenda' (Pannu 1996: 98), the link between capitalism and democracy will be weakened. Although the job of the state is to manage the unequal economic and social effects of globalization, to prevent the lid blowing off, the task is hampered by the forces of global neoliberalism: 'neo-liberal solutions simultaneously create the need for a strong state while crippling the capacities that the state needs for carrying out these solutions' (Pannu 1996: 97).

Neoliberalism not only legitimizes globalization, it promotes the stability that global capital needs by constructing a strong state which, while no longer (if ever) in control of its economy, nevertheless controls, through the welfare and education systems, the people – or more accurately controls *some* of the people. Yet, importantly, the discourse of neoliberalism is not one of control and restraint, but one that appears to enable choice and empowerment through opportunity. This neoliberal regionalized and nation state merges with late twentieth-century neocolonialism to serve the interests of globalization – economic, military and cultural – and to maintain the impoverished position of working-class women.

Neocolonialism brings the previously colonized country into the international political economy. The 'independence' of these countries with their own nation state government enables an apparent compliance with global economics, which might not have been possible under the old colonial system where imposed restraints inevitably led to unrest and resistance. This involvement of the previously colonized countries in globalization is, Pannu (1996) argues, vital to it – not only because it provides a continual (and competing) pool of low-cost labour enabling cheap production, but also because it itself exists as a hungry market for the consumption of goods and services. This 'freedom' of the postcolonized countries is controlled, at the end of the twentieth century, primarily by the United States and the old colonizing states of Europe, who no longer operate through military occupation (although importantly they retain the potential to do so) but through the agencies of the World Bank and the General Agreement on Tariffs and Trades (GATT) to create a debt-relationship and control of capital. Surveillance, control and threat are key concepts within the neocolonial relationship.

As neocolonialism relates to global labour, so neoliberalism relates to the internal labour of the EU, North America, Australia and New Zealand. Market forces and surplus labour keep down the wages of the peripheral and casual workers; undereducated working-class people, particularly women, are the western world's answer to low-cost global labour. Furthermore, as within neocolonialism, the working classes of the western states provide both a source of cheap labour for production and also a market for the consumption of goods and services – whether this is the 'official' market or alternative markets. Crucially, as will be shown in the following sections of this chapter, surveillance, control and threat are key concepts within neoliberalism and, as within neocolonialism, they are gendered, classed and racialized.

Working-class women and the previously colonized countries are, from within the discourse of neoliberalism, assumed to be within the norm of the state: working-class women as citizens, and the previously colonized countries as independent nation states. They are also both assumed to be within the norm of the global market. Yet within both the previously colonized countries and the working classes there are parallel markets, some explicitly gendered, that operate tangentially to the official market – the markets of 'helping someone out', of 'seconds', 'pass-ons', barter, 'knock-offs' and car-boot sales, as well as the markets in prostitution, drugs and stolen cars. These parallel markets have their own sets of rules and regulations, which bear little relationship to the official market, and furthermore operate, for the most part, in the spaces and gaps of official state bureaucracy. Yet the expressions of state or neocolonial control are an ever present reality: financially through welfare benefits, world aid and debt; physically through the threat or presence of the police or the military. What we see in both cases is the state and colonial control of those who, in the global market, are left to survive on the crumbs while others bask in plenty. A major task of the regionalized and nation state then is to mitigate the social effects of the class and colonial power relations of globalization.

The gendered welfare state, education and training

It has been argued that the gender exclusivity of the equality discourse has led to a persistent focus on traditional occupational under-representation from which there are few opportunities for training-related employment. This appears to be heading for a feminist heresy by suggesting that working-class women be trained only in traditional occupational areas. This is not a suggestion – or rather not the totality of a suggestion. Ideally, a range of training should be available to unemployed working-class women, training related to both traditional and non-traditional occupations, where women are both over-represented and under-represented. Moreover, in those occupations where women are over-represented, training should relate more particularly to hierarchical under-representation, building on the skills and experience that women have, rather than further devaluing their own skills and adding to their sense of worthlessness by so exclusively providing training in the traditional *male* skill areas.

Such an extended range of training opportunities could be achieved by mainstreaming gendered equal opportunities, yet as shown in the previous chapters, the exact opposite is happening; provision for women is being marginalized into the EO-pathway, further restricting women's opportunities to occupations where they have been traditionally under-represented. Unemployed working-class women want neither DIY skills nor a hobby – they want paid employment. However, as shown in the early chapters on globalization and as I pointed out in Chapter 4, training itself will not actually create jobs; if it were so easy to address the problem of unemployment there would be no unemployment.

I have shown that social policy is an important feature of the policy of regionalized 'states' and emerges from the concern of two major discourses – economic growth and peace. We return now to the welfare state and the concept of dependency, which were introduced in Chapter 3.

It has been argued that a central role of both the nation and regionalized state is to mitigate the social effects of globalization despite clear material and social inequalities to maintain internal peace, to prevent social unrest and maintain the conditions for effective economic growth. This concern of the state focuses on unemployed people.

Benefits are effectively set at a societal subsistence level – barely enough to house, feed and clothe the recipients, not enough to replace items like sheets or shoes, yet alone cookers or furniture, and most certainly not enough to enable any leisure pursuit that costs money, such as holidays or travel where even the bus fares from peripheral estates to city centres can be prohibitive. The daily struggle suggested here is increased where children are involved. It could be argued that despite state rhetoric, the benefit system is based not on the official economy or market place, but on the alternative economies and markets described above. Yet to remove state benefits altogether is to run the risk of increased social unrest, increased theft, prostitution and drug dealing. Nevertheless, some current recipients of state benefit will *choose* to reject compulsory training, lose their benefits, and have no alternative but to turn to begging or to another of these semi- or illegal means of economic survival.

Threats to the economic and social system come most from those who feel themselves to be not part of it, excluded from it, gaining no benefit or reward from it. If the clear potential for social unrest and dissatisfaction is to be curtailed then the first strategy open to the state is ideology. Yet if the ideology, in this case the discourse of equal opportunities, is, as discussed in Chapter 4, 'flawed' or unbelievable, then another strategy is needed. Although the state can always draw upon the physical force of the police or military it is, within neoliberalism, a later rather than an earlier strategy. Another option is to incorporate or tie the 'excluded' into the state. This is the currently favoured strategy: unemployed people are being tied to the state through training-related benefits and the compulsory occupation of their time. In North America, Australia, New Zealand and the EU such ties are currently in force. Within the neoliberal state, as discussed in Chapter 6, welfare benefits and compulsory training programmes have become discursively and practically intertwined. However, state benefits and compulsory training are only two of the three sides of the triangle, the third is the compulsory, effectively unpaid, work experience that is built into the benefit and training programme.

This leads to the question of why there has been this compulsion towards government training schemes? This is a particularly pertinent question given the overwhelming evidence presented in Chapters 1 and 2 that the processes of globalization, along with demographic changes, have led to increased long-term unemployment – often generational. Training is highly unlikely to lead to employment because 'the unemployed' are not needed in a world where marketization and the increased profits of shareholders are the defining feature. The global, national and (frequently) local labour force is surplus to requirement. It is true that some women will leave training programmes and find employment – there must, as I have argued elsewhere in relation to equal opportunities (Brine 1995a), be some success in order that the discourse be believable. However, if there is no employment for the majority, what then is the purpose of such compulsion towards training programmes? At one level they show politicians tackling 'the problem of unemployment' and they enable unemployed people to feel that they are 'doing something'. The relationship between training and state benefit suggests another reason for the increased emphasis on training provision. Government training programmes, I suggest, represent the interface between the benefit system and the state control of unemployed people. It is this assertion that I now wish to explore, specifically in relation to working-class women.

Benefit-linked training programmes for unemployed women and men have become a key part of the state discourse on 'the unemployed' and, despite in some instances being educationally or economically 'empowering', they represent a punitive state policy towards unemployed people – a policy that enables state surveillance.

The discourse of 'the unemployed' is constructed for the benefit of both the employed and unemployed. It is primarily a discourse based on class inequality, for most but certainly not all unemployed people are undereducated and working class. It is also a strongly racialized discourse. Finally, cutting across class and race, as shown throughout this book, is gender. The discourse, as for example expressed recently within the UK (DfEE 1996a) pathologically constructs the unemployed person as lacking work experience, an understanding that is translated to mean that employers are reluctant to employ them. The discourse suggests that, as unemployed people are 'dependent' on state benefits they need 'encouragement' into work. This discourse of the pathologized 'unemployed' is a late twentieth-century take on the concept of dependency explored in Chapter 3. Crucially, not only is this pathologized representation generally accepted by those in employment, it is frequently internalized by unemployed individuals as well, so that they too see themselves as responsible for their own 'failure'. Beverley Skeggs (1997: 37) recounts her research work with a group of working-class women on a college 'care' course:

> They had already been classified as academic failures when I met them. Along with unemployment this was experienced at an immediate intimate level. They blamed themselves for the lack of jobs and their lack of interest in schooling.

This pathologization fits happily at home within the wider 'discourse of derision' described by Stephen Ball (1994b) in which the policy failures of the state (education policy, the criminal justice system and the economy) are blamed on individuals.

On an individual level, of course, women and men will continue to respond to training programmes in a variety of ways, from those who are so desperate for any change, opportunity or social activity that they will immediately seize whatever training is offered, to those who gather information on which to make a choice, to those who, often in passive resistance, accept what seems inevitable, and even to those who resist and explicitly challenge – playing the system for as long as possible.

The effects of this discourse and its accompanying actions are punitive in two ways. The first is economic: the threat of loss of benefits. The second is the compulsory occupation of unemployed people's time, not as a means of progress towards employment but as a refined version of the qualifying criteria for state benefit. In the UK it is said that if you wish to claim unemployment benefit you must be unemployed and you must be available, any and every day, for work if it were offered to you. It now says you must prove you are available for work through attendance on a training course or by involvement in 'work experience'.

The linkage of benefit entitlement with compulsory training programmes enables the state surveillance of unemployed people. This databased surveillance will, in the UK, exist alongside current publicity, which on bill hoardings and sides of buses, exhorts the public to phone a free number and report suspected 'benefit frauds'. Acting on the information given by such anonymous informers the state investigates each complaint. Frequent amongst the complaints made about women claimants are those which allege a live-in lover. The system, echoing that perfected by the Nazis, is fraught with the possibility of harassment and injustice, for it places all claimants in the position where with no warning and with no identifiable accuser, their finances and their lifestyle are opened to state scrutiny. Moreover, the power of such surveillance is that it is maintained within the neighbourhood and the daily life of the accused, who must inevitably suspect (with or without proof) those around her.[1]

It is not the intention here to imply that prior to the benefit-linked training policies unemployed women and men on welfare benefits had an easy, 'free' time, but that the significant change is that the state now exercises the compulsory occupation of their *time*. Despite the rhetoric of educational and employment 'empowerment', the discourse of 'the unemployed' is one in which people are actively pathologized and constructed as individually responsible for their own state of unemployment. The cumulative effect of benefit-linked training programmes is the state control of unemployed people.

The equality discourse and lone mothers

Within this recent increased control of unemployed women and men there has been, within the UK, a further questionable development. Until recently, disabled people and lone parents (overwhelmingly women) were viewed as legitimately excluded from the labour market and therefore as 'deserving' recipients of state benefit. From within an equal opportunities discourse both disabled people and lone mothers are now being targeted for 'inclusion' in the labour market.

The first step in the reconstruction of 'legitimate' disability was a change in name of the relevant benefit, and harsher qualifying medical criteria. Those who did not meet these criteria were moved from the 'deserving' category of disability to the 'undeserving' category of unemployment. The latest move is that people who until recently were seen as disabled are now included in the benefit-linked training system.

Lone mothers have, in one policy step, been discursively shifted from the deserving to the undeserving recipients of state benefit, from being legitimately excluded from the labour market to being 'encouraged' into it. Beverley Skeggs's exploration of the connection between state stability and the moral purity of women is pertinent here. She quotes Tilt, who writing in 1852, stated:

> In civilised nations matrons give the tone to society; for the rules of morality are placed under their safeguard. They can try delinquents at their own tribunal, expel the condemned from their circle, and thus maintain the virtue and the country of which it is the foundation; or they can, as in France in the eighteenth century, laugh down morality, throw incense to those who are the most deserving of infamy, and, by the total subversion of all public virtue, lead to sixty years of revolution.
>
> (Skeggs 1997: 42)

Skeggs argues that the nineteenth-century perception of women as potentially dangerous enabled the linkage between degeneration, virtue, responsibility and social order. In short, 'working class women, especially (potential) mothers, are both the problem and the solution to national ills. They can be used and they can be blamed' (1997: 48). Moreover, this understanding has informed, and *continues to inform* 'the education and control of working-class women' which began in the early twentieth century with schools for mothers (1997: 42). This construction has not only gender and class connotations but is also strongly racialized: black women, unlike white women, tend not to be seen as a 'civilizing force', a 'solution' to society's ills. They are a prime target for blame, as evidenced in the US targeting of black lone mothers within the Workfare programme.

Lone mothers thus appear to epitomize the fears of patriarchal society – especially when they are working class and dependent on state benefits. Not only is a lone mother seen as having been 'irresponsibly' sexually active but she is, by definition, not in a formal economic arrangement with a man, supported instead by the state, and free to use her time as she chooses. Discursively shifting lone mothers to the status of 'undeserving' recipients of welfare reflects several significant late twentieth-century changes. First, heterosexual and lesbian women are increasingly choosing to become lone mothers. It can no longer be viewed as a 'victim' status resulting from accidental pregnancy, desertion, divorce or widowhood. Lone motherhood thus directly challenges the patriarchal control of women's sexuality, and of children. Second, it accords with the prevailing discourse of equal opportunities – why should lone mothers (or disabled people) be hindered from working? Why should the state not give them equal opportunities to compete in the labour market? Third, as discussed in Chapter 3, the welfare state is under considerable attack, with greater demands made upon (apparently) insufficient resources; lone mothers can be removed from state responsibility. Yet the chances of employment are slim, especially the chances of employment that would pay enough for them to be removed completely from benefit. The repositioning of lone mothers is yet another example of that opportunity–punitive dichotomy I have already discussed in relation to benefit-related training programmes in general. Similarly, training programmes for lone mothers will, through compulsory work experience, provide a cheap source of labour. The punitive nature of benefit-related training programmes is seen most clearly in the 'W2' programme of the US state of Wisconsin where the Republican governor asserts: 'you work or you don't get paid'. Women on this programme, which began in September 1997, are paid less than the state minimum wage for working up to 30 hours a week on community service. Non-attendance results in no cash, only food coupons for their children. Both President Clinton and the UK Labour government have already shown considerable interest in this programme.

What is significant is that the movement of some disabled people and lone mothers from the deserving to the undeserving poor is framed by the discourse of equality. Yet this latest shift in the equality discourse represents an interesting separation between equal and opportunity. The UK government makes repeated references to 'employment opportunities for all' but they no longer prefix them with 'equal' (Brown 1997).[2] Neoliberal benefit-linked training programmes no longer relate explicitly to employment, but to the *opportunity* for employment.

I have written elsewhere that a common-sense belief in the equality discourse and its possibilities is a vital part of its power, enabling the alignment of various, otherwise conflicting, groups and individuals within it (Brine 1995a). Belief in the possibilities of the equality discourse is thus vital to its success. There is a widespread understanding that unemployed people need jobs; an understanding that we cannot be complacent about unemployment; that unemployment is linked to social exclusion and poverty, and conversely that employment is linked to self-esteem, greater economic independence, social inclusion and freedom of movement. The neoliberal equality discourse speaks of increasing opportunities for employment and removing barriers to employment; the discourse says 'why shouldn't lone mothers (or disabled people) have the opportunity to work', 'they need help with understanding the opportunities for training, for employment, that are open to them'. This is a powerful position to take, apparently enabling a discourse that explicitly addresses issues of dependency, lack of opportunity, and inferred assumptions of inability. It speaks of a route towards economic and social respect, of the self and of others. Yet, crucially, this route demands enough employment opportunities for there to be 'full employment'. The key point is that such employment opportunities do not exist – at least on the scale needed. Instead of employment opportunities we have *opportunities* for employment – a highly significant discursive difference.

A speech by the British Labour Prime Minister, Tony Blair, epitomized the position of the late twentieth-century neoliberal nation state, even a relatively left-wing state, as it deals with the social consequences of a globalized economy.

> A strong society cannot be built on soft choices. It means fundamental reform of our welfare state, of the deal between citizen and society . . . The new welfare state must encourage work not dependency. We are giving young people and the long-term unemployed the opportunity . . . We want single mothers with school-age children at least to visit a Job Centre, not just stay at home waiting for the benefit cheque every week until the children are 16.
>
> (Blair 1997)

From within this neoliberal discourse, benefit-linked training programmes construct a falsehood of opportunity, and the discourse's compulsion disguises its punitive actions. A British unemployed lone mother states:

> Maybe what they're really about is trying to make, more so than it is already, being a lone parent a very unpleasant exercise. If they start establishing that if you have children this is the way its going to go,

maybe what they're really hoping to do is cut down the amount of lone parents we have – by hook or by crook.

(Pickard 1997)

Under the guise of economic realism, working-class lone mothers will no longer be economically 'protected' by the patriarchal state. In making lone motherhood a difficult option, the linkage between parenthood, marriage and patriarchy is reinforced once more.

While this section has highlighted the state control of 'the unemployed' in general and of lone mothers in particular, I nevertheless continue to resist the temptation to present an overly deterministic reading, for even here there will be educational practitioners, policy interpreters, unemployed women, lone mothers, femocrats and feminist activists who will continue to search for the gaps and spaces within which to exercise their own agency and resist loss of control and autonomy. Of course, there is always the possibility of forming new associations and allegiances from which to mount a counter-discourse or resist both the state and market forces.

Education, training and unemployed women

Literature exploring the connection between globalization and education continues, like the 'globalization' literature of the early chapters, to be dominated by men, as for example in the work and bibliography of Andy Green (1997) and James Avis *et al.* (1996).[3] Furthermore, much of the literature appears to reflect either a position of global economic determinism or an idealistic liberal education that ignores economic realities and people's economic and social need for paid employment. Notwithstanding these criticisms of the existing literature, I draw on writers who have explored the possibilities of future educational responses to globalization.

As we have seen, Raj Pannu (1996) for example, considers, within the framework of neoliberal globalization, the directions in which educational provision might move and suggests privatization or dualization. Privatization would lead to an emphasis on cost-recovery policies and the encouragement of private educational institutions. This was clearly the route of the UK's Conservative government of the 1980s and 1990s and was itself intricately linked to dualization. Pannu sees dualization as consisting of one strand of poor quality, poorly-funded provision aimed at the majority, and another strand of superior quality, well-funded provision aimed at the privileged minority. An example of dualization is provided by the European Commission's *White Paper: Education and Training* (EC 1995a) discussed in Chapter 5. This shows the EC proposals for a 'traditional' academic route and a 'modern' practical competency-based route.

Educational dualization has a clear relationship to the labour market, and needs further exploration, particularly in relationship to post- and neo-Fordism. Phillip Brown and Hugh Lauder (1992) provide a comparison of Fordism and post-Fordism and, in a later work, politically align neo-Fordism with the New Right and post-Fordism with the New Left modernizers (Brown and Lauder 1997). They describe Fordist labour as reflecting a typical production line that is fragmented into separate standardized tasks. The Fordist labour force is shown little trust and is required to show little discretion, but essentially to do the required tasks within a clearly hierarchical structure. On the other hand post-Fordist labour, they say, is specialized, multiskilled and flexible. The post-Fordist labour force is highly trusted, required to show discretion, to problem solve and act upon initiative within a 'flat' managerial system in which they are likely to be part of the growing managerial and professional class. This is however a somewhat simplistic model that suggests a stereotypical view of the labour market that does not take into account differing organizational cultures and nuances. Disputing this binary model, and arguments such as those of Friedman (1977) that we are all now part of the post-Fordist world, I suggest that both neo- and post-Fordism are perfectly coexistent within neoliberal globalization.

Post-Fordism appears to apply mainly to managers, administrators, professionals and other core and peripheral workers. Both Dennis Gleeson (1996) and James Avis (1996) critique what Avis calls the myth of post-Fordism. Sue Willis and Jane Kenway (1996) consider the restructuring of post-compulsory education and training within Australia and offer a gendered critique of post-Fordism in which they focus on the concept of flexibility. They suggest that many women want flexibility – of function as well as working hours. Functional flexibility is reflected in multiskilled jobs that are seen to offer variety, training and progression. They argue that, instead of functional flexibility women get 'contingent, insecure, low-paid jobs with no career prospects and few benefits' (1996: 243). Similarly, Jill Blackmore (1997) argues that post-Fordism, despite its attractions of flexibility and its emphasis on generic skills, continues to gender skills and does not alter existing unequal gender relationships.

The late twentieth-century post-Fordist tale of the labour market centres on the highly skilled, computer literate, flexible labour force. Such a labour force will, it is said, be needed as much on the factory floor as in the offices and boardrooms. However, demands for such a labour force of working-class women will not be achieved through the current training policies. There is a clear disjuncture here between the stated needs of the labour market and the training being given to the labour force – particularly to white and black working-class women. The obvious conclusion is that this training is not, after all, concerned with employment – or at least it's not concerned with employment in this post-Fordist version of the labour market, from which I argue, working-class black and white women are already excluded. Admittedly, the basic skills provision within training projects ensures the necessary minimal standards of literacy, but other than this, the lack of relevance between training and the labour market seems to suggest that it does not actually matter what specific skill training is given. If this is so, why are women not encouraged back into the home (as in Britain in the 1950s) to have and care for children?

In Britain and the US, the opposite is the case: women, especially lone parents, are being actively 'encouraged' into the labour market – or more accurately into training and compulsory 'work experience'. There is, apparently, a definite attempt to get lone parents off state benefit and into paid employment. So, is it that working-class women are, after all, needed by the labour market? Or is it, as just argued, that women are to be discouraged, as in the case of unemployed lone mothers, from being dependent on the state? If working-class women cannot be cared for by the state, and if working-class women are actually needed by the labour market, where exactly are they needed? If they are needed at all, it is only in those peripheral jobs that border on the formal and informal labour markets. Despite technological advances, cleaners for example (industrial, urban and domestic) are still needed, and, furthermore, an ageing population will need many (generally unqualified) carers, and educated middle-class women will need childcarers.

Post-Fordism bears little relationship to the employment reality of working-class women, other than in its emphasis on employee flexibility, or rather, employment insecurity. A reworking of Fordism, a neo-Fordist fine-tuning of the fragmented production line approach to fit it to turn of the century globalization, provides a more fitting account of the situation for women and men of the working classes. Within the globalized market, post-Fordism and neo-Fordism coexist, maintaining class, gender and race inequalities, within the nation and regionalized state, and within the neo-colonial global economy. Current training provision for working-class women is clearly not concerned with training for a post-Fordist labour market, and neither, despite neo-Fordist realities of working-class employment, is it concerned with a neo-Fordist labour market. The suggestion here is that training policy is applying neo-Fordist principles of control and surveillance to the state benefit-related training of 'the unemployed'. The principles of regulated control and diminished individual 'rights' structure the lives of both the employed and unemployed working-class women and men.

While focusing primarily on the construction of education and training policy for unemployed working-class women, I have argued against a determinist reading, and for an understanding of state, institutional and individual intervention, interpretation and pragmatism to take and make opportunities, to find or make the spaces and gaps necessary for alternative readings. The attempt to keep working-class women undereducated or inadequately trained actually creates the space for the feminist discourse of gender equal opportunities and for late twentieth-century feminist activism.

Constructed within a generally educated middle-class framework, both discourse and activism uncritically perpetuate class-based and racialized assumptions, unintentionally limiting women's training and employment opportunities. Yet, at the same time, in the hands of feminist educators, opportunities have been provided for working-class women to gain access to a radical adult *education*.

The distinction between education and training creates an important space for feminist intervention. The training curriculum has been built on notions of competency – related to vocational skills, to 'key' skills of literacy, numeracy and communication, and even to self-confidence. Yet the postcompulsory education system has also included a clear strand of radical adult education which, despite being consistently attacked through the withdrawal of funding, has nevertheless continued in a variety of sites and forms. For example, as we have seen, Chapter 8 considered radical education within UK training programmes for unemployed women.[4]

Radical adult education has a long history of working in the gaps and spaces between liberal and vocational education and of working beyond the reaches of the state. It has a tradition of placing inequalities and injustices at the centre of the curriculum and, perhaps most importantly, it has a history of addressing the inadequacies of the compulsory educational system. Whereas compulsory education and liberal postcompulsory education have often been the means of ensuring social stability, they nevertheless also hold powerful possibilities for social change. Radical adult education is a broad tradition that is often found associated with trade unions, black and feminist movements. As it is essentially an education for change, it is not surprising that it is found connected to those who most desire that change. The strong tradition of radical adult education that can be found in the UK is illustrated by the following examples.

Andy Green (1990) recounts the struggle of British working-class men, especially the Chartists, for literacy and political education. Similarly, E.P. Thompson (1968) depicts British working-class women and men fighting within trade unions for political education, for an understanding of the class-based power-structures and a language with which to critique it. June Purvis (1991) tells of British working-class women, under the cloak of religion (particularly the Quakers), educating themselves, and struggling to gain acceptance into the previously male working-class dominated Mechanics Institutes. She tells also of the political and liberal education programme of the Women's Co-operative Guild.

During the last 30 years, in Britain, the consciousness-raising groups of the women's liberation movement have engaged in a process of conscientiation similar to that expounded by Paulo Freire (1972) in his extensive work with poor, illiterate and oppressed people in South America. The significance of Freire for radical adult education continues.[5] Within Britain, despite hostile and restrictive policy and funding, and in contrast to the government's own policy for training programmes, this radical tradition continues amongst the government agencies, colleges and voluntary organizations currently funded through the ESF and working with groups of long-term unemployed working-class women, many of whom continue to struggle with literacy and grapple for political understanding and active citizenship. Whereas the increased surveillance of the unemployed and the increased state control of training programmes will undoubtedly have an impact on the possibilities for radical adult education, history suggests that they are unlikely to be stopped.

The fundamental problem of unemployment and social exclusion remains economic. Education, even radical education, can only enable us to adapt to its social consequences, or at best, and mainly from within localized arenas, resist, challenge and subvert. Although from within a framework such as this, writers have continued to consider the relationship of education and training, the old debate surrounding education's relationship to employment has been overtaken by the economic, social and moral consequences of *un-employment*.[6] Philosophically turning the argument on its head John White (1997) offers a radical alternative, that is provocative, interesting and suggestive of a more equitable and probably enjoyable life. However, it minimizes or ignores several crucial factors. The first is the economic necessity to work, which although to some extent is addressed by his suggestion of 'assured life-time income' avoids those thorny issues of pay differentials and consumerist aspirations. Second, he ignores the capitalist economic context within which work takes place, and the interests of shareholders in maintaining and strengthening their economic power. Third, although he specifically includes women in his 'activity society' he ignores gendered power relations and the interest of men, sometimes individually and certainly collectively, in maintaining that. As with all suggestions for a fair and equitable society, the redistribution of power, privilege and reward means that some of these must be relinquished by, or taken from, those who already have too much. This is, of course, unlikely to happen without an enormous struggle.

I conclude that compulsory and postcompulsory education needs to address the social and economic consequences of undereducation, of long-term unemployment and of its resulting economic poverty and social exclusion. While the funded provision of postcompulsory education continues to be vital, funds and attention need also to be turned to the compulsory sector. Postcompulsory education and training have continuously been placed in the position of trying to shut the stable door, which is determinedly fixed open as each cohort of undereducated girls and boys leave school with impoverished futures. In referring to undereducation, this does not mean simply literacy, numeracy or other competencies and qualifications, as vitally important as these are. More importantly I am advocating an education that encourages a critical and questioning understanding of the world and that provides people with the intellectual abilities not only to cope with long periods of unemployment (even continual unemployment) but with an education that enables each of us to critically engage with and even change (in numerous small and larger ways) our world.

The neoliberal debate on (under)education is focused on standards, competencies and other measurable indicators of educational success. New qualifications and new levels have been introduced to ensure that everyone leaves school with 'qualifications'. Qualifications provide a clear indicator of status, of educational attainment and, by inference, social and economic class. Qualifications also attest to the success of the educational system. But as Arnot has written, 'It is one thing to obtain large numbers of educational certificates, it is another to convert them into economic capital within hierarchically organised labour markets' (Arnot 1997: 291). The discourse that is constructed around qualifications and (un)employment states that qualifications will lead to a job; more qualifications and higher status qualifications will lead to better jobs. No qualifications means no jobs and it's your own fault; you can see it's not the fault of the education system because all around you, you can see other people gaining qualifications. Therefore, it's up to you, if you want a job, get qualified. The causes of unemployment are thus shifted away from education and onto the individual. Using the metaphor of the north face of the Eiger, it was argued in Chapter 4 that even if all those waiting to climb the Eiger were equally well equipped they would not all reach the summit, but would be staged, individually scattered and collectively grouped along the way. That is to say if all people left compulsory education extremely well qualified, other criteria would be inserted in order to distribute limited employment. All the evidence suggests that such criteria would continue to maintain and reflect unequal power structures based on gender, class and race. For, as Iris Marion Young (1990a) has argued, even if certain material resources, such as education, were more equally distributed they would still be affected by the dominant social and economic structures and power relations. The task of educators must be to encourage a critical engagement with, and questioning of our world, and to demand accountability for the choices and decisions that are made by the nation and regional state within the complex and conflicting processes of globalization where the local and the global are so intricately linked.

Notes

1 Extending further the notion of surveillance, in September 1997 the UK's new Labour government announced plans for setting up a free phone line upon which parents can tell of 'poor' teachers, with supposedly similar guarantees of anonymity and unquestioned investigation.

2 The UK Chancellor of the Exchequer, Gordon Brown, has persistently used this

phrase, resisting all attempts by interviewers to get any further clarification in respect of actual jobs. See for example the BBC *Newsnight* interview by Jeremy Paxman on Monday 29 September 1997.

3 This is despite Avis *et al.* (1996) own critique of the homogeneity inherent in Labour's education policies.

4 Referring to the impact of globalization on Canadian adult education, Jane Cruik-shank (1996) argues that adult educators should take an explicitly politicizing role, activity engaging with their students in collaborative action.

5 See for example, Paula Allman (1988), Kathleen Weiler (1991), Floresca-Gawagas (1996) and Peter Mayo (1996).

6 See for example, Terri Seddon (1994), James Avis (1996) and Sue Willis and Jane Kenway (1996).

Appendix I:
The countries of the
regionalized blocs

Asia–Pacific Economic Cooperation (APEC)

Australia	Indonesia	Philippines
Brunei	Japan	Singapore
Canada	Malaysia	South Korea
Chile	Mexico	Taiwan
China	New Zeland	Thailand
Hong Kong	Papua New Guinea	United States

Association of South East Asian Nations (ASEAN)

Brunei Darussalam	Philippines	Vietnam
Indonesia	Singapore	
Malaysia	Thailand	

European Free Trade Association (EFTA)

Austria*	Liechtenstein	Switzerland
Denmark*	Norway	United Kingdom*
Finland*	Portugal*	
Iceland	Sweden*	

[*have left EFTA to join EU]

European Union (EU)

Austria	Germany*	The Netherlands*
Belgium*	Greece	Portugal
Denmark	Ireland	Spain
Finland	Italy*	Sweden
France*	Luxembourg*	United Kingdom

[*original member states]

North American Free Trade Association (NAFTA)

Canada	Mexico	USA

Appendix II:
The Lomé Convention and the African, Caribbean and Pacific states

The African, Caribbean and Pacific (ACP) states included within the Lomé Convention are:

Angola
Antigua
Bahamas
Barbados
Belize
Benin
Botswana
Burkina Faso
Burundi
Cameroon
Cape Verde
Central African Republic
Chad
Comoros
Congo
Cote d'Ivoire
Djibouti
Dominica
Dominican Republic
Equatorial Guinea
Eritrea
Ethiopia
Fiji
Gabon

The Gambia
Ghana
Grenada
Guinea
Guinea-Bissau
Guyana
Haiti
Jamaica
Kenya
Kiribati
Lesotho
Liberia
Madagascar
Malawi
Mali
Mauritania
Mauritius
Mozambique
Namibia
Niger
Nigeria
Papua New Guinea
Rwanda
St Kitts–Nevis

St Lucia
St Vincent
São Tomé and Principe
Senegal
Seychelles
Sierra Leone
Solomon Islands
Somalia
Sudan
Suriname
Swaziland
Tanzania
Togo
Tonga
Trinidad and Tobago
Tuvalu
Uganda
Vanuatu
Western Samoa
Zaire
Zambia
Zimbabwe

Appendix III:
European legislation and documentation

Apart from adopting detailed rules that supplement agreed Council legislation, European law is not made by the European Commission. The Commission carries out preliminary research and makes proposals for Directives and Regulations, which then go through extensive consultation in Parliament, the Economic and Social Committee, and the Council of Ministers. The legal measure is finally adopted by the Council of Ministers and after adoption by individual member states in accordance with their own parliamentary procedures, it becomes law.

- An **Opinion** and a **Recommendation** are European Commission documents that carry no legal force. They simply express the Commission's recommended action or opinion on a particular issue.
- A **Directive** and a **Regulation** are European Commission documents that supplement existing legislation and have the legal force to demand the compliance of a member state.
- A **Decision** is a European Commission statement on a specific aspect of policy and it is legally binding on the addressee.

References

Allen, J. (1990) Does feminism need a theory of 'the state'? in S. Watson (ed.) *Playing the State: Australian Feminist Interventions*. London: Verso.

Allman, P. (1988) Gramsci, Freire and Illich: Their contributions to education for socialism, in T. Lovett (ed.) *Radical Approaches to Adult Education: A Reader*. London: Routledge.

Altbach, P.G. (1995) Education and neocolonialism, in B. Ashcroft, G. Griffiths and H. Tiffin (eds) *The Post-colonial Studies Reader*. London: Routledge.

Amin, S. (1997) Reflections on the international system, in P. Golding and P. Harris (eds) *Beyond Cultural Imperialism: Globalization, Communication and the New International Order*. London: Sage.

Andersen, B. (1983) *Imagined Communities: Reflections on the Origin and Spread of Nationalism*. London and New York: Verso.

Anthias, F. (1995) Cultural racism or racist culture? Rethinking racist exclusions. *Economy and Society*, 24 (2): 279–301.

Anthias, F. and Yuval-Davis, N. (1992) *Racialized Boundaries: Race, Nation, Gender, and Class and the Anti-Racist Struggle*. London: Routledge.

Appadurai, A.(1993) Disjuncture and difference in the global cultural economy, in P. Williams and L. Chrisman (eds) *Colonial Discourse and Post-colonial Theory: A Reader*. Hemel Hempstead: Harvester Wheatsheaf.

Apple, M. (1996) *Cultural Politics and Education*. Buckingham: Open University Press.

Arendt, H. (1958) *The Origins of Totalitarianism*. London: George Allen and Unwin.

Arnot, M. (1994) Feminist values and democratic education: rethinking equality and difference. Conference paper, University of Valencia 'International Congress on Coeducation', October 1994.

Arnot, M. (1997) 'Gendered citizenry': new feminist perspectives on education and citizenship. *British Educational Research Journal*, 23 (3): 275–95.

Asia–Pacific Economic Cooperation (APEC) (1991) *The Seoul Declaration*. Singapore: APEC Secretariat.

Asia–Pacific Economic Cooperation (APEC) (1994) *The Bogor Declaration*. Singapore: APEC Secretariat.

Asia–Pacific Economic Cooperation (APEC) (1995) *The Osaka Action Agenda*. Singapore: APEC Secretariat.

Association of South East Asian Nations (ASEAN) (1967) *The Bangkok Declaration.* Jakarta: ASEAN Secretariat.

Association of South East Asian Nations (ASEAN) (1976) *Declaration of ASEAN Concord.* Jakarta: ASEAN Secretariat.

Avis, J. (1996) The myth of the post-Fordist society, in J. Avis, M. Bloomer, G. Esland, D. Gleeson and P. Hodkinson. *Knowledge and Nationhood: Education, Politics and Work.* London: Cassell.

Ball, S.J. (1994a) Researching inside the state: issues in the interpretation of elite interviews, in D. Halpin and B. Troyna (eds) *Researching Education Policy: Ethical and Methodological Issues.* London: Falmer.

Ball, S.J. (1994b) *Education Reform: A Critical and Post-structural Approach.* Buckingham: Open University.

Barnett, T. (1997) States of the state and third worlds, in P. Golding and P. Harris (eds) *Beyond Cultural Imperialism: Globalization, Communication and the New International Order.* London: Sage.

Barron, R.D. and Norris, G.M. (1976) Sexual divisions and the dual labour market, in D.L. Barker and S. Allen (eds) *Dependence and Exploitation in Work and Marriage.* London: Longman.

Bates, I. (1990) 'No bleeding whining minnies': some perspectives on the role of YTS in class and gender reproduction. *British Journal of Education and Work,* 3 (2): 91–110.

Bauman, Z. (1992) *Intimations of Postmodernity.* London: Routledge.

Beechey, V. (1978) Women and production: a critical analysis of some sociological theories of women's work, in A. Kuhn and A.M. Wolpe (eds) *Feminism and Materialism: Women and Modes of Production.* London: Routledge.

Bergsten, F.C. and Noland, M. (1993) *Pacific Dynamism and the International Economic System.* Washington, DC: Institute for International Economics.

Billig, M. (1995) *Banal Nationalism.* London: Sage.

Blackmore, J. (1997) The gendering of skill and vocationalism in twentieth century Australian education, in A.H. Halsey, H. Lauder, P. Brown and A.S. Wells (eds) *Education, Culture, Economy, Society.* Oxford: Oxford University Press.

Blackmore, J. and Kenway, J. (eds) (1993) *Gender Matters in Educational Administration and Policy.* London: Falmer Press.

Blair, T. (1997) Speech to Labour Party Conference, 30 September, Brighton.

Bourdieu, P. (1997) The forms of capital, in A.H. Halsey, H. Lauder, P. Brown and A.S. Wells (eds) *Education, Culture, Economy, Society.* Oxford: Oxford University Press.

Brine, J. (1992) The European Social Fund and the vocational training of unemployed women: questions of gendering and regendering. *Gender and Education,* 4 (1–2): 149–62.

Brine, J. (1994) A women's training centre considered as a 'site of localised power': thoughts on Foucault. *Studies in the Education of Adults,* 26 (2): 201–18.

Brine, J. (1995a) Equal opportunities and the European Social Fund: discourse and practice. *Gender and Education,* 7 (1): 9–22.

Brine, J. (1995b) Educational and vocational policy and the construction of the European Union. *International Studies in Sociology of Education,* 5 (2): 145–63.

Brine, J. (1996a) *Integration of women into the labour market within the framework of ESF objective 3 in the UK,* Summary and Full Report (including commissioned research from Benelux and Germany). Brussels: European Commission.

Brine, J. (1996b) The ESF and new technology training for unemployed women, *ERIC ED 392 928, CE 071 058*. Eugene, OR: Educational Resources Information Centre (ERIC), University of Oregon.

Brine, J. (1997a) European education and training policy for under-educated unemployed people, *International Studies in Sociology of Education*, 7 (2): 229–45.

Brine, J. (1997b) Over the ditch and through the thorns: accessing European funds for research and social justice. *British Educational Research Journal*, 23 (4): 421–32.

Brine, J. (1998) The European Union's discourse of 'equality' and its education and training policy within the post-compulsory sector. *Journal of Education Policy*, 13 (1): 137–52.

Brine, J. (in press) Mainstreaming European 'equal opportunities': marginalizing UK training for women, in J. Salisbury and S. Riddell (eds) *Gender, Policy and Educational Change*. London: Routledge.

Brown, G. (1997) Speech to Labour Party Conference, 29 September, Brighton.

Brown, P. and Lauder, H. (1992) Education, economy and society: an introduction to a new agenda, in P. Brown and H. Lauder (eds) *Education for economic survival: from Fordism to Post-Fordism?* London: Routledge.

Brown P. and Lauder, H. (1997) Education, globalization, and economic development, in A.H. Halsey, H. Lauder, P. Brown and A.S. Wells (eds) *Education, Culture, Economy, Society*. Oxford: Oxford University Press.

Brown, S. (1988) Feminism, international theory and international relations of gender inequality. *Millennium*, 17 (3): 461–75.

Burton, L. (1986) *Girls into Maths Can Go*. London: Holt.

Byrne, E. (1978) *Women and Education*. London: Tavistock Publications.

Choi, S. (1992) Ageing and social welfare in South Korea, in D. Phillips (ed.) *Ageing in East and South East Asia*. London: Edward Arnold.

Cockburn, C. (1985) *Machinery of Dominance: Women, Men and Technical Know-how*. London: Pluto.

Cockburn, C. (1986) The relations of technology: what implications for theories of sex and class?, in R. Crompton and M. Mann (eds) *Gender and Stratification*. Cambridge: Polity Press.

Cockburn, C. (1987) *Two-track Training: Sex Inequalities and the YTS*. London: Macmillan.

Cockburn, C. (1988) The gendering of jobs: workplace relations and the reproduction of sex segregation, in S. Walby (ed.) *Gender Segregation at Work*. Milton Keynes: Open University Press.

Cockburn, C. (1990) The material of male power, in T. Lovell (ed.) *British feminist thought*. Oxford: Blackwell.

Cooper, D. (1995) *Power in struggle: feminism, sexuality and the state*. Buckingham: Open University Press.

Coulby, D. and Jones, C. (1995) *Postmodernity and European Education Systems*. Stoke-on-Trent: Trentham Books.

Council of Europe (1992) *The Unemployment Trap: Long Term Unemployment and Low Educational Attainment in Six Countries*. Strasbourg: Council of Europe Press.

Cruikshank, J. (1995) Economic globalization: which side are we on? *International Journal of Lifelong Education*, 14 (6): 459–75.

Cruikshank, J. (1996) Economic globalization: a need for alternate visions. *Canadian Journal of University Continuing Education*, 22 (1): 49–66.

Cumming-Bruce, N. (1998) Misery for migrant millions: turmoil in Tiger nations as 3m foreign workers face forced return to poverty and despair. *The Guardian,* 7 January.

Dean, M. (1995) Governing the unemployed self in an active society. *Economy and Society,* 24 (4): 559–83.

Department of Employment (DE) (1990) *European Social Fund: Guidance on Applications for 1991.* London: DE/ESF Unit.

Department of Employment (DE) (1991) *European Social Fund: Guidance for 1992 Applications.* London: DE/ESF Unit.

Department of Employment (DE) (1992a) *European Social Fund: Guidance for 1993 Applications.* London: DE/ESF Unit.

Department of Employment (DE) (1992b) *New Earnings Survey – Part A: Streamlined and Summary Analyses.* London: Government Statistics Office.

Department of Employment (DE) (1993a) *European Social Fund: A Plan for Objective 3 in Great Britain: 1994–1999.* London: DE/ESF Unit.

Department of Employment (DE) (1993b) *European Social Fund: Guidance for 1994 Applications.* London: DE/ESF Unit.

Department of Employment (DE) (1994) *European Social Fund: Guidance for 1995 Applications.* London: DE/ESF Unit.

Department for Education and Employment (DFEE) (1995) *European Social Fund, Guidance for 1996 Applications (Objective 3).* London: DfEE/ESF Unit.

Department for Education and Employment (DFEE) (1996a) *Objective 3, United Kingdom, 1997–1999, Single Programming Document.* London: DfEE/ESF Unit.

Department for Education and Employment, (1996b) *European Social Fund, Objective 3, 1997 Applications Guidance,* London: DfEE/ESF Unit.

Department for Education and Employment (DfEE) (1997) *European Social Fund Objectives 2, 3, 5b and Regional Community Initiatives: 1998 Applications Guidance.* London: DfEE.

Diamond, I. and Quinby, L. (1988) *Feminism and Foucault: Reflections on Resistance.* Boston, MA: Northeastern University Press.

van Doorne-Huiskes, A., van Hoof, J. and Roelofs, E. (eds) (1995) *Women and the European Labour Markets.* London: Chapman.

Edwards, R. (1990) Connecting method and epistemology – a white woman interviewing black women. *Women's Studies International Forum,* 13 (5): 477–90.

Eisenstein, H. (1990) Femocrats, official feminism and the uses of power, in S. Watson (ed.) *Playing the State: Australian Feminist Interventions.* London: Verso Press.

Ellsworth, E. (1989) Why doesn't this feel empowering? Working through the repressive myths of critical pedagogy. *Harvard Educational Review,* 59 (3): 297–324.

English, H.E. and Smith, M.G. (1993) NAFTA and Pacific partnership: advancing multilateralism? in F.C. Bergsten and M. Noland (eds) *Pacific Dynamism and the International Economic System.* Washington, DC: Institute for International Economics.

Enloe, C. (1989) *Bananas, Beaches and Bases.* London: Pandora.

Esping-Andersen, G. (1990) *The Three Worlds of Welfare Capitalism.* Cambridge: Polity Press.

Esping-Andersen, G. (1996) After the golden age? Welfare state dilemmas in a global economy, in G. Esping-Andersen (ed.) *Welfare States in Transition: National Adaptations in Global Economics.* London: Sage.

European Commission (EC) (1957) *Treaty of Rome.* Brussels: European Commission.

European Commission (EC) (1963) *OJ 63, 10 April 1963: Decision 63/226/EEC: Common Vocational Training Policy.* Brussels: European Commission.

European Commission (EC) (1971) *OJ L28: Council Decision of 1 February 1971 on the Reform of the European Social Fund, (71/66/EEC, 4 February 1971).* Brussels: European Commission.

European Commission (EC) (1975) *Directive 75/117: Equal Pay for Work of Equal Value.* Brussels: European Commission.

European Commission (EC) (1976a) *Vocational Guidance and Training for Women Workers,* Luxembourg: Office for the Official Publications of the European Commission.

European Commission (EC) (1976b) *Directive 76/207/EEC: Equal Access to Vocational Training.* Brussels: European Commission.

European Commission (EC) (1977) *Reform of the European Social Fund.* Brussels: European Commission.

European Commission (EC) (1978) *Background Report, 21 July 1978: Encouraging Equality for Women: The Community Record.* London: European Commission.

European Commission (EC) (1981) *Women of Europe Supplement 6: Women and the European Social Fund.* Brussels: European Commission.

European Commission (EC) (1983a) *The Stuttgart Declaration of 19 June 1983 Promoting European Awareness in Education.* Brussels: European Commission.

European Commission (EC) (1983b) *Council Decision 7709/83, 21 June 1983: Reform of the ESF.* Brussels: European Commission.

European Commission (EC) (1984a) *The Fontainebleau Declaration of 25–26 June 1984 Promoting European Identity.* Brussels: European Commission.

European Commission (EC) (1984b) *European File 2/84: The European Social Fund: A Weapon Against Unemployment.* Brussels: European Commission.

European Commission (EC) (1984c) *Council Recommendation of 13 December 1984: Promotion of Positive Action for Women.* Brussels: European Commission.

European Commission (EC) (1985) *Equal Opportunities for Women: Second Medium-Term Community Programme 1986–1990, (COM(85)801).* Brussels: European Commission.

European Commission (EC) (1986) *Single European Act.* Brussels: European Commission.

European Commission (EC) (1987a) *New Forms, New Areas of Employment Growth: A Comparative Study.* Luxembourg: Office for the Official Publications of the European Commission.

European Commission (EC) (1987b) *Directive 76/207/EEC: Recommendation on Vocational Training for Women.* Luxembourg: Office for the Official Publications of the European Commission.

European Commission (EC) (1987c) *COM(87)376/2/final 8251: Reform of the Structural Funds.* Brussels: European Commission.

European Commission (EC) (1987d) *The Re-insertion of Women in Working Life: Initiatives and Problems.* Luxembourg: Office for the Official Publications of the European Commission.

European Commission (EC) (1988) *Resolution on the European Dimension in Education.* Brussels: European Commission.

European Commission (EC) (1990a) *Annual Report on the Implementation of the Reform of the Structural Funds, COM(90)516*. Luxembourg: Office for the Official Publications of the European Commission.

European Commission (EC) (1990b) *Equal Opportunities for Women and Men: Third Medium-Term Community Action Programme: 1991–1995 (COM(90)449)*. Brussels: European Commission.

European Commission (EC) (1990c) *European File 5/90: Education and Training in the Approach to 1992*. Brussels: European Commission.

European Commission (EC) (1992a) *Treaty on the European Union*. Brussels: European Commission.

European Commission (EC) (1992b) *The Position of Women in the Labour Market*. Luxembourg: Office for the Official Publications of the European Commission.

European Commission (EC) (1993a) *White Paper: Growth, Competitiveness, Employment: The Challenges and Ways Forward into the Twenty-first Century*. Luxembourg: Office for the Official Publications of the European Commission.

European Commission (EC) (1993b) *Community Structural Funds, 1994–99: Regulations and Commentary*. Luxembourg: Office for the Official Publications of the European Commission.

European Commission (EC) (1993c) *OJ L193: Council Regulation (EEC) No 2084/93 of 20 July 1993*. Brussels: European Commission.

European Commission (EC) (1994a) *European Social Policy: A Way Forward for the Union: A White Paper, (COM(94)333final)*. Luxembourg: Office for the Official Publications of the European Commission.

European Commission (EC) (1994b) *Social Europe Supplement 4/94: Wage Determination and Sex Segregation in Employment in the European Community*. Luxembourg: Office for the Official Publications of the European Commission.

European Commission (EC) (1995a) *White Paper: Education and Training: Teaching and Learning: Towards the Learning Society*. Luxembourg: Office for the Official Publications of the European Commission.

European Commission (EC) (1995b) *The Fourth Framework Programme 1995–1999: Targeted Socio-Economic Research: The Work Programme*. Brussels: European Commission.

European Commission (EC) (1995c) *The Fourth Medium-Term Community Action Programme on Equal Opportunities for Women and Men (1996–2000), (COM(90)381final)*. Luxembourg: Office for the Official Publications of the European Commission.

European Commission (EC) (1996a) *COM(96)491 final: Report on the Development in Relations with Turkey Since the Entry into Force of the Customs Union*. Luxembourg: Office for the Official Publications of the European Commission.

European Commission (EC) (1996b) *Background Report B/11/96: The Lomé Convention*. London: European Commission.

European Commission (EC) (1996c) 1997 will be the European Year against racism. *The Week in Europe WE/28/96 25 July 1996*. London: European Commission.

European Commission (EC) (1997a) *Background Report B/3/97: The Enlargement of the European Union*. London: European Commission.

European Commission (EC) (1997b) *The Week in Europe, WE/02/97, 16 January 1997*. London: European Commission.

European Commission (EC) (1997c) *Amsterdam Treaty.* Brussels: European Commission.

European Free Trade Association (EFTA) (1960) *Stockholm Agreement.* Geneva: EFTA Secretariat.

Eurostat (1992) *Europe in Figures,* third edition. Luxembourg: Office for the Official Publications of the European Commission.

Evans, J. (1995) *Feminist Theory Today: An Introduction to Second-wave Feminism.* London: Sage.

Eviota E.U.Y. (1992) *The Political Economy of Gender; Women and the Sexual Division of Labour in the Philippines.* London: Zed Books.

Fiske, J. (1995) *Media matters: everyday culture and political change.* Minneapolis, MN: Minnesota University Press.

Floresca-Gawagas, V. (1996) Empowerment of the people: insights from the Philippines. *The Alberta Journal of Educational Research,* XLII (2): 161–9.

Folbre, N. (1992) *Women's Work in the World Economy.* New York: New York University Press.

Foucault, M. (1970) *The Order of Things.* New York: Random House.

Foucault, M. (1977) *Discipline and Punish.* New York: Pantheon.

Foucault, M. (1980a) *Power-knowledge: Selected Interviews and Other Writings 1972–1977.* New York: Pantheon.

Foucault, M. (1980b) *History of Sexuality,* vol. 1. New York: Vintage.

Franzway, S., Court, D. and Connell, R.W. (1989) *Staking a Claim: Feminism, Bureaucracy and the State.* Cambridge: Polity Press.

Fraser, N. and Gordon, L. (1994) A genealogy of dependency: Tracing a keyword of the US welfare state. *Signs: Journal of Women in Culture and Society,* 19 (2): 309–36.

Freire, P. (1972) *Pedagogy of the Oppressed* (1993 edn). Harmondsworth: Penguin.

Freire, P. (1985) *Politics of Education.* London: Macmillan.

Friedman, A.L. (1977) *Industry and labour.* London: Macmillan.

Funnell, P. and Müller, D. (1991) *Vocational Education and the Challenge of Europe.* London: Kogan Page.

George, S. (1996) *Politics and Policy in the European Union.* Oxford: Oxford University Press.

Ghosh, R. (1996) Economic liberalization and its impact on women and women's education. *The Alberta Journal of Educational Research,* XLII (2): 115–20.

Giddens, A. (1985) *The Nation-state and Violence.* Cambridge: Polity Press.

Giddens, A. (1990) *The Consequences of Modernity.* Cambridge: Polity Press.

Golding, P. and Harris, P. (1997) Introduction, in P. Golding and P. Harris (eds) *Beyond Cultural Imperialism: Globalization, Communication and the New International Order.* London: Sage.

Gore, J.M. (1993) *The Struggle for Pedagogies. Critical and Feminist Discourses as Regimes of Truth.* New York: Routledge.

Gramsci, A. (1971) *Selections from the Prison Notebooks,* Q. Hoare and G. Nowell-Smith (eds). New York: International Publishers.

Grant, R. and Newland, K. (eds) (1991) *Gender and International Relations.* Buckingham: Open University Press.

Green, A. (1990) *Education and State Formation.* London: Macmillan.

Green, A. (1997) *Education, Globalization and the Nation State.* London: Macmillan.

Green, S. (1997) *Urban Amazons: Lesbian Feminism and Beyond in the Gender, Sexuality and Identity Battles of London.* London: Macmillan.

Griffin, C. (1985) *Typical girls?: Young women from School to Market Place.* London: Routledge & Kegan Paul.

Gunew, S. (1990) Feminist knowledge: critique and construct, in S. Gunew (ed.) *Feminist Knowledge: Critique and Construct.* London: Routledge.

Hall, C. (1992) Missionary stories: gender and ethnicity in England in the 1830s and 1840s, in L. Grossberg, P. Treichler and C. Nelson (eds) *Cultural Studies.* London: Routledge.

Halsey, A.H., Lauder, H., Brown, P. and Wells, A.S. (eds) (1997) *Education, Culture, Economy and Society.* Oxford: Oxford University Press.

Hamnett, C., McDowell, L. and Sarre, P. (eds) (1989) *The Changing Social Structure.* London: Sage Publications with the Open University Press.

Hannah, J. (1989) 'Worker co-operatives as a response to unemployment: the impact upon participants', unpublished PhD thesis. Department of Applied Social Sciences, Newcastle-upon-Tyne Polytechnic.

Hao Li (1987) Introduction, in L.G. Martin (ed.) *The ASEAN Success Story: Social, Economic and Political Dimensions.* Honolulu, HI: East–West Centre.

Harcourt, W. (1994) The globalization of the economy: an international gender perspective, in IRIS (eds) *Reflections on Women's Training: A Wider Vision,* Brussels: IRIS Publications.

Hart, M.U. (1992) *Working and Educating for Life: Feminist and International Perspectives on Adult Education.* London: Routledge.

Harzing, A.K. (1995) The labour-market position of women from ethnic minorities: a comparison of four European countries, in A. van Doorne-Huiskes, J. van Hoof and E. Roelofs (eds) *Women and the European Labour Markets.* London: Chapman.

Hashimoto, A. (1992) Ageing in Japan, in D. Phillips (ed.) *Ageing in East and South East Asia.* London: Edward Arnold.

Heater, D. (1990) *Citizenship: The Civic Ideal in World History, Politics and Education.* London: Longman.

Her Majesty's Stationery Office (HMSO) (1996) *Social Focus on Ethnic Minorities.* London: HMSO.

Hewlett, S. (1986) *A Lesser Life: The Myth of Women's Liberation in America.* New York: Morrow.

Higgins, A. (1998) Uncle Sam disturbs Asia's dreams, *The Guardian,* 18 January.

Hill, J. (1986) *Sex, Class and Realism: British Cinema 1956–1963.* London: British Film Institute.

Hirst, P. and Thompson, G. (1995) Globalization and the future of the nation state. *Economy and Society,* 24 (3): 408–42.

Hirst, P. and Thompson, G. (1996) *Globalization in Question: The International Economy and Possibilities of Governance.* Cambridge: Polity Press.

Hockenos, P. (1993) *Free to Hate: The Rise of the Right in Post-communist Eastern Europe.* London and New York: Routledge.

Holden, R. (1988) *Understanding Liberal Democracy.* Oxford: Philip Alan.

Holland, J. (1988) Girls and occupational choice: in search of meanings, in A. Pollard, J. Purvis and G. Walford (eds) *Education, Training and the New Vocationalism,* Milton Keynes: Open University Press.

Hoogvelt, A. (1997) *Globalization and the Postcolonial World: The New Political Economy of Development*. London: Macmillan.

hooks, b. (1982) *Ain't I a Woman: Black Women and Feminism*. London: Pluto Press.

Home Office (1970) *Equal Pay Act*. London: HMSO.

Home Office (1975) *Sex Discrimination Act*. London: HMSO.

Hufbauer, G.C. and Schott, J.J. (1993) *NAFTA: An Assessment* (revised edition). Washington, DC: Institute for International Economics.

Huggan, G. (1995) Decolonizing the map, in B. Ashcroft, G. Griffiths and H. Tiffin (eds) *The Post-colonial Studies Reader*. London: Routledge.

Hutchings, K. (1996) *Kant, Critique and Politics*. London: Routledge.

Hutton, W. (1995) *The State We're In*. London: Jonathan Cape.

Jagger, A. (1983) *Feminist Politics and Human Nature*. Brighton: Harvester.

Jameson, F. (1984) Postmodernism, or the cultural logic of late capitalism. *New Left Review*, 146: 53–91.

Janadas, D. (compiler) (1994) *Southeast Asia: Challenges of the Twenty-first Century*. Singapore: Institute of Southeast Asian Studies.

Kaplan, G. (1992) *Contemporary western European feminism*. London: Allen and Unwin.

Kenway, J. (1991) Feminist theories of the state: to be or not to be, in M. Muetzelfeldt (ed.) *Society, State and Politics in Australia*. London: Pluto Press.

King, E. and Hill, M. A. (eds) (1993) *Women's Education in Developing Countries: Barriers, Benefits and Policies*. Baltimore, MD: Johns Hopkins University Press.

Kristeva, J. (1993) *Nations Without Nationalism*. New York: Columbia University Press.

Kuhn, A. (1988) *Cinema, Censorship and Sexuality, 1909–1925*. London: Routledge & Kegan Paul.

Larrain, J. (1979) *The Concept of Ideology*. London: Hutchinson.

Levitas, R. (1996) Fiddling while Britain burns? The 'measurement' of unemployment, in R. Levitas and W. Guy (eds) *Interpreting Official Statistics*. London: Routledge.

Lister, R. (1998) From equality to social inclusion: new Labour and the welfare state, *Critical Social Policy*, 18(2): 215–25.

Lovenduski, J. (1986) *Women and European Politics: Contemporary Feminism and Public Policy*. Brighton: Wheatsheaf.

McDowell, L. (1989) Gender divisions, in C. Hamnett, L. McDowell and P. Sarre (eds) *The Changing Social Structure*. London: Sage Publications with the Open University Press.

McGinty, J. and Fish, J. (1993) *Further Education in the Market Place: Equity, Opportunity and Individual Learning*. London: Routledge.

MacKinnon, C. (1989) *Towards a Feminist Theory of the State*. London: Harvard University Press.

McMichael, P. (1995) The new colonialism: global regulation and the restructuring of the interstate system. *Contributions in Economics and Economic History*, 1 (164): 37–55.

McRobbie, A. (1978) Working class girls and the culture of femininity, in Women's Studies Group, Centre for Contemporary Cultural Studies (ed.) *Women Take Issue: Aspects of Women's Subordination*. London: Hutchinson.

Mahoney, K. and van Toen, B. (1990) Mathematical formalism as a means of occupational closure in computing – why 'hard' computing tends to exclude women. *Gender and Education*, 2 (3): 319–31.

Mahony, P. and Zmroczek, C. (1997) Why class matters, in P. Mahony and C. Zmroczek (eds) *Class Matters: 'Working-class' Women's Perspectives on Social Class*. London: Taylor and Francis.

Marshall, T.H. (1950) *Citizenship and Social Class*. Oxford: Oxford University Press.

Martin, L.G. (ed.) (1987) *The ASEAN Success Story: Social, Economic and Political Dimensions*. Honolulu, HI: East-West Centre.

Mayo, P. (1996) Transformative adult education in an age of globalization: a Gramscian-Freirean synthesis and beyond. *The Alberta Journal of Educational Research*, XLII (2): 148–60.

Meehan, E. (1992) Researching women in Europe: European Community policies on sex equality. *Women's Studies International Forum*, 15 (1): 57–64.

Meehan, E. and Sevenhuijsen, S. (1991) Problems in principles and policies, in E. Meehan and S. Sevenhuijsen (eds) *Equality Politics and Gender*. London: Sage.

Mies, M. (1986) *Patriarchy and Accumulation on a World Scale: Women in the International Division of Labour*. London: Zed Books.

Miliband, R. (1973) *The State in Capitalist Society*. London: Quartet.

Mill, J.S. (1859) *On Liberty*, Harmondsworth: Penguin.

Mill, J.S. (1869) *The Subjection of Women*. Harmondsworth: Penguin.

Mishra, V. and Hodge, B. (1993) What is Post(-)colonialism? in P. Williams and L. Chrisman (eds) *Colonial Discourse and Post-colonial Theory: A Reader*. Hemel Hempstead: Harvester Wheatsheaf.

Mitter, S. (1986) *Common Fate, Common Bond: Women in the Global Economy*. London: Pluto Press.

Morgan-Gerard, F. (1980) *Equal Opportunities and Vocational Training: Catalogue of Training Innovations in the EC Member States*. Berlin: European Centre for the Development of Vocational Training (CEDEFOP).

National Council for Voluntary Organizations (NCVO) (1995) *NCVO European Social Fund Guidance: A Guide to ESF Applicants in 1996*. London: NCVO.

Neave, G. (1991) Policy and response: changing perceptions and priorities in the vocational training policy of the EEC Commission, in G. Esland (ed.) *Education, Training and Employment: Vol. 2: The Educational Response*. Wokingham: Addison-Wesley and Open University Press.

Need, L. (1988) *Myths of Sexuality: Representations of Women in Victorian Britain*. Oxford: Blackwell.

Network Women in Development Europe (WIDE) (1996) *A Gender Perspective on European Union Trade Polices: With Case Studies of the Philippines and Vietnam*, Briefing paper for the First World Trade Organization Ministerial Meeting, Singapore, 9–13 December.

Nicaise, I., Bollens, J., Dawes, L., Laghaei, S., Thaulow, I., Verdie, M. and Wagner, A. (1995) Pitfalls and dilemmas in labour market policies for disadvantaged groups – and how to avoid them. *Journal of European Social Policy*, 5 (3): 199–217.

Ohmae, K. (1990) *The Borderless World*. London: Collins.

Oppenheimer, V.K. (1970) *The Female Labor Force in the United States*. Berkeley, CA: University of California Press.

Organization for Economic Cooperation and Development (OECD) (1992) *Adult Illiteracy and Economic Performance*. Paris: OECD.

Organization for Economic Cooperation and Development (OECD) (1994) *Women and Structural Change: New Perspectives*. Paris: OECD.

Ozga, J. (1990) Policy research and policy theory: a comment on Halpin and Fitz. *Journal of Education Policy*, 5 (4): 359–62.

Paine, T. (1791/2) *The Rights of Man*. Harmondsworth: Penguin.

Palmer, J. (1991) Major signals concessions, but not over social policy, *The Guardian*, 10 December.

Palmer, J. (1997) EU fails to decide how best to decide, *The Guardian*, 19 June.

Palmer R.D. and Reckford T.J. (1987) *Building ASEAN: 20 Years of Southeast Asian Cooperation*. New York: Praeger Publishers.

Pannu, R.S. (1996) Neoliberal project of globalization: prospects for democratization of education. *The Alberta Journal of Educational Research*, XLII (2): 87–101.

Parvikko, T. (1991) Conceptions of gender equality: similarity and difference, in E. Meehan and S. Sevenhuijsen (eds) *Equality Politics and Gender*. London: Sage.

Pateman, C. (1980) *The Disorder of Women*, Cambridge: Polity Press.

Pateman, C. (1986) Introduction: the theoretical subversiveness of feminism, in C. Pateman and E. Gross (eds) *Feminist Challenges: Social and Political Theory*. London: Allen and Unwin.

Pateman, C. (1988) *The sexual contract*. Oxford: Polity Press and Basil Blackwell.

Peterson, V.S. (ed.) (1992) *Gendered States: Feminist (Re)visions of International Relations Theory*. Boulder, CO: Lynne Reiner.

Pickard, B. (1997) *Panorama*, BBC TV, 29 September.

Pollert, A. (1981) *Girls, Wives and Factory Lives*. London: Macmillan.

Polychroniou, C. (1995) Rise and fall of US imperialism. *Economic and Political Weekly*, 30 (130): 54–64.

Pool, H. (1997) Looking to the future, *Guardian Education*, 4 February.

Prechal, S. and Senden, L. (1993) *Equal Treatment after Maastricht: Special Report of 1993 of the Network of Exports on the Implementation of the Equality Directives*. Brussels: European Commission, DG V, Equal Opportunities Unit.

Purvis, J. (1991) *A History of Women's Education in England*. Buckingham: Open University Press.

Purvis, T. and Hunt, A. (1993) Discourse, ideology, discourse, ideology, discourse, ideology . . . *British Journal of Sociology*, 44: 473–99.

Raab, C.D. (1994) Where are we now: reflections on the sociology of education policy, in D. Halpin and B. Troyna (eds) *Researching Education Policy: Ethical and Methodological Issues*. London: Falmer.

Ramazanoglu, C. (ed.) (1993) *Up Against Foucault: Explorations of Some Tensions Between Foucault and Feminism*. London: Routledge.

Ramprakash, D. (1994) Poverty in the countries of the European Union: a synthesis of Eurostat's statistical research on poverty, *Journal of European Social Policy*, 4 (2): 117–28.

Ramsay, H. (1995) *Le défi Européen*: Multinational restructuring, labour and EU policy, in A. Amin and J. Tomaney (eds) *Behind the Myth of European Union*. London: Routledge.

Rauner, F. (1985) *Women Study Microcomputer Technology: A Report About Initial Survey Findings Concerning Information Technology/Microcomputer Projects for Women in EC Countries.* Berlin: European Centre for the Development of Vocational Training (CEDEFOP).

Rifkin, J. (1995) *The End of Work: The Decline of the Global Labor Force and the Dawn of the Post-market Era.* New York: Putnam.

Rowan, D. (1998) Meet the new world government, *The Guardian,* 13 February.

Rowntree Trust (1995) *Income and wealth,* Report of the Joseph Rowntree Enquiry Group, Vols 1 and 2. Poole: BEBC Distribution.

Said, E. (1978) *Orientalism.* London: Routledge and Kegan Paul.

Sarre, P. (1989) Recomposition of the class structure, in C. Hamnett, L. McDowell and P.Sarre (eds) *The changing social structure.* London: Sage Publications with Open University Press.

Schiller, H. (1976) *Communication and cultural domination.* New York: International Arts and Science Press.

Seddon, T. (1994) Reconstructing social democratic education in Australia: versions of vocationalism. *Journal of Curriculum Studies,* 26 (1): 63–82.

Seeland, S. (1980) *Equal Opportunities and Vocational Training: A Survey on Vocational Training Initiatives for Women in the European Community.* Berlin: European Centre for the Development of Vocational Training (CEDEFOP).

Sewell, T. (1994) Black British youth culture and its relationship to schooling, Conference paper, Oxford University, British Educational Research Association conference, September.

Skeggs, B. (1997) *Formations of Class and Gender.* London: Sage.

Smart, V. and Coman, J. (1997) Europe's new axis looks for a third way on jobs, *The European,* 19–25 June.

Social Europe (1988) *Supplement 3: The Role of Education and Training in the Completion of the Internal Market.* Luxembourg: Office for the Official Publications of the European Commission.

Social Europe (1989a) *Supplement 8: Activities of the Commission of the European Communities in the Fields of Education, Training and Youth Policy During 1987 and 1988.* Luxembourg: Office for the Official Publications of the European Commission.

Social Europe (1989b) *Supplement 3: The Toledo Seminar on the Evaluation of Community Policy on Equal Opportunities for Women and Men: Outlook for 1992.* Luxembourg: Office for the Official Publications of the European Commission.

Social Europe (1993) *Supplement 3: Occupational Segregation of Women and Men in the European Community.* Luxembourg: Office for the Official Publications of the European Commission.

Social Europe (1994a) *Supplement 1: European Integration and the European Labour Market.* Luxembourg: Office for the Official Publications of the European Commission.

Social Europe (1994b) *Supplement 4: Wage Determination and Sex Segregation in Employment in the European Community.* Luxembourg: Office for the Official Publications of the European Commission.

Social Europe (1995) *No 2: Racism and Xenophobia: A Tale of Violence and Exclusion.* Luxembourg: Office for the Official Publications of the European Commission.

Sreberny-Mohammadi, A. (1997) The many cultural faces of imperialism, in P. Golding and P. Harris (eds) *Beyond Cultural Imperialism: Globalization, Communication and the New International Order.* London: Sage.

Stedman Jones, G. (1971) *Outcast London: A Study in the Relationship Between Classes in Victorian Society*. Oxford: Clarendon.

Sung, S.J. (1997) 'Colonialism and language: a case study of Korea', unpublished part submission for the MEd in Educational Studies, University of Sheffield.

Thompson, E.P. (1968) *The Making of the English Working-class*. Harmondsworth: Penguin.

Thompson, J. (1983) *Learning Liberation: Women's Response to Men's Education*. London: Croom Helm.

Thompson, R. (1994) *The Pacific Basin Since 1945*. London: Longman.

Thornton, M. (1986) Sex equality is not enough for feminism, in C. Pateman and E. Gross (eds) *Feminist Challenges: Social and Political Theory*. London: Allen and Unwin.

Tickner, A. (1992) *Gender in International Relations: Feminist Perspectives on Achieving Global Security*. New York: Columbia University Press.

Troyna, B. (1994) Blind faith? 'Empowerment' and educational research, Conference paper, University of Sheffield, International Sociology of Education conference, 4–6 January.

United Nations (UN) (1986) *Construction Statistics Yearbook 1984*. New York: United Nations.

Walby, S. (1986) *Patriarchy at Work*. Cambridge: Polity Press.

Walby, S. (1988) Segregation in employment in social and economic theory, in S. Walby (ed.) *Gender Segregation at Work*. Milton Keynes: Open University Press.

Walby, S. (1994) Is citizenship gendered? *Sociology*, 28 (2): 379–95.

Walkerdine, V. (1990) *Schoolgirl Fictions*, London: Verso.

Wallace, C. (1986) From girls and boys to women and men: the school reproduction of gender roles in the transition from school to (un)employment, in S. Walker and L. Barton (eds) *Youth Unemployment and Schooling*. Milton Keynes: Open University Press.

Wallace, H. and Wallace, W. (1996) *Policy-making in the European Union*. Oxford: Oxford University Press.

Wanandi, J. (1987) Political development and regional order, in L.G. Martin (ed.) *The ASEAN Success Story: Social, Economic and Political Dimensions*. Honolulu, HI: East–West Centre.

Waters, M. (1995) *Globalization*. London: Routledge.

Watson, S. (1990) The state of play: an introduction, in S. Watson (ed.) *Playing the State: Australian Feminist Interventions*. London: Verso Press.

Weiler, K. (1991) Freire and a feminist pedagogy of difference. *Harvard Educational Review*, 6 (4): 449–74.

Weiner, G. (1994) *Feminisms in Education: An Introduction*. Buckingham: Open University Press.

Whalley, J. (1993) The Uruguay Round and the GATT: whither the global system? in F.C. Bergsten and M. Noland (eds) *Pacific Dynamism and the International Economic System*. Washington, DC: Institute for International Economics.

White, J. (1997) *Education and the End of Work: A New Philosophy of Work and Learning*. London: Cassell.

Whitty, G., Edwards, T. and Gewirtz, S. (1993) *Specialization and Choice in Urban Education: The City Technology Experiment*. London: Routledge.

Wilkjman, P.M. (1993) The existing bloc expanded? The European Community, EFTA and Eastern Europe, in F.C. Bergsten and M. Noland (eds) *Pacific Dynamism and the International Economic System*. Washington, DC: Institute for International Economics.

Willis, S. and Kenway, J. (1996) Gender and the restructuring of work and vocational education in Australia: some perilous possibilities, *Journal of Education Policy*, 11 (2): 239–58.

Wollstonecraft, M. (1792) *A Vindication of the Rights of Women*. Harmondsworth: Penguin.

Women of Europe (1992) *Supplement 36: The Position of Women in the Labour Market*. Brussels: European Commission, Women's Information Service.

Wong, A.K. and Cheung, P.P.L. (1987) Demographic and social development: taking stock for the morrow, in L.G. Martin (ed.) *The ASEAN Success Story: Social, Economic and Political Dimensions*. Honolulu, HI: East–West Centre.

Yeatman, A. (1990) *Bureaucrats, Technocrats and Femocrats*. Sydney: Allen and Unwin.

Yeatman, A. (1993) Contemporary issues for feminism: the politics of the state, in J. Blackmore and J. Kenway (eds) *Gender Matters in Educational Administration and Policy*. London: Falmer.

Young, I.M. (1990a) *Justice and the Politics of Difference*. Princeton, NJ: Princeton University Press.

Young, I.M. (1990b) Polity and group difference: a critique of the ideal of universal citizenship, in I.M. Young (ed.) *'Throwing Like a Girl' and Other Essays in Feminist Philosophy and Social Theory*. Bloomington, IN: Indiana University Press.

Yuval-Davis, N. (1993) Gender and nation, *Ethnic and Racial Studies*, 16 (4): 621–32.

Yuval-Davis, N. (1997) *Gender and nation*. London: Sage.

Index

GENDER IN THIRD WORLD POLITICS

Georgina Waylen

This book puts forward a gendered analysis of Third World politics. It uses a wide definition of the political to examine both 'high politics' and political activity at the grass roots, focusing particularly on women's organizations. It also examines the impact of policy and politics on gender relations and on different groups of women. After a general discussion of the major theoretical questions involved in the study of gender in Third World politics, and the nature of the Third World and development, the analysis is developed through the in-depth study of different political formations. These are colonialism, revolution, authoritarianism, and democracy and democratization and uses examples from much of the Third World.

Gender in Third World politics

- is the only book to provide comprehensive coverage of gender in Third World politics;
- provides a gendered analysis of both 'high politics' and different women's political activity at the grass roots;
- weaves together material from a wide range of disciplines such as politics, sociology, history, development studies and women's studies.

Contents

176pp   0 335 15770 X (Paperback)   0 335 15771 8 (Hardback)

FEMINISMS IN EDUCATION
AN INTRODUCTION

Gaby Weiner

Gaby Weiner presents an overview of recent developments in feminist educational thinking and practice in Britain, exploring the ethical and professional challenges which now face feminist teachers and educators. She
relates feminist thinking and practice to her own autobiographical experiences, to research and practitioner perspectives on gender, and to a variety of
teacher and policy gender initiatives. She examines how the curriculum is
implicated in the construction of gender relations, for example, in defining
gender appropriate behaviour and/or in shaping perceptions of the appropriate place for girls and women in the family, school and employment. Throughout, she offers suggestions for feminist practice and the book concludes with
specific proposals for developing educational politics out of poststructural
feminism, and for creating a feminist praxis as a basis for feminist action in
education.

> This timely book takes stock of past and present feminist educational
> thinking and practice in Britain. It is the range and clarity of the descrip-
> tions of past feminist activities in education, combined with an unflinch-
> ing engagement with the complexities of contemporary feminist ideas,
> that make this book essential reading for a wide range of people.
> Weiner's style is direct and intellectually interactive.
>
> *Gender and Education*

Contents
*Preface – Introduction – From certainty to uncertainty: an autobiographical
narrative – Teacher-proof or teacher-led: universal or specific (discourses on
the curriculum) – Feminisms and education – Eradicating inequality: feminist
practitioners and educational change – The gendered curriculum: producing
the text – Developing a feminist praxis in pedagogy and research – References
– Index.*

176pp   0 335 19052 9 (Paperback)   0 335 19053 7 (Hardback)